AT THE

BIRTH

OF

TEXAS

The Diary of
William Fairfax Gray
1835~1838

Copano Bay Press
2015

First published in 1909 under the title *From Virginia to Texas*.

New material copyright 2015
Copano Bay Press
ISBN 978-1-941324-77-6

Introductory Preface

Having occasion to examine my father's record of his experiences and observations during his visit to Texas in 1835-6, I found the ink of a large part of it so faded and dim as to render it certain that in a comparatively short time it would become unreadable. I felt therefore that prudence required it should be put into a more durable form, to preserve the information contained in it for the benefit of his descendants, and possibly for the use of the future historian. I therefore determined to print it, just as he wrote it, changing nothing; and, while doing so, I was impressed with the conviction that it was due to his memory that, being the last survivor of his immediate family, and the only person living who could now do so, I should put into the same permanent form along with his diary, the reason for his coming to Texas at that time, why he returned to Virginia when he did, and why he again came out before he determined to make Texas his permanent home. It is with a loving reverence for his memory that I endeavor to do so.

The panic which spread over the United States in 1833 and 1834, consequent upon the withdrawal of Government deposits from the National Banks, was widespread in its results, and reduced thousands of prosperous people to straitened circumstances, and many more to absolute poverty, if not penury. My father was one of the sufferers. The distress was greatest in the Atlantic States, and a great many of all walks in life sought new fields of enterprise in the Middle West—Kentucky, Tennessee and Missouri; in the Northwest, as Ohio, Indiana and Illinois were then designated; and in the Southwest, as Alabama, Mississippi and Louisiana were grouped. Large numbers migrated to these new fields of enterprise, and reports from them of the great fertility of the soil and the rapid advance in land values, consequent upon this migration, induced many of the comparatively few who had suffered less from the financial panic to embark in land speculation; and Texas just then loomed up as a land of promise, and shared in the general movement.

Among the more fortunate alluded to were two friends of my father Tom Green and Albert T. Burnley, of Washington City, D. C., both of whom were "well to do," and both had been bitten by the stegomia which inoculates the land speculation virus. They had already invested to some extent in Mississippi, and wanted to invest more, either in Mississippi, Louisiana or Texas; but they desired reliable information, and the judgment of one on whom they could rely more implicitly than upon the land agents generally of that day. With this in view they opened negotiations with Col. Gray, and his trip to the Southwest and Texas was the result.

With these facts kept in mind, the motives which controlled his actions may be clearly understood. No man was ever more devoted to what he believed to be duty; and no man ever held more sacred any phase of duty than fidelity to trust. Hence his actions were more often contrary to his inclinations and desires than in accord with them. Thus, when he found affairs in Texas in a state of turmoil, almost the entire country abandoned by its white inhabitants, and but a handful of armed men between them and the invading army which so far had swept all before it, the result of the impending conflict hardly even doubtful, however much he desired to stay and take part in that conflict (and I know he did ardently so desire), he felt that duty to his employers, to say nothing of the large family in Virginia dependent upon him, required that he take no more risk than was necessary, and that he return as soon as possible, and by the shortest route, and report the result of his mission. He did so, and in so doing realized to the full that it ofttimes requires more courage to do right than to do wrong. His silence on the subject proves to me that he felt it too deeply to talk about, though he was at no time given to explaining the motives of his actions.

It seems that persons enrolled as citizens of Texas at that time were required to obtain permission to leave the country, and to show good cause for so doing before the leave was granted. I gather this from the fact that my father secured from the Department of State the necessary permit, which reads as follows:

DEPARTMENT OF STATE
REPUBLIC OF TEXAS
28th March, 1836

William F. Gray having made application to this Department for leave of absence from the Republic of Texas, and having shown that his business is of such a nature as to justify his absence. Be it known to all persons, That the said William F. Gray has leave to be absent from the Republic of Texas for and during the term of * * * from date hereof.

By order of the President.
SAM P. CARSON,
Sec'y of State

To assign timidity as the cause of his leaving when he did would run counter to the course of his whole life, for he had a great fondness for military tactics, and when very young became a member of a volunteer company of riflemen called the Lafayette Cadets. In 1811, in view of probable war with

Great Britain, Virginia began in earnest the organization of her militia, as the State troops were then called; and on the 21st day of March, 1811, Commission "No. 1," signed by James Monroe, Governor of Virginia, afterwards President, was issued, appointing him Captain in the Sixteenth Regiment, First Brigade, and Second Division, * * * "to rank as such agreeably to the number and date hereof." He was then a little over twenty-three years of age; and during the war which followed—1812-14—he was ordered with his company to the mouth of Occoquon Creek, a stream in northeast Virginia, which empties in the Potomac about twenty-five miles below Washington, where it was learned the British intended to land, with instructions to resist the landing. He obeyed orders so effectively the enemy was driven off and forced to land on the Maryland shore, and Virginia escaped the threatened invasion. His grandson, Dr. E. N. Gray, of Houston, Texas, has the original of that commission, and also the commissions appointing him Major of the Sixteenth Regiment, dated "the 5th day of November, 1819," signed by Gov. James P. Preston, and Lieutenant Colonel of the same regiment, dated "26th day of May, 1820," signed by Gov. Thomas M. Randolph. He has also another commission signed by Gov. John Floyd, naming him as "Captain of Riflemen in the Sixteenth Regiment, First Brigade and Second Division," dated "27th day of September, 1831," which bears the following endorsement:

> *To this commission I did not qualify. I was, at the time, Postmaster at Fredericksburg, and by the laws of Virginia incapable of holding a commission under the State. This was understood by the Rifle Company when they elected me to the captaincy. I commanded the company until the winter of 1834, when I resigned. W. F. G.*

This company was called the "Rifle Greys," and in accepting his resignation made him an honorary member, and on his return from Texas, in 1836, turned out at midnight, in full uniform, with a band of music, to welcome him home—an occasion of which I have a very distinct remembrance, though I was then but six years of age.

He was a devoted Mason, and among the old papers we have are his commissions as District Deputy Grand Master for each year from 1825 to 1832, inclusive, and his dimit from Fredericksburg Lodge, No. 4, in 1838, on the eve of his departure with his family to make their home in Houston, Texas, on which occasion, after granting the dimit, "the Lodge expressed its approbation of his zeal and ability as a Mason, and its wishes for his future welfare and happiness." Afterwards:

On motion made and seconded, ordered that Brother William F. Gray, late a member of this Lodge, be enrolled among the list of members of this Lodge as an honorary member, entitled to all the privileges of the Lodge. From the minutes—a copy—teste J. J. Chew, Secretary.

When General Lafayette visited the United States in 1824, as the "Guest of the Nation," he evinced his respect and devotion to the memory of Gen. George Washington by a visit to his tomb at Mount Vernon. Fredericksburg Lodge, in which Washington was "entered, passed and raised," and was for a long time a member, took advantage of the opportunity to invite Gen. Lafayette to visit Fredericksburg, in which it was cordially joined by the town authorities. On notification of his acceptance, and that he should arrive on the 20th of November (Saturday), and remain over until the evening of Monday, the 22nd, preparations for a grand civic and military reception were at once begun, and the following programme formulated, which I copy from the official bulletin, because I think it both interesting and worthy of preservation:

At a meeting of the La Fayette Committee, convened in the Mayor's Office, on the 12th November, 1824: It was resolved,

*That the proceedings of said meeting, so far as they related to the
regulation of the military and civil escort, should be published in
the Virginia Herald; and the Committee designated individuals
to perform that duty, who respectfully report—*

*That General La Fayette and suite will be received at the di-
viding line of Orange and Spotsylvania counties, on Saturday
the 20th instant, by a deputation from the Committee of Arrangements, accompanied by two Marshals, who will provide
the necessary carriages and baggage wagons, for their accommodation. A corps of officers, associated for the purpose, will
meet the Guest at the Wilderness Tavern, and form an escort to
the town of Fredericksburg, and will march in rear of the carriages to the parade ground on the hill, west of the town, when
they will advance to the front, preceded by the two marshals—the
military will be formed in line on the parade ground adjoining
the turnpike road, and salute by presenting arms—as the General
and suite attain the right of the whole, a signal will be given by
a marshal, and communicated by him in the same manner to
the Commandant of Artillery, who will, on its reception, fire a
federal salute.*

*When the General and suite shall have cleared the right of the
military, they will in such order as shall be adopted by them,
wheel into column in rear of the junior volunteers, who will
follow the carriages—and such citizens or strangers as may be
on horseback, shall wheel into column in sections of four, and
follow the rear of the military. The whole procession will then
proceed towards the town, and such of the citizens as choose
(and all are requested to unite in the procession), shall assemble
on each side of the street, opposite the residences of I. H. Williams and John T. Lomax, Es'rs, and as the rear of the aforesaid
procession pass them, wheel into column in sections of four, and
follow on.*

*The procession will then proceed to the main street—wheel to
the left, thence to Henderson's corner, and wheel again to the*

left, and proceed to Princess Ann street, wheel again to the left, and proceed to the Town Hall. When the carriages in which the General and suite are conveyed arrive in front of the Town Hall, the whole procession will halt, and the General and suite be conducted to the platform in front of the Hall, where he will be met by the Mayor and Council and Justices of the Peace, and an address will be delivered.

At the conclusion of these ceremonies, of which the commandant of artillery will be advised by signal, a national salute will be fired, and the General and suite conducted into the Town Hall, where the Revolutionary officers and soldiers, distinguished visitors, the mayor, common council, and justices of the peace, strangers, the committee of arrangements, and all the officers of the day, will be permitted to enter, and all other persons excluded. The General and his suite will then be conducted to his carriage, and the procession will resume the foregoing order and Proceed to escort him down Princess Ann street to the Masonic Hall, thence to the main street, and thence up Main street to his lodgings, when the military will again salute.

It is particularly requested, that upon the reception of the General and suite, and throughout the whole procession, the strictest silence be preserved until the Guest shall have been saluted by the military at his lodgings, when if desired by the assembled multitude, three cheers may be given.

All parents and guardians are earnestly and respectfully solicited to keep their children and wards within their respective lots, to avoid the danger to which they would be exposed, and the interruption and inconvenience to which all in the procession will be exposed by their neglect of this request.

Owners of slaves are respectfully solicited to keep their slaves within their lots, and not to suffer them to go into any of the streets through which the procession will march, on any pretence whatever.

11

And all coloured persons are warned that they are not to appear in any of the streets through which the procession will pass, under the penalty of immediate punishment, from those conducting it.

And owners of drays, wagons, carts, carriages and horses are requested not to permit them to be placed in any of the streets through which the procession will march.

The General and his suite are confidently expected to arrive in Fredericksburg on the 20th instant, between the hours of 3 and 5 o'clock p.m., and will remain in Fredericksburg on Sunday, and be attended to the Episcopal Church by a Masonic procession. On Monday it is confidently expected that the drawing room of the Guest will be open for the reception of the ladies, only, from 10 to 12 o'clock a.m., when the Guest will be conducted to the Town Hall by a military procession, and be introduced to such citizens as may desire it. The Guest will be entertained at a dinner at Mr. W. F. Gray's, on Monday, and during the evening of that day proceed to Potomac Creek, and there embark in a steamboat for Washington.

In addition to the foregoing the Lodge extended the following invitation, which was accepted:

Fredericksburg, Nov. 19, 1824
To Gen'l La Fayette,
Sir and Brother:

Understanding that you will sojourn with us on the approaching Sabbath, the Brethren of Fredericksburg Lodge, No. 4, anxious, as a body, to manifest the grateful respect and fraternal regard, which, as individuals, they, in common with their countrymen, feel for your person and character, will hold a Lodge on the morning of that day, and form a procession to the church at which you may be pleased to attend Divine Service.

In the name of the Lodge I respectfully invite you to honor us with your presence, together with all the Masonic members of your family.

With sentiments of profound respect and fraternal regard,

I am, &c., &c.,
William F. Gray,
Master

This letter was sent to Gen. La Fayette at the Wilderness, the invitation was accepted, and the "Guest" attended Divine Service with the Lodge. On Monday he dined at my father's house. On the occasion of the public reception my father filled the position of Grand Marshal and Military Commandant.

Col. Gray left Houston in August, 1838, after making preparations for bringing his family out, such as buying a lot or lots on the west side of Courthouse Square, and contracting for the building of a house. On account of the scarcity and very high cost of lumber, the house was built of a concrete consisting of cement and shell, making a good, substantial building of one and a half stories, which served the family as a residence for ten or twelve years. In November, 1838, the family took the steamship *Rappahannock*, plying between Fredericksburg and Baltimore, for the latter city, where they embarked on the brig *Bertha*, for Galveston, arriving there the day before Christmas, having been six weeks making the voyage. We were detained at Galveston, on board the vessel, one full week, when the steamboat *Rufus Putnam*, Capt. J. H. Sterrett, brought us to Houston, arriving the first day of January, 1839, just after a soaking rain, and the climb of the hill—steeper then than it is now—from the bayou to Commerce street, by my brother Fairfax and myself, two little shavers nine and a half and eight years old, is still very vivid in my memory, for I was very tired of Houston before I reached level ground, notwithstanding we had on our first pair of top boots, and were accompanied by a negro man named Armistead, who pulled first one and then the other out of the red clay as we were alternately stuck in it.

My father was warmly welcomed by his many acquaintances, and for several years afterwards our house was headquarters for the distinguished men of that day.

It will be noticed that the Diary ends abruptly in the spring of 1837, while he is making preparation to go to Houston, to which place the Seat of Government was about to be moved, and the only authentic information we have of his life between that time and his return to Virginia, in the fall of 1838, to bring out his family, is derived from the statements of other, and the few official papers we have. Among the former, Lubbock, in his Memoirs, says he was Clerk of the House during the second session of the First Congress, and Secretary of the Senate the first session of the Second Congress, and this is to some extent confirmed by a note from Sam Houston, then President, relative to enrollment of bills. Among the papers we have are his license to practice law, appointment as Clerk of the Supreme Court of Texas, upon its organization, dated 29th May, 1837, and signed by "James Collinsworth, Chief Justice." This position he seems to have held until August 6, 1838, when he appointed Hamilton Stuart (afterwards a prominent citizen of Galveston, and editor of note), his Deputy, to serve for him during his absence; and his re-election to the same office January 7, 1840, his commission being signed by "Tho. J. Rusk, Chief Justice Supreme Court." Among the papers is also the official notification of his appointment of District Attorney for the district embracing Houston. In March, 1841, in the discharge of his official duties, he visited Galveston, and while there he contracted a severe cold, which, on his return to Houston, developed into acute pneumonia, terminating in his death on the 16th of April, 1841.

Singularly enough, my mother, almost exactly ten years after, also visited Galveston, was taken sick with dysentery, returned to Houston, and after several weeks of suffering, died on the 1st of July, 1851.

My father has often been called the founder of Christ Church Parish of Houston. I know that it was through his efforts that the first missionary clergy of the Episcopal Church were sent here, and that he was very active in bringing about the organization of the parish; but, at the time of his death, there was no clergyman in Houston, and he was buried by the Masonic Fraternity in the old City Cemetery. On the death of my mother, their son, Judge Peter W. Gray, had his remains taken up and buried with those of our mother in the Episcopal Cemetery; but, on the opening of Glenwood Cemetery, the remains were again disinterred and reburied there.

Of the entire family that accompanied my father from Virginia, I am the sole survivor, and all of the rest, save two, repose in Glenwood, and, according to the laws of nature, it can be but a few more years at most before I join them there. May they rest in peace, together with their children and children's children, until the Archangel's trump, through the mercy of God and the intercession or His Son, calls us to a glorious resurrection.

A. C. Gray
1909

AT THE BIRTH OF TEXAS

DIARY

VOL. I

MEMO ON INSIDE FRONT COVER:

Memo. of Persons to enquire for—Elijah Wilmore, or Whitmore, of Mississippi—relations live in King and Queen, Va.; he lives somewhere in the upper part of Miss., near the river. Is a small settler.

Tuesday, October 6, 1835.

Stage fare to Charlottesville, $5.

Left Fredericksburg at ½ past 12 o'clock, in the stage. Passengers—a Mr. S. T. Wharton, a lawyer from New Orleans, and his lady; Mr. Ficklin, a mercht. of Charlottesville, and daughter; a Mr. Roome, of New York, who is going to the White Sulphur Spgs. to take the body of his sister, a Mrs. Oakley, of N. Y., back to that place. She came to the Springs in July, in low health, and died; 3 Cornish miners and 1 Scotchman, who have been working at the Gold Mines about Fredbg. and are now going to Galena, in Illinois. The Englishmen came over in the *William IV,* which arrived at Tappahannock this summer. The Scot has been in the country 6 years. He is a shrewd, but rough fellow, and rather forward and conceited, named John Hyne. The English more modest and well behaved—Chappell, Hall, Collins.

Dined at Chancellors (dinner excellent, 50 cts.). Met here F. W. Taliaferro, wife and daughter, returning home from upper country.

Supper at Terrell's, good (50 cts.). Arrived at Orange C. H. after 9 o'clock. Lodging good, 25 cts., at Rawlings'.

Had a shower of rain this afternoon—weather becoming cold. Company agreeable. The Scot talkative, fond of controversy, and of showing his reading, which is greater than could be expected from a man of his vocation and rude exterior. Tried to engage with me on Universalism, which I avoided. He was taken up and overcome, but not silenced, by the old merchant—who I take to be a Baptist.

Wednesday, October 7, 1835.

Left Orange C. H. at 3 a.m., passed Barboursville, on the west side of S. West Mt. Before arriving at Barboursville, gear broke and leaders ran off; retaken, hurt, and after repairing, went on to breakfast (indifferent, at 50 cts.). Charlottesville—got a new stage. Fare to Staunton, $3. Left the merchant and his daughter and took in 3 new passengers—one, Mr. Wiley, of Pattonsburg, a wild young man, apparently intoxicated; Mr. Clark, of Waynesburg, and Mr. Perry, of Staunton, both older and genteel.

Dinner good at Lewis's—50 cts.—5 miles from top of Blue Ridge. Our only lady passenger, Mrs. W., who is a very handsome and lovely woman, left a little box at the dining house. Did not discover it until the tavern was a mile behind. The Scot, with ready alacrity, offered to go back for it on foot. This they would not allow. A horse could not be had, and we went on. I promised to write to a friend to bring it on.

Crossed the Blue Ridge at Rockfish Gap, about sunset. Saw Jos. F. Maury and wife—they keep the hotel on the top of the mount.

At the western foot of the Ridge, passed the Town of Waynesburg, on a branch of the Shenandoah. Here we dropt Mr. Clarke. Arrived at Staunton about 8 o'clock—supper and lodging, 75 cts—stage to Lewisburg, $6. Sent my card to my friend, Dr. Edw. Berkeley; he was at church, but came, in a little time, and sat with me until 11 o'clock. The New Orleons lady also had a lady and gent. to see her. Tavern kept by McClung. A very good house. Shaved by a black, who claimed an old acquaintanceship with me and tore my face to pieces—(Robert Campbell). Passage today altogether agreeable. The young Blood from Pattonsburg, a furious Jackson man, disputed with Clarke, of Waynesburg, who was cool, sensible and anti-Jack. Attempted to quiz the raw-looking miners; failed and silenced by the Scot and a little Englishman, who is a fine personification, in appearance and manner, of the Bonnet Maker in the *Fair Maid of Perth*.

Thursday, October 8, 1835.

Breakfast at Frazier's, very good, 50 cts. Left Staunton at 3 a.m. Dinner at Brooks', 50 cts., poor—very rude establishment. Supper and lod., 75 cts., at Shumate's, on Jackson's Riv. A rude estab't kept by a tall, rough hunter-looking man—but very polite in his way.

Company today altogether agreeable. At Staunton dropt Mr. Perry, of Staunton, a gentle young man, and the *Blood*, of Pattonsburg. Took in a Kentuckian of Boone County (James Crisler, a Dutchman, who left Madison, Va., about 10 years ago), and a sober-looking gent. from the mountains, entered only to Callahan's. The Kentuckian had been a wagoner in Madison—shrewd, sensible—a humorist, and a decided acquisition. Our New Orleans fr'ds also improve on acquaintance. Mr. W., a lawyer, has been all over the southwest, and in Texas; prefers U. S. lands to Texas for immediate speculation. Thinks great speculations may be made in Texas with capital that one can lay out of for a time. They appear to be newly married. The lady, a Virginian by birth, lived lately in Tennessee. She is a Jackson man—he, anti.

Arrived at Warm Springs about 4 o'clock; found Hudgins and Farrish and Miss Hardin waiting. They could not get a seat the day before, and we are now too full, having 10 passengers—9 inside, 1 outside; took up Farish, outside, which makes 11. Saw Geo. B. Richards—no time to see his family or to view the place. About sunset, passed the Hot Springs, a very pretty place—more so than the Warm Springs—owned and kept by a Dr. Good. The Warm Springs owned by Dr. Brokenbrough, of Richmond, and kept by * * * Fry.

Friday, October 9, 1835.

Left Shumate's at 2 o'clock a.m. Weather intensely cold. Snow has fallen on the mountains, as the travellers from the West inform us, 3 inches deep. Changed horses at Pat. Callahan's, at the east foot of the Alleghany, before day. Our sober way-passenger here got out, and poor Farish, who had been on the outside, got in, almost frozen. Crossed the Backbone about sunrise. I suffered very much with cold, having on thin stockings and shoes, thin vest and hat—my cap snugly packed in trunk. Breakfast, 50 cts., good—at the White Sulphur Springs.

Here I got thawed—put on thick stockings and boots and cap. Dropt Mr. Roome, from New York. No time to view the place, which appears to be extensive and of great capabilities.

Arrived at Lewisburg, in Greenbrier, about * * * and paid stage fare to Guyandotte, $10. Went to printing office; got a paper (The Lewisburg Alleghanian, edited and published by Edw. B. Bailey); contains a long advertisement of H. O. Middleton, as commissioner for public sale of H. Banks' lands, under a decree Greenbrier Court, in favor of Wm. Duval. Sales to be in Mason, Jackson, Nicholas and Harrison. This, I fear, will interfere with the Doyle claim. Memo. to write to P. Harrison and send him the paper. Dinner rude and poor, 50 cts., at Mount Pleasant, a little tavern on roadside, in Greenbrier, kept by Josh. Remley. Supper and lodging, 75 cts., at John Deem's on the side of the Big Swede—a wretched, rude, uncomfortable place. Found here, Law. Ashton, of Fauquier, who has been lying sick ever since the 14th September; arrived here, in a barouche, with his brother Richard and his bride; they had gone to Greenupsburg, in Kentucky, and left him. Dr. (or Gen'l) Dan'l Smith, has attended and nursed him, and, he says, saved his life. Has been out of his senses for 3 weeks; now very low; has to be lifted out of his bed. Dr. says wants nothing but nursing and society. Furnished him with a box of seidlitz powders (suffered for medicine), and wrote to Thos. L. Ashton, his brother at Warrington, to come for him, informing of his condition, and requesting him to come for him. Richard has been written to. I promised to call at Greenupsburg and see him, if possible; also to write to J. Metcalfe, Fredericksburg. Poor fellow, rejoiced to see me, and very grateful for the powders.

Saturday, October 10, 1835.

Left Deem's at * * *. Breakfast at Mc Vey's or New Haven, 50 cts. Passed Hawksnest; the driver stopt for us to get out -and see it. The road passes within 100 yds. of the cliff which overhangs New River, perpendicular 860 feet. Scenery grand, sublime, awful. Crossed Gouley Branch just at the junction of Gouley and New River. Dined at Falls of Kenawha (river formed by New and Gouley), 50 cts.; very good. At the Kenawha Salines, the Scot left us, intending to get work there. Stopt to see the Burning Spring—a great curiosity. Puddle about 12 feet diameter, continually boiling from the escape of gas, which ignites on the application of flame. It was night, and seen to great advantage. Our New Orleans fellow traveler was unwell and would not leave the stage. At his request, I escorted his fair wife, with whom I have become much interested. She is beautiful, well-bred and intelligent, but mischievous and daring. Would go to the brink of the cliff, at Hawksnest, in spite of her husband's remonstrance and my entreaties. I like her—but fear for her.

Road today descending all day; mountain left behind. Approaching Great Valley. Temperature milder. My cap and thick stockings no longer wanted. Arrived at Charleston about 9 o'clock. Supper and lodging at Wilson's, 75 cents. Poor accommodations, bad attendance and plenty of dirt. Our New Orleans friend, Wharton, quite sick; has taken cold, lost rest; has high fever and pains in his limbs. I insisted on his having a doctor, which he at last consented to. Sent for Dr. Spicer Patrick, who immediately bled him and prescribed medicine. He suffers much pain, and his mind wanders. His lovely wife is now the "Ministering Angel." I was desirous of sitting up with him, as she had lost much rest on the journey; this she would not permit. We must now certainly leave them here. I was half inclined to stop a day with them, and try to be serviceable. But it is very doubtful, if I stop one day, whether I can get on the next. This would throw me back, and be very inconvenient; besides, I am a stranger, of only 4 days stage acquaintance. Would they not consider me obtrusive? His wife is with him—they have the means of commanding and rewarding services—their carriage and two servants are coming on, and will be with them in a few days. On the whole I must go on, against my inclination.

One of our Englishmen also is sick, and the whole three stop here for a day. Our party will be sadly diminished. It has hitherto been very agreeable. The dry humor and good nature of our Dutch Kentuckian has enlivened us much.

He cracked his jokes all around, but leveled the heaviest of his fire on the poor Scot, whom he almost used up—he was dumbfounded, silenced, cowed.

Sunday, October 11, 1835.

Left Charleston at 3 a.m. I was not called up until the other passengers were dressed, owing to the stupid negligence of the clown who acted as barkeeper—the driver shouting and railing about waiting for one passenger so long. He is a savage, insolent fellow—and the only one of the description that we have had on the journey. My *compagnons de voyage* are now reduced to the Kentuckian and Farish; a young man from the Salines rides on the outside, and we had 3 decent black boys inside for 12 miles to Cool Bridge, going to pay a Sunday visit.

Breakfasted at Morris's; 50 cts. Had a long grace said by a truculent-looking Baptist, which the landlord, I was told, also professed to be, and the rascal made us pay 50 cents apiece for a bad breakfast, whilst the man from the Salines only paid 25 cts. This, our new companion told us, and I learn it is the common practice all through the mountains, to make the same distinction between stage passengers and other travellers. This is a vile imposition, which will be corrected only by competition. Our new companion very talkative and not unpleasant; but we are dull. We all think and talk of the interesting company we have just left: The Kentuckian is as much pleased with them as I—says she is a first-rate lady. He had made a bet with her, of a big apple, which she was to go home with him to receive if he lost, against a quart of buttermilk, his favorite drink, which he was to go to New Orleans to receive. He says the first thing he will do, when he gets home, will be to put up a barrel of his best apples and send to them.

Arrived at Guyandotte at 2 o'clock, in time for dinner. Here we wait for a boat to take us down the river. The Ohio is rising rapidly, and they may be expected every hour.

On looking back at the incidents of the last 5 days, there is much to cause reflection, as there has been to excite. The roads were good; the accommodations, on the whole, good; my health excellent; my spirits also good, as they generally are in a stage coach; our company has been delightful—but here I am, at the end of my journey (that is, across Virginia), without one of the companions that I set out with! What a picture of the wayfare of human life!

8 o'clock p.m.—The steamboat *Tuscumbia* came up and landed a number of passengers-among them Henry Brooke and a Mr. Tabb, of Richmond, on their return from the Northwest, where they had been to buy lands. They left Richmond, 11 August, by the way of New York and the Lakes. Brooke in fine spirits—speaks extravagantly of the land of Illinois and Indiana, but badly of the people—population vile.

10 o'clock—Steamboat *Coquette* came down, and Farish and our Kentucky companion Crisler both went off for Cincinnati. So, here I am, left alone, on the banks of the Ohio! I remain to see a Mr. Laidley, a lawyer, on Jerome's business, and to await the arrival of Hudgins, tomorrow.

Monday, October 12, 1835.

This tavern is kept by John G. Wright, a cousin of J. Metcalfe. He married a Miss Holloway, step-daughter of John Crump's sister, Mrs. H. of Staunton, who is now here, and recognized me. The barkeeper is * * * Fulton, a young man who once lived with W. R. Smith at the Orange mine. He also recognized me.

Saw Mr. Laidley—says the estate of Jerome, and of the company of which he is trustee, is worth nothing to the heirs. Jerome died much in debt. Had also incurred large debts for the company, on which judgments have been obtained, which will swallow the whole concern. He mortgaged the whole of the lands to one Garnier, for $80,000. This has been set aside in favor of other creditors, but is good as to J. and the company. A hopeless concern.

Hudgins and Miss Hardin arrived at 2 o'clock; also one of our English miners. Reports his sick companion, at Charleston, better; Mr. Wharton also mending. In stage, also, Wm. M. Peyton, bound for the Southwest, and a Mr. Archer, going to Mississippi, and Dr. Best, of Mississippi.

At 8 o'clock, the steamboat *Argo*, from Pittsburg, came to, at the wharf. She was full of goods and passengers, and our company determined to wait for the *Wave*, which is expected in a short time. At 10 o'clock the *Wave* arrived, and we embarked. Only 1 lady passenger and 6 gents. Bill at Guyandotte, $1.75; porter and boots, 12 ½ cts.

Tuesday, October 13th, 1835.

Found ourselves, this morning, lying at the wharf at Portsmouth, a town in Ohio, at the mouth of the Scioto, and at the termination of the Ohio and Erie Canal, 103 miles above Cincinnati, 62 miles from Guyandotte; 1,000 inhabitants; 45 miles from Chilicothe and 90 from Columbus, both on the Scioto. As the boat lay here until 1 o'clock, taking in freight, went over the town, and a short distance up the canal. Locks of fine masonry, freestone of a superior fineness, and of a brownish cream colour; much of the building in this place and Guyandotte also ornamented with the same, taken from the neighboring hills. Churches—Episcopal, Presbyterian and Methodist, one building. An extensive rolling and stilling steam mill and nail factory, owned by T. G. Gaylord. The *Argo* lying here, taking in freight. She went on at 10 o'clock. The *Fame*, from Pittsburg, stopt a few minutes, and went on. A number of canal boats from Cleveland, on Lake Erie, with goods from New York, lying here. Emigrants from all parts of the civilized world to be seen. Here is a number of Germans, from Saxony, coming on our boat as deck passengers. They have a great deal of baggage, and the leader is said to be rich—going to Indiana.

We passed a great number of emigrating parties in Virginia, most of them bound for Missouri. Where they had slaves, they were uniformly for Missouri; those that were without, were for Indiana, or some other State north of the Ohio. This remark is applicable to all that we passed west of Staunton. Those bound for the Southwest took a south course in the valley of the Shenandoah. It is a melancholy sight to see so many wealthy, intelligent and useful citizens leaving old Virginia, and many poor families, women and children, going to unknown parts, to encounter untried difficulties and hardships.

A merchant at Portsmouth told me the expense on goods from New York, by the Lakes and canal, was $2 per cwt.; time, generally * * * days. He thinks a railroad from Fredericksburg to Guyandotte or Sandy would be preferred—that there would be employment for as many cars as could be put on the road. Goods could be got from New York to Portsmouth in 8 or 9 days.

Had a pleasant passage down the Ohio; passed several little settlements that figure on the maps as towns, without any of the characteristics: Vanceburg, Ky., Manchester, Rockville, etc., in Ohio. From the hills about Rockville all the fine freestone is taken, which makes and ornaments so many of the buildings in Cincinnati.

Wednesday, October 14, 1835.

Arrived at Cincinnati in the night. Awakened in the morning (October 14) by the reveille of the little garrison at the U. S. Armory in New Port, a little town of about * * * inhabitants, in Kentucky, opposite to Cincinnati. On looking out, found ourselves surrounded by steamboats; the City of Cincinnati above us on the north, and the towns of New Port and Covington on the opposite side of the river, on the south. The morning was foggy, and none but the nearest objects could be distinctly seen.

Steamboat from Guyandotte to Cincinnati, $5; boots and porter, 37 ½ cts.

Found Farish at the Broadway Hotel, where Hudgins and self also took a room. H. had to cross the river to New Port, and take Miss Hardin to her friends, some distance in the country. Peyton stopt at the Cincinnati Hotel. I missed him and Farish and crossed the ferry to New Port by myself. Was attracted to a large manufacturing establishment, which I found to be owned by the Kentucky Manufacturing Co., of which Gov. James Taylor is President. His son-in-law, Mr. Harris, who is clerk to the concern, politely showed me over the whole. It is a large and splendid establishment. They make their own machinery. Of cotton bagging they can make 1650 yds. per day—present price, 35 to 36 cts. They also make Kentucky jeans, a mixture of wool and cotton, and card, spin and weave cotton. A great number of women and girls employed. Women's wages, 87 ½ cts. to $1.25 per day. Girls of 12 yrs. earn 50 to 62½ cts. One woman wove 600 yds. of bagging in 1 day and received a handsome dress as a premium for it. This establishment has been in operation but 3 yrs., and they contemplate enlarging it by the erection of another bagging house, to cost $100,000.

Thursday, October 15, 1835.

Took passage on board the steamboat *Algonquin*, bound for New Orleans, but to stop at Louisville. The advertisement said to sail at 8 o'clock, but did not get off until half past 10. The *Algonquin* is a beautiful new boat, built at Pittsburg, to ply between Pittsburg and New Orleans; this is her first trip. Accommodations fine, but not a large boat. Capt. Cadwallader, a very young and genteel-looking man.

Fare at Broadway Hotel, including the washing of 6 pieces	$1.52 ½
Porter	.25
Map of Illinois	.50

The banks of the Ohio increase in beauty as we descend. Numerous gentlemen's seats, of taste and elegance, adorn the banks, and villages also appear, but they generally present a decaying aspect. The introduction of steamboats has taken away their business, which was mostly with the boats.

At the north bend of the Ohio, passed the residence of Gen'l. Harrison, a modest but neat white wooden house, in the midst of a fine, thrifty-looking orchard.

Just below the mouth of Miami, passed Lawrenceburg, the first town on the Ohio, in the State of Indiana. Has some good buildings; guess some 500 inhabitants.

The steamboat *Genl. Pike*, with the U. S. mail, which left Cincinnati soon after us, has several times come close upon us, notwithstanding her stoppages with the mail. At half past 1 we stopt to wood, and she passed us. Captain said the two boats have the same power, viz., 160 lbs. to the inch, but the *Algonquin* has only 60 lbs. on today—machinery new, and don't like to force her—at which I am well pleased—slow and sure.

Passed the Village of Vevay, in Indiana, and Ghent, on the Kentucky side, just before night. Vevay is in Switzerland County, and was settled by emigrants from Switzerland, whose object was to found a colony of Vignerons. After night, rounded to at the Town of Madison, in Indiana. Among the passengers on board I recognized Dan'l Somers, an old schoolmate in Alexandria. He has been living, for 10 years, in New York, and is now going to reside in New Orleans. Was introduced by him to John R. Davis, of Vicksburg. On board Major Flournoy, from near Lexington, Ky., a fine specimen of the Kentuckian; a great resemblance of H. Clay. A Mr.

Silman, of Germany, on his travels; been through much of the United States; intelligent, modest, prepossessing. Several ladies going to Vicksburg. Fare to Louisville, $4. Distance, 132 miles from Cincinnati. Conversed with * * *, originally from Maine; has lived some years in Suffolk, Va.; the last 2 years in Louisiana. He settled, without purchasing, on U. S. lands, on an island in the Red River, below the Raft. Inhabitants French. His brother has bought in Texas. He does not like Texas; thinks the titles insecure and the Gov't unstable.

Friday, October 16, 1835.

This morning found ourselves at the wharf at Louisville, having arrived during the night. Was awakened at daybreak by the ringing of what I thought was a church bell; learned that it is a part of the police regulations of the place to ring this bell (court house bell) at day break every day. They call it the Day Bell. Walked about town early; not market day; no one in the market house. The *Algonquin* is advertised to sail today at 2 p.m.; resolved not to go today. Our party went to the Louisville Hotel, a large and well-kept house, by Drake & * * * .

Fell in with J. F. Scott, who is going down to Yellow Banks today. Hudgins and Farish resolved to go with him. I will stay to see some gentlemen here, and will overtake them at Yellow Banks, as Scott cannot leave there until Sunday or Monday, when we will all proceed down the river together.

Called to see Judge Browne, and was most affectionately received by him. Found at his office Mr. Minge and Mr. Adams, both of Virginia, on their way to Southwest. Judge laments having stopt at Louisville; has not met with encouragement; thinks he would have done better by going farther. Judge's family reside in country. Called to see Horace B. Hill, who is now one of the most prominent merchants of this place (H. B. Hill & Co.). Walter Cox lives with them. Was cordially received; invited to dine with him, a bachelor, and boards at Throckmorton's. After dinner took me, in his gig, a drive all around the city—to the race field, to the canal, where I saw the steamboats passing through, under the bridge. Afterwards we ascended to the top of a new hotel—the Galt House—just built, and had a beautiful panoramic view of the city. I now have a clear perception of the external features of the city and its locality. It is regular, and level to a fault; streets at right angles, and very little inequality in the surface, and that little they are making less.

Fell in with John B. Shepherd, who is living with * * * and gets $700 per annum, $200 of which he pays for board; also, with Robt. Hume, who is likewise here at a salary of $500. The barkeeper is a son of Bartlett Gutline, and gets $720 per annum. There are many Virginians here. Saw G. M. Long, who is married a second time, lives in Louisville, and went down in the steamboat *Boston* today. Also saw his brother, B. B. Long. Saw Mr. Arthur H. Wallace, of New Orleans, who very politely pressed me to call on him in New Orleans.

Dr. H. Hall is physician to the Hospital here—a good berth. Could not call to see him. John S. Allison is also doing business here—Allison & Anderson. Saw Wm. D. Payne; he has married a lady of wealth; lives out of the city; practices law.

Saturday, October 17, 1835.

The *Algonquin* did not steam yesterday. To start this morning at 9, positively. Got baggage on board after breakfast; on wharf met Mr. Carlin. The family just arrived in the *Patrick Henry*. She lay at Cincinnati while I was there, but did not then know they were on board. Mr. C. went with me to H. B. Hill & Co.; introduced him to Hill and to W. Cox. Hill gave me a letter to * * * Pescard, Esq., Vicksburg. Went on board *Patrick Henry* and saw Mrs. Chewning, Jane and little Sylvan. Mr. Chewning on shore; did not see him. Mrs. Carlin has been sick; looks badly. While thus occupied, the *Algonquin* started from the wharf and left me. But I knew she would be delayed in passing the canal and locks, and that I might there overtake her. Mr. Carlin walked with me down to the canal. The *Algonquin* did not get through the locks until half past 12 o'clock. Several large steamboats are lying below the falls, being refitted and repaired, viz., the *Mediterranean, Homer*, etc. They are of the largest class. The *Algonquin* is a second-rate boat. She measures 240 tons, and will carry 350 * * *.

The weather, for several days past, has been excessively warm. We have a large number of passengers, upwards of 100, and accommodations for only about half that number (some 60 or 70 passengers also on the deck below); only 28 berths in the cabin; 10 state-rooms of 2 berths each; and, I suppose, 8 or 10 berths in ladies' cabin. We have about 25 or 30 ladies and several children. I fear we shall be uncomfortably crowded. I have a good berth. We had a pleasant company from Cincinnati to Louisville—a number of ladies from Pittsburg. They had been very merry, and some of the ladies sang agreeably for an hour or two in the evening, in which I joined them.

While passing the locks, a passenger who had come on board at Louisville informed the captain that one of the lady passengers that he had brought down with him was not *comme il faut*, and the captain unceremoniously caused her to be put on shore, to return to the city as she could. Below the falls passed Shipping Port, on the Kentucky side, and New Albany, on the Indiana side. This day passed the mouth of the famous Salt River, where is a little town called West Point. A great number of wagons and emigrants here, with sheep, etc., crossing the river into Indiana. Passed, also, Buck Creek, Northampton, Indian Creek, etc., in Indiana, and Brandenburg, in Kentucky. The captain is very cautious, and lay to at night near * * * on the Indiana side. Hitherto I have enjoyed excellent health. I now feel a little indisposed-stomach disordered, and headache. A little feverish.

At the Birth of Texas

Sunday, October 18, 1835.

The boat got under way at daylight. I passed a restless and uncomfortable night, altho' I have a good berth, but rose at the usual hour, shaved, etc.; head and stomach very uncomfortable. Chewed rhubarb, and ate a slight breakfast—bad appetite. Weather drisley and uncomfortable; it had rained hard during the night. At 4 o'clock, came to at Owensboro, or Yellow Banks. Here we were joined by J. Scott, Hudgins and Farish. R. Triplett and A. T. Burnley came on board to see me, and expressed regret at my not stopping. Phil. Triplett had gone to Breckenridge Ct.; he lives in Owensboro. R. Triplett lives a few miles further up the river. Came to at night on the Kentucky shore. A number of wood-cutters came to the bank, and there was an encounter of wits, in the Kentucky boatman style, between them and the hands of our keel, and some of the deck passengers. One of them preached a sermon and made a mock prayer, with all the external demonstrations of earnest devotion. They also sung a mock hymn or two, with much vociferation. My indisposition continues; but has not yet made me omit a meal, although my appetite is bad. Stomach very squeamish and bowels a little affected—I hope by the rhubarb.

Monday, October 19, 1835.

Boat started, as usual, at early day. My uncomfortable feelings rather mitigated, but not removed. Head still sympathizes with the stomach, which I apprehend is offended with the dinner that I ate in Louisville. Besides eating of various things, drank one or two glasses of Madeira wine and one of Champagne. Regret that I did not take medicine as soon as I felt unwell. Today the steamboat *Patrick Henry*, which we left at Louisville, came down and passed us while we were at dinner. I went out and recognized Mrs. Chewning and Jane, and exchanged a wave of handkerchiefs with them. Did not see Mr. Ch., nor Mr. Carlin. Before night the *Patrick Henry* stopt to wood, and we passed them; another wave of handkerchiefs. Passed today, Evansville and Mt. Vernon, in Indiana, and the Wabash, which divides Indiana from Illinois, and Shawnee-town, one of the oldest towns on the river, but in a decaying state. Came to on the Illinois side, near the Cave in Rock. Went, with a number of passengers, to see the cave. It opens face to the river, with a beautiful elliptical arch, of about 30 or 40 feet span, and about the same pitch; runs back into the limestone rock, perhaps 100 feet or more; the floor rising regularly, by an easy ascent, until it meets the roof, which is nearly horizontal from front to rear. The banks around the mouth have a rugged and wild appearance, imperfectly seen, as they were, by candle and lamp light. These remarks are hastily made, without measurement, of course, and may be erroneous. My head, stomach and bowels still uncomfortable; no appetite. Ate no supper, and resolved to take physic in the morning. The steamboat *Patrick Henry,* passed us in the night, and expect to see her no more. Met today several steamboats coming up the river, among them the *Rob Roy*, which was at Cincinnati when we arrived there. She has since been to St. Louis and is now on her return. A great deal of gambling on board—no less than 6 card tables at one time. Some playing high. Most of the passengers gentlemen and men of business; some blacklegs, with hang-dog looks, fit only for the gallows. Made acquaintance with several gentlemen, among them a Capt. Cardoza, of New Orleans (introduced to him in Louisville), whose family is on board. He introduced me to a Mr. and Mrs. Satterfield, of Alexandria, La. She is young and pretty and newly married, and a Mr. * * *.

VOL. II

MEMO ON INSIDE OF FRONT COVER:

Col Jeremiah Strode.

David Imboden.

Northern mail arrives at Vicksburg, Sun., Wed., Fri.;
closes same days at 4 p.m., Southern mail arrives Mon., Th.,
Sat.; closes at 9 p.m.

Tuesday, October 20, 1835.

This morning my uncomfortable symptoms are much mitigated, and I shall not take physic. Fare is becoming very indifferent, and I eat but sparingly; made my breakfast on crackers, without butter, a small piece of fresh fish of the kind called here the Buffaloe—inferior to our Perch or Pan Rock. At half past 10 we grounded on a sand-bar, at the head of Cumberland Island. The largest part of the stream (two-thirds) and the main channel formerly ran on the Illinois side. Capt. Shreve threw a dam of rock across that, for the purpose of diverting the stream to the Kentucky side, believing that it would deepen the channel and open a direct route to the town of Smithland, at the mouth of Cumberland River, which now lies in sight. It has not had the desired effect, but has increased the difficulty of the navigation at this place While we lay here had the mortification to see the steamboat *Lady Byron*, which we had passed in the morning, pass us on one side, and the *Free Trader* on the other. About half past 2 o'clock, we got off by rocking, and rounded to at Smithland— a small town just below the mouth of Cumberland River, in Kentucky. Started at 4, and at lower point of Cumberland Island, passed the *Free Trader*, grounded on the bar, which we scraped, but passed over by putting all the passengers on board the keel, which is still lashed alongside. Gave three cheers. A fine afternoon. Sun set gloriously as we approached the mouth of Tennessee River, 12 miles below Cumberland. Rounded to at Paducah, a small town which has just sprung up below the mouth of Tennessee, in Kentucky. Went ashore and walked over the town; all new; stumps of the forest still standing in the streets. *Free Trader* has come up with us. Our fare has become intolerable. The steward execrable. Servants dirty, lubberly fellows. Here the captain discharged the steward and one waiter, and put a smart, active white man in his place. Supplies, of fowls, etc., pigs, etc., obtained. Left this place about dark, and soon after rounded to on the Illinois side, and stopt for the night. *Free Trader* still near us. A fine night. Comet visible; has traveled rapidly to the southwest. Lightning playing beautifully at a distance; said to be south. I have got confused, and cannot readily realise the points of the compass. Cincinnati is on the north, Louisville on the south side of the river; and the course of the boat changing with the devious course of the stream every minute. Without the aid of a compass it is impossible to tell the points of the heavens. Ate but little at supper; tea bad; appetite bad—nothing to tempt it. Our new steward has got good loaf bread, and milk for tea and coffee—the first of either that we have had on board. Gambling still going on to excess. Much disturbed in the night by some of the company who had been on shore gambling, and came in about 2 or 3 o'clock, very noisy. Unwell ever since I left Louisville. A Major Flournoy, who came with us from Cincinnati, complains of the same. He is sick every night. Hudgin also complains. Archer, of Petersburg, the same. A lady sick in the night (Mrs. Taylor); her son occupies berth under me. He was called up to her. Our company increases at every town. There are now 200 souls on board; upwards of 100 cabin passengers; great scuffling for mattresses. I am happy in having a good and very comfortable berth. Most of the gentlemen sleep in pants. I change as at home. Astonished to find in how small a compass I can arrange and perform all the economy of the toilet.

Wednesday, October 21, 1835.

Our boat and *Free Trader* both under steam at early day. A fine, bracing morning. Not entirely well, but up and on deck. No appetite for breakfast. Introduced to a Mr. Marshall of Natchez, a nephew of Geo. Rothrock; recalled his father and mother in Alexandria. He went South when young; has become very wealthy; married a rich Widow Ross; he is now between 35 and 40, handsome, plain and gentlemanly. Invited me to see him in Natchez, and proffered information about lands. Is president of the National Bank. Passed the Grand Chain, a ledge of rocks across the river, which has been really improved by Shreve; 10 ft. water on the bar. At 10 we entered the Great Mississippi, the Father of Waters. Disappointed again. Size not wider than the Ohio, and the two united do not add to the greatness of the stream in appearance. A general expression of disappointment from those who see it for the first time. Can see nothing of the country beyond the banks. One side presents a steep bank of 30 to 50 feet, the other a wide and dreary beach of sand—these alternating as the channel crosses from side to side, as it continually does. The background wood, wood, wood!

One o'clock, come to at Mill's Point, in Hickman County, Ky., the first settlement we have seen on the Mississippi. Only 2 or 3 stores, and about 1 dozen houses; 5 years old; houses built about 100 yards from first bank, which is frequently overflowed; growth of cypress prodigious. Country poor and sickly; grows nothing but corn. This can never be much of a place. Numerous flocks of geese seen on the shores. No human dwellings beyond the size of a wood-cutter's shanty. The water has a very muddy appearance, but is pleasant to the taste, and said to be more salubrious than that of the Ohio. The water of the Ohio always disagrees with Southern people. I hope that has been the cause of my bad feelings. Passed several remarkable bends, twists, islands and shoals in the river. Had to heave the lead, and slacken the speed of the boat. Another glorious day. The sun very warm about dinner time; turns cool towards night. The foliage becoming greener as we go down. No hard frosts here yet. Came to, for the night, soon after nightfall. I played drafts with the ladies. Mrs. Satterfield and myself vs. Mrs. Dunning and Mr. S. We beat them 3 games. Mr. S. a merchant of Alexandria, and lady, formerly of Edenton, N. C., just married—his wife pretty, modest, new. Ate no supper—stomach still weak.

Thursday, October 22, 1835.

Under steam again at early day. Passage a slow one; passengers grumble. Fare becoming every day worse. Much disturbed last night from the noise, blackguardism and profanity of a few passengers—evidently shameless and abandoned blacklegs. Conversed with Mr. Satterfield about Alexandria; says there is a fine opening for lawyers. C. died there this summer. Mr. Dunbar living there; might have made a fortune if he had kept sober. About 1,000 population; seat of Justice—not increasing. Inhabitants obliged to leave it from 3 to 4 months every summer—from June to October.

Weather is very warm today. Stopt at the Town of Randolph, situated on the 2nd Chickasaw Bluff, in Tipton County, Tennessee. A new place—great anticipations entertained by its inhabitants of its future growth. Marshall thinks it can never be great. Too far north for cotton. Make 1,000 to 1,200 lbs. per acre. Sometimes destroyed by frost—bit this fall. About 400 inhabitants, wretched looking, sit about the wharfs. Drunkenness, vice and cholera pictured in their faces. We are now opposite the northern part of Arkansas. Large flocks of wild geese, swans and pelicans to be seen on the sand flats.

At 10 o'clock, came to at Memphis, in Tennessee. A place of some note. Here many emigrants from Virginia and North Carolina cross into Arkansas. It is situated on a high bluff, very inconvenient to reach from the river. Went ashore for half an hour, to look at the town by star light. Appearance not favourable. Hudgins being very unwell and anxious to get on shore, and Scott having business there, they two and Farish left the boat, intending to wait here for the passing of some other boat. Having no business at Memphis, and desirous to stop at Helena, resolved to go on, and wait for my company at that place. Major Flournoy, of Lexington, Ky., who has purchased and settled near the mouth of White River, in Arkansas, also stops there; also Mr. Obediah Small, living on the West Francis, 15 miles from Helena. Mr. S. went from near Edenton, N. C.; lived in Alexandria 3 years. Says the lands, for 40 or 50 miles around him are very fine; all taken up, he thinks.

Friday, October 23rd, 1835.

The boat did not get far from Memphis before daylight. Weather warm. uncomfortable, threatening rain. I am quite well. Paid fare from Louisville to Helena, $20. Invited by Capt. Cardoza to visit him in New Orleans, and by Mr. Satterfield to visit him at Alexandria, and by Mr. Small to call at his home in Arkansas. Mr. S. says he knows Wm. R. Horner; that he is doing a good law business. About 10 o'clock a.m. passed the steamboat *Geo. Colyer*, from New Orleans to St. Louis; a fine, large looking boat.

Passengers on board whose names I have ascertained and shall recollect: Cooke, an engineer, and wife; Crog Ker, son of Dr. D. C. Ker; A. H. McClung, Jackson, who shot Allen; Dr. Carter, of Lexington, Ky.; J. H. Bush, Natchez, to whom I was introduced in Louisville; Dr. Merrill, of Natchez; Sam'l Toby, New Orleans; R. A. Striker, New Orleans; Dr. L. Bradford, Vicksburg; H. Connolly, Natchez; S. A. Meredeth, Natchez; Mrs. Graham Kerr, from Pittsburg to Vicksburg. At 11 o'clock, passed steamboat *Alert*, coming up; at 1 o'clock met and passed steamboat *Mountaineer*, coming up, a few miles from Helena. Arrived at Helena to dinner.

Helena, October 23, 1835.

Put up at the home of Col. Wm. B. R. Horner, who keeps a tavern and practices law. The court is held in his house, there being no court house built. Tavern a very common and rough house; no bar; a large additional building, by Mr. Sandford, Horner's brother-in-law. Horner and wife gone to Virginia, to Clarksburg, Harrison County, where his brother lives, and his son goes to school. In their absence the tavern is kept by their son-in-law, Dr. Wherry. Saw Mr. Sandford, who is building an addition to the tavern. Was kindly received by the family as a far-off connection. John Sandford is clerk of the court, and practices in trade with his brother-in-law, Hanks. Advertises as land agent. Introduced by Major Flournoy to the Register of the Land Office, Dr. Cabeen. The Receiver, Littleberry Hawkins, has just been displaced, account of default, but Flournoy, who was one of his sureties, says he will pay up, and save his sureties harmless. His successor, * * * Thompson, of Kentucky, has been appointed two months, and has not yet arrived. Mr. Chas. Morehead, Attorney-General of Kentucky, is here, entering land; also, a Mr. Gaston and Miles, from Chicot County. Met a land hunter named Isaac S. Boone, of Columbia, Chicot County, who says there is yet some good land, not entered, on Bayou Bartholomew and Bayou Mason. His price, $200 per section, for showing.

Saturday, October 24. 1835

The steamboat *Revenue* came down this evening, and I got on board, but finding my company had not come, I returned. Major Flournoy, Dr. Carter, Miles, Boone, Gaston, etc., went off.

Sunday, October 25, 1835.

Had a long conversation this morning with Peter G. Rives, of Helena, a hunter. His price for locating, one-fourth of the land. He says that much of the military bounty lands are very good. They lie between the Arkansas and St. Francis. A speculation may be made in bounty land warrants. The sales for taxes, which are made annually, are not good. The owner may always regain possession by paying the expenses and 50 per cent damages. The County Courts will set the sale aside. Morehead, Flournoy and Sandford all concur in saying that sheriffs' sales do not pass an indefeasable title, but a purchaser is always safe. If the land is reclaimed, he gets 50 per cent, and if never reclaimed, he will ultimately get a title by possession. If the original owner of the patent finds his land badly located, not arable, he can claim another patent, or float, to be laid on good land.

Lovely claims are floats for 320 acres, given to the former citizens of what was Lovely County, in lieu of the settlements which they had made there, and which were taken from them when that county was surveyed and sold. They now sell for about $1,000. Col. Ashly is accused of having forged some of those claims, and has been indicted for it.

At 1 o'clock the steamboat *Superior* came down. I had barely notice enough to get my baggage down to the skiff, the boat lying off. I was so certain that Scott, etc., were on board, that I made no inquiry until it was too late to retract. They were not there, and J. M. Bernard had gone ashore, expecting to see me. We passed on the bank without recognizing each other. Found on board Lt. L. Smith, on his way to Fort Jessup. Mrs. Dr. Kerr and family, and Major Anderson Miller, to whom I had been introduced in Louisville. He politely introduced me to several gentlemen, W. Nickolson, Mr. Worthington, Mr. Pearce, of New Orleans; the latter is the son-in-law of Dr. Kerr—a widower.

There was also on board a Col. Jeremiah Strode (he said his father and old John Strode, of Culpeper, were brothers' children.) He was an officer in Harrison's command at the Battle of the Thames. Major Miller recognized him. He is now a surveyor in the Mexican service, and living in Texas. Had some conversation with him respecting Texas. He thinks there is a negotiation on foot, if it has not been concluded, for the sale of that country to the enited States for $14,000,000, and if the United States does not buy it, that it will soon be independent, for that it is fast settling with people from the United States, who know their rights, and are determined to defend them; and they will never submit to Santa Anna's project of a central government. He has not been on the coast, and is not acquainted, personally, with the southern part, but says the middle region is highly salubrious, and very productive. He has surveyed a great deal, and acquired land. He offers a one-fourth league, 1107 acres, for $500, about 50 miles from Nacogdoches, on the upper waters of the Trinidad. He ran the line between the United States and Texas, and says the maps are all wrong—that the line strikes the Red River about the middle of the Raft, instead of at Pecan Point. He says that the titles derived from the Empresarios and confirmed by the government are indisputable. Mr. Pearce read his papers, and says that his title to the one-fourth league is clear; but it requires a settlement to be made on it by the 1st of June next. Major Miller thinks it will be a good speculation. I think better of Texas than I did heretofore.

Monday, October 26, 1835.

Monday afternoon, came to at Princeton, a new settlement of about seven or eight houses, in Washington County, Miss. Major Miller speaks highly of the country, and offers to show me the plantations on Lake Washington and Lake Jackson. I determined to stop and see the vicinity. This is the seat of justice, but as yet no court house nor other public building is erected. One store, one poor tavern, a postoffice, three doctors, two lawyers, one tailor, one blacksmith. Boat from Helena, $5.

Tuesday, October 27, 1835.

Major Miller politely borrowed a horse for me; rode with him to his mill on Lake Jackson. A steam engine of very simple construction, 25-horse power, designed to work an oil mill (cotton seed), a saw mill and a grist mill. The saw mill only in operation as yet. The oil mill will be at work in four weeks. He calculates to make 300 gallons of oil per day, saw 3,000 feet of plank, and grind * * * bushels of meal; oil worth * * *, plank $2 to $2.50 per hundred. He says the saw mill will make him $30 per day. Cost of engine, $1,500. Whole cost of machinery and houses, $14,000; capital invested in machinery, buildings, negroes, land, transportation, etc., $30,000. The saw mill may be made to pay 30 to 33 per cent on the whole investment. Seed costs nothing, except a small gratuity to the negroes for saving it. The timber grows in abundance all around—costs nothing but the hauling. The planters will thank him for taking it off. It grows so heavily that the labor of clearing their land is very great. It is a rich country, and will settle rapidly; he says it is the center of the cotton region, and his mills must be immensely profitable. He has made some improvements in the oil mill.

We went to several plantations on the Lake Washington, John A. Miller's, David Knox's, where we dined. Family agreeable. Mrs. Shelby, a widow planter, and sister of Mrs. Knox, present. Went on to Ward's. He lives in Louisville. Overseer sick. Crossed the lake to Dunbar's. Dunbar sick. Was recognized by an old negro, who told me his name was Peyton, and that he had belonged to General Minor's estate, in Fredericksburg. He is well pleased with his situation. Has lost his wife and two children. Went on to Fred Turnbull's. The best improved place I have seen. House neat but plain, furniture good, supper elegant. Mr. Turnbull out electioneering. Mrs. Turnbull, a fine woman, sensible, spirited, handsome, a good manager, a nullifier; has two sweet little daughters, Mary, about three years old, and Laura, under one year. Their first got drowned as they were coming to settle at this place; the second died here afterwards. Mrs. Turnbull generally stays here all summer. Went up to Kentucky this summer, but returned home on 15th of August. Has had no sickness in the white family, and only lost one black, and that an infant. The plantations around here have been very sickly this summer. Most of them have lost some slaves. Turnbull and Johnston have lost none, and that may be fairly ascribed to difference of treatment, good houses and good nursing. One planter in this county is said to have lost fifty slaves. Major Miller lost a blacksmith worth $3,000, and several of his white mechanics are now laid up sick. The crop of cotton is backward, and will be short, in consequence of a rainy season from June to August, which lasted forty-three days. This is also said to have caused the unusual sickness. Lake Washington is a beautiful sheet of water, fifteen miles long, one-half to one mile wide; believed to have been once the bed of the Mississippi. Only discovered about ten or twelve years ago. Thickly settled. Land on the lake valued at $100 per acre. That has been refused. A railroad will soon be built from the lake to Princeton, five miles, and connected with a bank at Princeton; proposed capital, $500,000. If that is granted, Princeton will become a flourishing and distinguished place. The neighborhood will be wealthy, intelligent and refined every way desirable. Lodged at Turnbull's. A Mr. Howell, a relation of the family, present. Saw for the first time a "Bowie knife." Five or six rose bushes in full bloom. Saw the pecan tree for the first time; ate pecans; saw numerous flocks of paraquets. The lake abounds in fish and wild fowl.

Much pleased with Mrs. Turnbull and all I see here. Major T. says she is all woman. Her maiden name was Fitzpatrick; not one of your fainting ladies. Children named Mary and Laura. Saw an evergreen in the yard, which she called *Laura Mundi* a good deal like myrtle, but much larger. Setts. 25 cents.

Wednesday, October 28, 1835.

Breakfasted at Turnbull's. Road up the lake on the eastern side. Saw the plantations of Major Ely, Dunbar, Julius Ward, the Johnstons, etc. Dined at Johnston's, with Morris, the overseer. Gave us the best milk I have drank since I left home. Crossed the swamp at the head of the lake; near getting swamped; horrible traveling. Tobacco growing spontaneously along the lake and in fence corners. Saw the palmetto growing for first time. Saw numerous canebrakes. Returned to Princeton about 2 o'clock, having left the Major at his mill. The steamboat *Iberia* went down yesterday, and the *Chariton* today, about one hour before my return. I must now wait for another, which I fear will not come speedily. I have, within the last two days, witnessed the operation of picking, ginning and packing cotton, on a large scale. I have seen fields of it growing, of two, three and four hundred acres. This, I suppose is a fair sample of cotton growing, and the life of a planter. It is worth the trip. Between 9 and 10 retired to bed. At half past 10 was roused with the notice that a boat was coming down. It proved to be the *Chief Justice Marshall.* I got on board, and found Dr. Cantwell, J. M. Macor, and Mr. Newman, of Orange, and Mr. Nalle; the latter about to settle at Vicksburg. He brought on my umbrella from Guyandotte, and gave it to me. Bill at Princeton, $1.62 ½.

Thursday, October 29, 1835.

Arrived at Vicksburg at 10 o'clock. Passed several very fine plantations above Vicksburg, with fine, neat looking houses.

Vicksburg beautifully situated on the Walnut Hills. High and rugged hills, much resembling old Stafford. Scott, Hudgins and Faust not yet arrived. Saw Dr. Jackson and the Camps, and Barnett, Chewning, the two Skinkers, Horace Carter, J. M. Smith, Ben Camp, Morehead, and Wm. Moss; was urged by the latter to accompany him to Clinton. Would have gone, but wish to await here the arrival of my party, who may be expected by every boat. Borrowed Dr. Crump's horse, and rode with Jackson all around the town, and to the old Spanish Fort, on the highest point of the Walnut Hills, about one mile above Vicksburg. The main city of Vicksburg exceedingly rugged and picturesque, buildings going up on every side. No letter from home. Fare from Princeton, $4. Porterage, 50 cents. Barber, 37 ½ cents.

Friday, October 30, 1835.

Bad night's rest; room dirty and dark; much annoyed by mosquitoes; no bars to my bed; got room changed. Chewning says all the good lands in Mississippi that are subject to entry have been taken up, except some in the interior, which are hard to find; must pay the hunters well for finding them.

Hudgins, Farish and Archer arrived about noon in steamboat *Rob Roy*. Hudgins has been sick with scarlet fever, and looks badly. Scott is at Helena. Passed the day in seeing the place, and making inquiries about lands and the country generally. Saw Dr. Bower, who lives at Providence, in Louisiana, about fifty miles from here. Dr. Barnett, who has formed a partnership with a physician near this place, Dr. Birchett, who is about to settle at Mt. Albon. R. Crump arrived from Natchez. He has formed a partnership with a Mr. Garmin, of this place, and will return to Virginia for his family immediately. This is a busy place. All appear to be intent on making money, and most of them are doing it, truly. The style of living is coarse; tavern dirty and mean, cooking bad, table poor and in bad taste.

Saturday, October 31, 1835.

Day raining and uncomfortable. A horse race; a military parade, two companies, blues and greys, very much like those in Fredericksburg. Inferior in appearance and description; only about twenty men each. After drill and marching through the town, drew up in front of the hotel, and were harangued by Jesse Bledsoe, drunk and foolish—disgusting. This man was once a United States Senator, a Judge, and a rival of H. Clay. Now a common sot, and none so poor as to do him reverence. Introduced to William Piscod, to whom delivered letter from H. Hill. Mr. Piscod is President of the Commercial and Railroad Bank, a new institution; is to have three branches, one at Vernon, one at Clinton, and one at Manchester; capital, $4,000,000.00. It is expected that a great addition will be made to the banking capital of this State at the next session of the Legislature. A real estate bank is spoken of, such as is in operation in Louisiana, of ten or twelve millions. The banking capital of the State is already twelve millions. If that be done, a large portion of the real estate will be bound to the bank.

Sunday, November 1, 1835.

The Sabbath but little observed in Vicksburg. The streets full of wagons, loading and unloading with cotton, whiskey, etc. Many of the stores open and doing an active business, particularly near the wharves; steamboat business knows no Sabbath. There are here two small houses for worship, one for Presbyterians, in which Rev. McRoberts officiates; not at home; said to be an indifferent preacher, with a very small congregation; one for Methodists, Judge Taylor generally preaches, absent now. A Dr. Baker, from the country, preached; affected, noisy, uninteresting. Text, first twelve verses of the *Sermon on the Mount.* He called it a discourse on human happiness; not at all edifying to me. Congregation a fair one; many of them strangers. All well dressed; decently attentive; singing bad. Four or five members added to church by letter from other churches. Judge Taylor is a relation of the Orange Taylors. He has just purchased a home in town, and will reside here. Took tea and spent the evening with Chewning. Mrs. Chewning not very pretty, but pleasant. Introduced to Dr. and Mrs. Pallen. He is a son of old Pallen, of Richmond, a Jew; she was a Miss Cochran, of Baltimore; recently married; only here a few weeks.

Monday, November 2nd, 1835.

John F. Scott came into our room this morning, while dressing. He came during the night in the *Mohawk*. Says Miss Horner is to be married this week to Mr. Wherry, brother of Dr. Wherry. I have determined to commence operations in land in this State. Engaged all day in copying maps, lent me by Dr. Macklin, Chewning and Scott. Paid for parchment, $1.50. This paper, 50 cents. A Mr. Lee, of Fauquier, is engaged in the same business. Introduced to Simon, the brother-in-law of Chewning, and to Dr. French, late of Norfolk, now of Virginia. Dogwood, elm, scrub hickory, plum, redbud, are evidences that the land is not subject to overflow; also magnolia and stiff, heavy cane. The following is a schedule of an outfit for going up the Sun Flower River to hunt lands, furnished by Dr. Macklin:

One barrel flour (saw out two staves, don't break the head), corn meal, 25 lbs. sugar, 15 lbs. coffee, 1 coffee mill, 1 coffee boiler, 6 tin cups, 6 tin plates, 4 butcher knives, 1 tent cloth, 1 buffalo robe, 6 blankets, 3 round wood boxes, 1 bushel potatoes, black pepper, red peper, salt, half bushel onions, 4 canvas hams, mustard, belt, hatchet, cane knife, half gallon vinegar, 1 gallon molasses, a skiff, 2 oarsmen, 2 compasses, 2 guns, cheese, pickles, skillet, pot, frying pan, tin bucket, tin pan, ammunition, 10 gallons whiskey, in a keg.

R. Crump, Archer and Dr. Birchet all set off for Virginia this afternoon, in the steamboat. Wrote by them hastily to my wife and to T. Green.

The general election takes place to-day and to-morrow throughout the State. Went to the court house to see how it went on. Much order and decorum, no quarrelling, little apparent excitement; have seen much more confusion and disorder at an election in Virginia. Vote by ballot. All the officers of the State election, from the Governor and Chief Justice down.

Hudgins will remain and operate here with me for the present. Farish will go on with Scott. Archer has made a conditional purchase of a plantation of * * * acres; part open, for $30,000, three payments of $10,000, first on 1st of March, 1836, the balance in one and two years thereafter, and he returned to Virginia for his slaves, without seeing the land. A friend of his who goes in with him knows the place. No letter from home.

Tuesday, November 3, 1835.

My birthday; forty-eight years old, and just beginning the world anew, and in a new world. All day at work copying maps. Can hear of great speculations in lands in all parts of the State. All classes engage in the purchase of lands as soon as they can make a little money by other means; and as yet, while lands are rising, all do well. The election closed to-day, quietly. It will be several days before the result, even for this county, can be known, as there are several precincts to be heard from. The contest has been mostly for persons. This place is decidedly anti-VanBuren, and Poindexter being a candidate for the senate, the election as to members of the assembly will turn on that. McNutt, a candidate for the State senate, is a Jackson man, but pledges himself to vote for Poindexter. He is believed to be elected. No letter from home.

Wednesday, November 4, 1835.

Rained incessantly all day. Copied maps as long as I could see. At night received a letter from my wife, written 11th and 13th, postmarked 14th; twenty-one and a half days coming. All well. This town is built on a succession of steep hills, formerly called the Walnut Hills, very much washed and full of ravines, and the cost of grading and filling up will be great; very badly done, so far; streets not paved, very few footways even paved; full of dirt and rubbish, very slippery, almost impassable. The poor cattle that have to pull the wagons and drays up hill suffer much, and are ill treated.

The tavern at which I lodge is badly kept, dirty, ill furnished and mean.

T. 16 R 3 W.–T. 16 R. 4 W.

T. 15 R. 3 W.–T. 15 R. 4 W.

T. 18 R. 6 W.–

Scott thinks are worth examination; also, T. 17 R. 3 W., south fraction.

Thursday, November 5, 1835.

Still raining all the forenoon; cleared up in afternoon, sun set clear; effect on the river very fine. Copied maps all day. In the afternoon Farish reported a fight in the street between two lawyers, Templeton and Guyon, rough roll and tumble in the mud; no deadly weapons used! I have not seen a fight, nor heard a quarrel approaching to a fight since I have been in the State. The quantity of liquors drank at the bar is immense.

Friday, November 6, 1835.

Morning cloudy, cleared up finely; weather delightful. A headache all day, otherwise well. Still engaged in copying maps. Scott very busy arranging his business to depart for Red River. Arranged our business so as to negotiate draft on T. Green at the Planter's Bank, drawn in favor of W. H. Simms, who will indorse without charging commission. Saw Paul Ward, of Culpeper, who has just arrived, going to settle a plantation for G. W. Latham. Saw also John Dean; says he now lives in * * * County, Miss., and is a planter.

Memorandum to obtain at Clinton a memorandum of the townships that have not been offered for sale, to be marked on the general map of the district.

An old raftsman, who had his camp on Bogue Phaliah, thinks there is some excellent land in T. 17 R. 6 W. Scott thinks the sections are 14, 15, 22, 23, 26, 27. Chewning recommends looking at 15/3, 15/* 16/3 and 16/4 W.

Saturday, November 7, 1835.

Intended to-day to go to Clinton to correct my maps and get some new ones. Met Dr. Barnet, who said he would to-morrow bring me Dr. Birchet's horse, which I might use until the Doctor returns from Virginia; determined to wait until to-morrow for the horse, rather than hire one at $2 per day, which is the regular price here. Sorry to lose the good weather, which is very fine to-day. Got some more maps, and continued copying until a late hour. Scott and Farish packed up, and are ready to start on a steamboat which goes to-morrow morning. Scott wrote letters until a late hour. The two uniform companies paraded again this evening, preparing for the reception of the Natchez Fencibles, which are to visit here on the 11th. Sorry that my trip to Clinton will prevent my seeing them. The two companies to-day turned out about fifty.

Sunday, November 8, 1835.

It rained heavily during the night, and in the morning everything was wet and uncomfortable. This is a very moist climate; everything feels wet, and grey mould, or mildew, is observable everywhere. Scott and Farish left us about 10 o'clock, in the steamboat *Walk-in-the-Water*. They will make a short stop in Natchez, and then proceed up Red River, Scott to settle a plantation on that river, and to return here in a few weeks. He is full of hope and pleasing anticipation, of course, in fine spirits. Poor Farish is rather low. His destination was for Texas. The state of the country there discourages him. He is in doubt and perplexity, and his way does not appear so attractive as at the outset, and his heart sinks as he breaks one by one his connection with kindred and friends. He appears to be a fine young man, amiable, and I trust will succeed.

The departure of our friends, a visit from Chewning, the bad weather, etc, prevented my going to church this forenoon. Went in the afternoon to the Presbyterian church. Minister, a Mr. McRoberts, an indifferent orator, but apparently pious and unaffected man. Congregation, twenty-six, and, what is uncommon, fewer women than men, being but six to twenty. Text: "We are ambassadors from God; and pray you in Christ's stead, be ye reconciled to God." After tea visited Mrs. Chewning. Read and wrote until 11 o'clock. Barnett has not come with the horse.

Monday, November 9, 1835.

A fine day. Barnett not yet come, and I am disappointed in going to Clinton to-day. Continue copying maps. About 11 o'clock steamboat * * * came up, with the Natchez Fencibles on board; come to pay a visit to the Volunteers of Vicksburg. They were invited for the 11th, and their arrival to-day was unexpected, and some delay took place in getting the Vicksburg companies under arms to receive them. They landed between 12 and 1 o'clock, and after exchanging salutes, both firing and marching, were escorted by the Vicksburg companies to the Vicksburg Hotel, where apartments were provided for them, at the expense of the Vicksburg Volunteers. Their arrival seems to have produced a relaxation among many of the citizens, who indulged freely in drinking. The tavern is a scene of riotous mirth, drunkenness and noise. The military, however, behaved very well. Before night the Fencibles paraded for drill, and marched to the court house yard. Commanded by Capt. Quitman, a lawyer of high standing, formerly chancellor of the State. Appears to be a man of firmness, and a gentleman, but not a good drill officer; voice and manner both bad. Lt. Loria, smart, active, soldierly, better drill officer than the Captain. Capt. Guyon, of the Vicksburg Volunteers, did not turn out; said to be sick; the men say he neglects the company, and seldom drills it. Commanded by Lt. BrunGaard, a good officer; Dr. Jackson, Sec. Lt. The rifle corps commanded by Capt. Bobb. A number of young ladies came up from Natchez, and at night they had a little dance in the tavern parlor, on the carpet. The Fencibles have a small black band, who play pretty well, but lack instruments. The Vicksburg companies also have a band, composed of a father and three sons, boys named Tetlow; very indifferent. The blacks make excellent music for the ball room. Ladies dance prettily, but are not handsome.

MEMO.—Request Peter to reserve for me all that remains of the ream of thin bank paper in his Uncle Robert's store.

Barnett has arrived with the horse and I will go to Clinton to-morrow.

Tuesday, November 10, 1835.

Engaged all the morning negotiating with an old raftsman, who has engaged to show us lands subject to entry. We are to equip and accompany him to the woods. All the afternoon it rained heavily, so could not go to Clinton. Dined by invitation with the Volunteers and Fencibles, at 4 o'clock p.m., at the exchange. Dinner given by former to the latter. The only others present in citizens' dress besides myself were Mr. Prentiss, the member-elect from Vicksburg, Major McNiel, and Mr. Angus McNiel, of Natchez. Capt. Quitman presided, contrary to all rule. Angus McNiel was the former partner of J. J. Chewning, "Wilkinson, McNiel & Co.," that failed about * * * ago. The concern is now nearly wound up, and will come out whole, and something to spare. He is a large landholder in Texas. Has travelled all over Texas, and is said to know more of the country than any other person in this State. A very intelligent man, but visionary. Major McNiel says his views are at least twenty-five years in advance of the state of things.

The military extremely boisterous, but great good feeling seems to prevail. Prentiss was toaster; made a speech; interrupted by the arrival of a reinforcement of Fencibles, who have just arrived in another boat. He waited until they were seated, and then went on with his speech. Declamatory, vehement—*ad captandum*—bad taste. Reputed a man of first rate talents. Think him overrated. Dining party broke up by command of the Captain about 6 o'clock. Returned to their quarters in order. House crowded. Major McNiel slept in our room. He and I sat up talking until 2 o'clock.

MEMO ON BACK INSIDE COVER:

MEMO. Given by T. Green—At Nacogdoches get all the information about Texas lands, in what grants the titles are best, and where are the most desirable lands, headrights and 11-league grants. Do not be in too great a hurry, but examine well, and be very particular. See the information of Thompson about the purchase of lands. Keep a diary. Write T. G. frequently, with a particular description of each tract of land, both before and after a purchase, with the field notes.

Route received by T. G.—Down the Nueces and Snow Rivers, and on the Trinity, then on towards Austin's Colony, and Robbinson's and Williams' grant.

VOL. III

MEMO ON INSIDE FRONT COVER:

Articles taken to the swamp, November 16, 1835.

Three pairs socks, 1 cotton close shirt, 1 flannel shirt, 2 linen shirts, 1 vest, 1 pair cloth pants, 1 pair cotton drawers, 1 pair flannel drawers, 6 collars, pencil, writing materials, 1 loaf sugar, pepper, coffee, salt, 40 lbs. ship bread, 1 ham, bacon, 1 black stock, comb, tooth brush, 3 pocket handkerchiefs, 2 blankets, 1 horse blanket, 1 towel, 1 tin cup, 1 tin pan, 1 frying pan, 1 hobble, man saddle, bridle, martingale, 1 pocket compass, 1 spoon, 1 cane knife, 1 pocket knife, 1 pistol, 1 double-barreled gun, India rubber coat, pants and cap, 1 casinet jacket, 1 watch, 2 pairs saddle bags, 1 pair boots, 1 pair shoes.

Wednesday, November 11, 1835.

Fine, clear morning; wind from northwest, and cold. Very like our Virginia weather. Preparing for Clinton. Our raftsman gave us some information which determined me to enter some land at once. This delayed my departure until half past 2 o'clock. This is the great day with the military; they have been out all the morning, and their songs and music are ringing in my ears. I am sorry to leave them, but business must be attended to. They are to have a ball tonight, and as I should not be at it, I shall escape the noise and confusion.

Rode twelve miles to Cowan's, on the road to Clinton, where I slept. A Mr. Samuel L. Moore, of Hinds County, and a Mr. Campbell, of Madison, also slept there; decent people. Mrs. Cowan is a little deranged at times, but now tolerably rational. She prepared supper and ate at table, but looks and talks silly. Had a brother concerned with the Vicksburg gamblers, which is said to have aggravated what was before an unsettled state of mind. Coarse fare; $1.50.

Thursday, November 12, 1835.

Started after an early breakfast, in company with Mr. Moore, who I find to be a sensible and moral man. Suspected him to be pious, but not a word dropt from him of cant. He lives five miles from Clinton, and as we rode slowly it was 2 o'clock when we reached his house. Gave me a cordial invitation to "light and take dinner," which, being desirous to see as much as possible of life here, I accepted. Table coarsely and frugally spread, but as he said a very devout and appropriate grace, I ventured to name the subject of religion to him, and he informed me he was a Methodist. The establishment is exceedingly coarse and rough, yet he owns several tracts of land, two of which he wishes to sell. He has four hearty looking children. He is only twenty-nine years old. I took him for forty. He supposed I was less than forty; I am forty-eight. One of his tracts in Madison County, * * * acres, he offers at $5, and a quarter section adjoining he says may be entered at $1.25; for a tract adjoining his residence of 320 acres he asks $17, one-third cash, balance in one and two years.

Arrived at Clinton about 4 o'clock. Went directly to land office, and entered two and one-eighth sections. Found here Mr. A. L. Dabney and his relation. He has determined to settle in Raymond and practice law, but has not yet determined where to settle his lands. Raymond is the seat of justice for Hinds County.

Jackson, Friday, November 13, 1835.

Not being able to get the maps that I wished at the land office promptly, and finding two gents yesterday evening who were going to ,Jackson, I determined to ride here to see the place. Distance from Clinton, 10 miles. Arrived here about sunset; walked over the place. This morning my travelling companions, who are a Major Riddle and a Capt. Rhea, of Knoxville, Tenn., pursued their journey to Madisonville, and I spent a few hours looking about the place, and making inquiries. Site a bad one. The Pearl River comes within one-fourth mile of the town, but is not navigable, except for flat boats, or in dugouts; river narrow, shallow and crooked. A small steamboat has been up this high, but none attempt to run regularly. The river is now up twenty feet, and the water backs over the low ground to within one or two hundred yards of the town. A new State house has been commenced, basement only put up, and the work stopt; said to be badly done; architect dismissed. The probability is, it will never be finished. The situation is a bad one, on sloping ground, overlooked by a tavern not 100 yards off. The site of the town is swampy, and must be sickly. A change of parties, which is just taking place, will probably transfer the government to Clinton, or elsewhere. Clinton is high, dry, and more healthy; I should think, in all respects, more eligible than Jackson. Population of Jackson, * * *; of Clinton, 1,500. Found in the county office a young man named John Murdaugh, who is from Williamsburg, a cousin of G. W. Bassett and of J. W. Murdaugh.

Clinton, Saturday, November 14, 1835.

Left Jackson at 12 o'clock yesterday; called to see Wm. Morson, who lives about two miles from Clinton. Not at home; gone to seek for a place to purchase. He only rents this at $1,000. Chinn, the overseer, received me very joyfully, and gave me a good dinner, a thing seldom met with in Mississippi. The negroes, also, that I met, knew me, and seemed delighted to see me. Returned to Clinton and adjusted my business at the land office. It was then too late to proceed on towards Vicksburg, as I had intended. I therefore called on Capt. Geo. House, to whom I had a letter of introduction from Chewning. He was absent when 1 arrived in Clinton, having gone to Vicksburg. I passed him on the road. He had now just returned from drilling the Clinton Guards, of which he is Captain. He is the partner of Mr. Geo. Bierne, the son of Col. Bierne, of the Vicksburg senate, in a store at Clinton. Very polite and agreeable. Sat with him an hour.

At supper, introduced by Dabney to Mr. Rives, a lawyer of Clinton, formerly of Virginia, who, Dabney said, knows more of Virginia and Virginians than any man in the State. Lodged at the Spring Hotel, a dirty house, with vile bedding, and extortionate charges, $3 per day for man and horse. Broke crystal of my watch, and was charged $1 for a very common one.

Tavern bill at Clinton	$4.50
Tavern bill at Jackson	4.00
Perry at Big Black	2.25
Apples and hostler	.25
Tavern bill at Cowan's	1.50
Tavern bill at Peebles, B. and horse	.75
Ferry, recrossing Big Black	.12 ½
Crystal to watch	1.00
Six new township maps	9.00
Examining and correcting 30 maps	5.00
Two and one-eighth sections land, * * * acres, at $1.25	1,700.65

Saw a man making tar. He could get none in Clinton to put on the axletree of his wagon, so he split up some pine knots in an old yellow pine plank, and placed them on a board two feet square, which had been previously scooped, and a drip made on one side, in the manner of a cider press. Over these he placed a common iron pot, and having stopt up with dirt all the apertures around, except a small one at the drip, he built a fire over the pot, and the heat distilled the turpentine from the pine knots, which ran out in the shape of tar. The fixture was on the ground. He dug a little pit under the drip deep enough to admit his tar bucket, in which he caught the tar as it ran. By this simple method he obtained tar enough for his wheels.

Sunday, November 15, 1835.

Left Clinton at quarter before 7 o'clock. Found a $10 note in the road. Breakfasted at Peebles', nine miles from Clinton, on the Ridge Road. Mr. Peebles has a fine crop of cotton. Met here Dr. Erskine and a Mr. * * * from Huntsville, Ala., who had started to go to Red River on horseback, but could not cross the swamps in Louisiana, and so abandoned the trip; now on their way back. Peebles and family, formerly of Huntsville. Mrs. Peebles knew T. B. Adams, who she says now lives in Copiah County, Miss. She does not like Mississippi. Says it is a fine place to make money in, but for nothing else. Passed a house where a poor negro was undergoing an unmerciful flogging. I think I must have heard forty or fifty lashes, severely laid on. Just here was overtaken by Ira E. Williams, who is clerk in the Receiver's office at Clinton, who rode with me several hours. Offered to enter land for me. Memo. to see him hereafter. He said he had no doubt the entry I made was a very fine one; but he thought a good deal entered by J. F. Scott was bad. Invited me to go with him to a widow lady's, Mrs. Wren, where he would pass the night. I would have done so, but had carelessly left my spurs at Cowan's on Wednesday night, and had to go by for them. I also left my leggings at Clinton. My umbrella I had left at Charleston, Va.; this I have recovered. My great-coat I left at Helena. This I have not recovered, and fear I never shall. My spurs I have got. Minus, great-coat and leggings.

Overtaken by night and a storm of rain, and put into Hensley's, a small, mean, house, five miles from Vicksburg. Very much crowded. I got a bed to myself in a small shed room, in which was a man beastly drunk, a planter of the neighborhood, who had just sent 80 bags of cotton to Natchez, and had as much more to send. The poor wretch suffered much in the night for water, which the landlord's son gave him, and much more from the agony of mind which his debauch had brought on; but he did not greatly disturb me. Some wagoners who were encamped near the house, and came in to get supper, had their wagons robbed while they were in the house. Negroes blamed, of course, and, I fear, some whipt. Bill, $1; hostler, 12 ½ cents.

Monday, November 16, 1835.

Arrived at Vicksburg to breakfast. Found Hudgins uneasy at my protracted stay. He is nearly ready to start to the swamp. I consumed the day in arranging my clothes, and making other preparations for the trip.

Found on my return a letter from my wife, which was written on the 18th and 19th of October, postmarked 20th. Hudgins says it arrived the evening that I left here for Clinton, which was the 11th, so the letter was on the road twenty-two days.

Neglected yesterday to note my singular luck, in finding a $10 note lying in the road a few miles from Clinton. It is of the "Grand Gulf Rail Road & Banking Company," Let. A, No. 827, May 21, 1835. J. C. Callender, Cashier; B. Hughes, president.

On the road from Clinton fell in with a Mr. Peebles, who lives in Attacapas; a sugar planter, just taking out a young wife. Says the sugar crops have been bad for last five years. Plenty of fine prairie lands yet to be entered, not taken owing to the scarcity of timber.

MEMO. from Col. Anderson of New Orleans—Just below Norconna lies Horn Lake, which connects with it by a slough, and there is a series of lakes—a most beautiful country.

Tuesday, November 17, 1835.

It rained all night last night, but having cleared up to-day, we continued our preparations, and started from Vicksburg about 3 o'clock. Still cloudy and threatening rain. Overtaken by dark, and our guide mistaking his way, we got into the plantation of Dr. Geo. Smith, formerly of Greenville County, Virginia. The Doctor not at home. Politely received by his wife, who was a Miss Avery. In a little time the Doctor returned from Vicksburg, and with him a Mr. Davis, a planter and neighbor. Our reception was hospitable and kind. House plain and small, fare and lodging excellent.

Wednesday, November 18, 1835.

It rained hard all night, and continued to rain at intervals all day, and at the Doctor's pressing instance we remained all day. The Doctor gave over the practice of medicine when he became a planter. Occupies a very hilly plantation. Makes about 150 bags cotton. This year will not make more than 75. Has a fine vegetable garden, and has the best fare that I have seen in Mississippi, except at F. Turnbull's, on Lake Washington, where the living was much the same. Here I ate the first salt herring that I have seen in Mississippi. The Doctor says he has a plenty of fine fish in a lake near to him, which connects with the Yazoo.

Thursday, November 19, 1835.

This morning the rain has ceased, but the weather is still uncertain. The Doctor pressed us to stay and take a hunt with him; we, however, thought we had imposed long enough on his kindness, and being anxious to get on, prepared to depart. After breakfast, Mr. Davis rode up and said a deer had just crossed the road before him. The Doctor, like a keen sportsman, called his dogs, and prepared for a hunt. We rode together about a mile to where the deer crossed the road, and put his dogs on the trail. He then told me if I was disposed to kill a deer, to take the rifle and stand, and the deer would certainly cross there; but, not wishing to stop, I declined, and

passed over a knoll, so as to be out of sight, and left the Doctor at the stand. In a few minutes he fired. The poor deer rose
a steep hill, followed by a single hound bitch, and fell dead
not fifty yards from where I was, having run about 100 yards
after it was shot. The other dogs had all taken the back track;
the bitch was the only one that followed the deer. She kept up
a sharp cry until it fell, and immediately ceased, and stood
by it. The Doctor, in a minute, came running up in search of
his victim. The place he knew with wonderful accuracy, by
the course it ran and by the cessation in the cry of the bitch.
It proved to be a fine buck. He insisted on our taking two
quarters along with us, but we were already overpacked, and
declined it. We left him, deeply impressed with the kindness
and hospitality of himself and wife.

Crossed the country and gained the Ridge Road. Land
very broken and unpromising, but, like Dr. Smith's hillside,
astonishingly productive. Stopt at night at Mrs. Chambers', a
filthy place; poor supper, poor house and mean beds, a vile,
filthy stable, the yard of which was ankle deep with mud; and
yet her son, a pert, forward puppy, bragged of their owning
fifty negroes, and having 400 acres of land in cultivation, and
that he could make as much money as he pleased, and lie
late in bed (he was the last to rise in the house); said there
was nothing to be made by rising early. And for this dirt and
meanness we were charged $1.25 each for supper, lodging and
horse. Annoyed all night with noisy negroes, dogs, bleating
calves, a cow with a bell on, which took a special fancy to the
house, cock crowing, landlady coughing, and a loud belled
clock, stuck on the wall just over our bed, which I heard toll
every hour through the night, except the hour of one.

Friday, November 20, 1835.

Left Mrs. Chambers' at sunrise, unrefreshed and out of
humor. Rode until 11 o'clock before we could get food for

our horses or ourselves, and then had to intreat for both, at a dirty cabin in the woods, the keeper of which is a Methodist and a Thompsonian doctor. He was from home, and his wife, a very slattern in dress and person, got our breakfast, which consisted of badly fried pork and eggs, bad coffee, good, coarse corn bread and milk. Ate heartily, although the table cloth was so foul that under other circumstances it would have spoilt my meal.

Missed our way, which we did not discover until within two miles of Sartartia; turned back, and regained the Ridge Road. This threw us back seven miles in our day's journey. Stopt at a Mr. Stamply's for the night. Found here Mr. Steptoe Picket, formerly of F* * * City, Va., now living in Alabama, near Huntsville. He is on his return home, accompanied by a young gent named Geo. Wilkinson, of Huntsville. Informed me that Dr. Clarkson and Arthur Payne had purchased on the road that we were travelling, and that we should pass by the Doctor's door. Here we had a pretty good supper and breakfast, but bad lodging. The house was crowded, and Hudgins and myself slept on the floor, very cold and comfortless. Poor house, open and shabby; fare $1.25 for supper, lodging, horse and breakfast, which is a meal for myself and horse better than at the rich Widow Chambers'.

Saturday, November 21, 1835.

Left Stamply's after an early breakfast. The wind, which has for many days blown from the south and produced warm rains, last evening chopped around to north, and now threatened a steady north or northeast storm, cold, damp and cheerless. Drew on an India rubber suit, and determined to reach Manchester tonight. Passed several emigrating parties, some of them from this State, having sold out their farms here and going to Red River and to Texas. One with whom I conversed, whose name was McKane, had a wife and five children along. He was originally from Tennessee; had gone to Texas last winter; spent three months there; purchased land in Robinson's Colony, on the Brazos; returned, sold his land in Tennessee at $9 per acre, and was now on his way out; would cross the Mississippi at Rodney and the Red River at Alexandria. He says the cost of land in Texas is about $95 per square league from the Empresarios, and a fee to some one to find out a good location brings the whole cost to about $100 per league. He was in high spirits, and spoke in glowing terms of the richness, salubrity and beauty of the country.

A little further on, came to Dr. Clarkson's settlement; found him hard at work putting up buildings for his negroes. He is much pleased with his purchase; has been lucky; has 1,200 acres, which he purchased of several persons at an average of $9; some cost him $20. Arthur Payne has bought about two or three miles from him, on the south, at $12 per acre. Stopping to talk with McKane and with Clarkson, I fell behind, and had to ride briskly to overtake Hudgins and our guide, whom I found waiting for me at Cullen's, a public house six miles from Manchester. It was now half past 3 o'clock, raining, with every prospect of a bad evening. The accommodations in Manchester said to be bad, and we determined to rest here for the night. Good accommodations, in a plain, coarse way. Joined after dark by a Mr. Jno. Speed, from Copiah County, who has recently sold a farm that he had improved, for $15 per acre, and is come here to look out for another place. Says lands here are all too high, and repents having sold; says if he had it back he would not sell for $45. Is acquainted with T. B. Adams and all his family; speaks highly of Adams. (T. B. Adams bought his place for a Dr. Shepherd, of Richmond, Va.)

Sunday, November 22nd, 1835.

It rained all day, and we determined not to go on. In the course of the day Dr. Clarkson and Arthur Payne called.

Cullen is a native of Snow Hill, in Maryland, and his wife of Louisa County, Virginia. He first moved to Alabama and began planting. Sold out to Steptoe Picket, and came to this place about five years ago. Since then he says the whole settlement has changed owners except one other and himself. The place that Dr. Clarkson has bought has been bought and sold four times in five years, the Doctor being the fourth. He has refused $25 per acre for the place where he lives. It was offered by A. Payne.

Monday, November 23, 1835.

Left Cullen's after breakfast, and we stopt in Manchester, at a tavern kept by a Frenchman, named Parisat, who, a few years ago, was riding in the stage to Clinton. The horses ran down a hill pretty fast, and he fancied they were running away, and leaped out, hurt his ankle, and the Doctor, who was called to him, cut off his foot. He goes on crutches, and keeps a very poor tavern; charges $3 per day for man and horse. The roads are horribly bad from the recent rains, and everybody warns us against the swamps; they say they are impassable; that all the land hunters have come out. This is discouraging, and we forebore making the attempt to-day. Like my usual bad luck, left my bunch of keys at Cullen's; had to ride back for them, and stayed there all night; fare, $1.25.

Tuesday, November 24, 1835.

Returned to Manchester after breakfast. Cullen came with me; also Mr. Speed, who is on a negotiation for a plantation and negroes with Dr. Dorsey and a Mr. Hughes, of Manchester, 640 acres, fourteen negroes; offered for $30,000, one-third cash; balance in two equal annual payments. I think Speed seems disposed to purchase, but wishes some modification of the payments.

The weather being fair and cold, and a likelihood of some days of fair weather, determined to attempt to cross the swamps and reach our land. There is no ferry over the Yazoo at this place, but learning that a settler in the swamp had, a few days before, passed over some negroes by means of a flat boat, kept at a saw mill a short distance above town, we applied for the same, and by a little coaxing succeeded in being put across about 3 o'clock in the afternoon, for which they charged us $1.50; gave the black oarsman 25 cents. Bill at Parisat's, $10.

NOTE—Manchester is a new place, of about forty or fifty houses, built on a small prairie flat, touching a bend of the Yazoo. It is a dirty and uncomfortable place; a place of considerable trade. Several large stores, a branch of the Planter's Bank. A great deal of cotton shipped here; very sickly; two Indian mounds here, the first that I ever personally saw; one about twenty or twenty-five feet high, and about thirty feet across; the other about half the size. They are built on the flat, about 100 yards from the river, and above overflow. There are high hills within one-fourth mile from them. Several that I saw a few miles above Vicksburg were similarly situated. At this place resides John Head, the son of Emanuel Head, who is doing well as a house joiner. E. Head, the father, is also here now, and intends coming out to live. He told me he has made an arrangement by which he will go to planting in connection with a landholder, who puts in as many hands as Head can put in, and the land and one additional hand, against Head's services as overseer, and divide profits equally.

After crossing the Yazoo we entered upon an unbeaten swamp road, marked only by the recent passage of wagon wheels, and an opening large enough for a wagon. The greater part of the way half-leg-deep in mud and water; uncertain where we should lodge. We passed a deserted cabin, almost roofless, and a suggestion was made for the occupation of it for the night, but went ahead in hopes of better quarters. At dusk came to an opening and a house. Informed by a negro that it was just taken possession of by Mr. White, from South Carolina. Rode up and asked for quarters; politely received, and every attention and comfort rendered that his situation would admit of. Arrived and took possession only last Thursday; bought 2,500 acres, 1,800 of which is warranted above overflow; $40,000, $10,000 in hand, $15,000 in 1838, $15,000 in 1839. Brought 100 negroes, large and small. He is from Columbia, S.C. (nullifier), named Jos. J. B. White; his nephew, who is with him, Augustus B. Faust; overseer, Gairry. He is an intelligent, well bred gentleman; supplied me with a pair of leggings in lieu of those I left in Clinton, and a box of Lunettes, or matches. Broached politics; regretted that we were not nullifiers. Has a portrait of Warren, of South Carolina, painted by his brother, whom he says has some celebrity as a painter; also, a portrait of his father, and of a child, which, I think he said, was the father of Mr. Faust. He says that in five years he thinks two-thirds of the negroes of South Carolina will be moved off to this or some other Southern State. The average yield of the cotton lands of South Carolina not more than 100 pounds, ginned, to the acre. His coming will start several other families. Dr. Lee, on Silver Creek, and Mr. Wm. H. Taylor, same place, are from South Carolina; they will start some of their friends also, and probably many will follow them into the Mississippi bottom.

Wednesday, November 25, 1835.

Left Mr. White's after an early breakfast. Our road lay all day through the Yazoo swamp; very low and wet; almost always over the horses' feet in mud; some deep sloughs; passed some very heavy cane brakes. In the middle of the swamp met Dr. Lee and his overseer riding (learned afterwards that he and his overseer had quarrelled, and the overseer had just left the plantation). He is going to Manchester to take steamboat for Vicksburg, to charter a boat to come up for his cotton. A negro was walking with him to bring back his horse. His plantation lies exactly in our path; did not ask us to call, but told us he had left a skiff on this side of Panther Creek, which we might use if we would direct one of his slaves to come to-morrow and bring it back to the east side, for the use of the negro who accompanied him, and who would return with the horse. At Panther Creek we found the skiff, by means of which we passed it dry, and swam the horses. Creek about 100 feet wide, and now full and rapid. Just before night came to Lee's plantation. Inquired for other houses, as we could not stop here. Informed that a Mr. Browner had a plantation two miles lower down the creek. I knew at once that this was my friend, H. B., of Port Tobacco, who settled a plantation last winter, I had not been able before to ascertain where. Resolved to go there, but our guide said it would put us four miles out of our way, and there was another plantation across the creek, where we once more determined to ask quarter. Again in luck; this plantation is owned by Mr. Hughes, last of the Br. Pl. Bank, Manchester. His overseer, Mr. Geo. Callahan, received us politely, and entertained us kindly in a plain bachelor's style. Found here also Mr. Browne, the nephew of H. Browne, who is his overseer. Said his uncle is expected here daily.

Thursday, November 26, 1835.

Left Callahan's after breakfast. His (Hughes') plantation is in T 12 R 4; also Lee's and Brawner's (Brawner bought of Lee). After a ride along the side of the creek, or bayou, of about four hours, came to where our guide had formerly encamped, and at his suggestion halted to examine some land in T 13 R. 3, which he had partially examined some months ago. Pitched our tent, hobbled the horses, and turned them loose. Our guide, who is a kind of Leather Stocking, rides a small, thickset Indian pony, which was unmercifully loaded, and the two make a singular and grotesque appearance. Pony was belled, by which we could always tell when they were near. After taking a snack, crossed the creek, and proceeded through the woods to find the lines and see the lands. Much swamp and cane; had to wade a good deal, and in one place got over my boot tops in a slough. Although a trace had been cut as far as we went, it was laborious travelling, and I returned to camp at night, wet, tired and dispirited, dreading the consequences to my health. Washed and dried my feet by the fire, and changed stockings and put on shoes, and did not take cold. Just behind our camp is a small lake or pond, in which Hudgins shot a duck, which we cooked for supper.

Friday, November 27, 1835.

A rain came on last night, which has made the woods and cane so wet that we would not venture in them to-day. Showery all day. I made an unsuccessful hunt on the creek. Shot once and missed. Hudgins killed another duck. He has fired five times and only killed two. Wrote a little in journal, the first chance I have had since last Sunday, at Cullen's.

Saturday, November 28, 1835.

A fine, clear day, white frost. All hands went into the woods. We were seven hours out; constant exertion in clambering through cane brakes, entangled with briars, vines, etc., and wading through sloughs. The general character of the land is good; a succession of cane brakes, holly groves and open woods, where the ground is generally covered with water, sometimes knee-deep. The fatigue consequent on such laborious exertion is excessive. Feet wet again. I could not walk through the cane with the rapidity of the others, and not wishing to retard them, I started to return on the trace, while they designed, after pursuing the line to a corner, to strike for the bayou on a western course. I missed the trace, and had to make my way for a mile alone through the thicket. I knew the course by a pocket compass, and that the bayou was on my left, so felt no apprehension; but the solitude of these deep recesses of wild nature was awful, and I could realize the horrors of being lost in a cane brake. By inclining to the west I avoided the sloughs, and got better ground than that we had cut through, the ground rising towards the bayou, the banks of which are fifteen to thirty feet above the bottom. In the midst of the thickest cane I discovered a mound, and, tired and belated as I was, could not avoid pausing to contemplate it. I walked or rather clambered over it, and, as nearly as I could judge, it was about twelve feet above the surrounding level, and forty or fifty feet across the top. Struck the cross trace much nearer the bayou than I expected, and reached the camp about three-fourths of an hour before the other party. Hudgins has killed another duck, Murphy also one, so we breakfast and sup, or dine, on stewed duck and coffee. We all keep well, but excessively sore and fatigued.

Sunday, November 29, 1835.

To-day I declined going out. I could do no good in the woods. I understand the general character of the land, and the only inquiry now is, how far does it continue. This Hudgins can report, and I can do some necessary work in camp. Shot two ducks at one fire in the pond, which excels the others. Hudgins has shot five times for two, and our woodman has missed several times. He blames the shot-gun. Hudgins returned at night, much wearied and dispirited. Says he fears the good land is nearly run out. Our horses strayed off to-day in search of pasturage. They live mostly on cane. We have no dry provender for them. I had to go and bring them up.

Could not catch the pony, so had to drive him up with his hobbles on, and it is amusing to see the uncouth gait he moves in. My mare is very gentle; a fine, beautiful animal. I am much pleased with her, and call her Bessy. I wish Evelina had her to ride on. Her size and qualities are suitable for a lady's riding, but she does not pace.

Monday, November 30, 1835.

Fine, clear, cold day. Both this morning and yesterday the ice in our vessel was as thick as a dollar, a degree of cold at which I am much surprised. The weather is now delightful. To-day we all started on horseback, and pursued an old Indian trace until we struck the corner we sought, which was in the midst of a slough a foot deep, at least. We then cut on through immensely heavy cane for some distance. As our guide and Hudgins wished to return by a nearer route, which they would accomplish by again striking for the bayou, I returned and took the horses back to camp. I rode the pony, led Hudgins' horse, and my mare followed as gently as a dog. Crossed the bayou on a log, and led the horses through. Got back about half an hour before sunset; the others soon after. Hudgins begins to flag and despond. I have clearly discovered that my physical powers are not equal to such exertions. Health, limbs and life are all endangered; but I have much cause to be thankful that thus far all have been most wonderfully preserved. The health of each one is very good, mine singularly so. Made a sad discovery. One of my saddle bags was wet, and on examination found that a little flask, in which I had got half a pint of good brandy in Manchester, had become uncorked, and all had run out. It was the only spirits we had. I designed it as a medicine, and not a drop had been tasted by either of us.

Tuesday, December 1, 1835

The first day of winter, and a very mild morning. It has clouded a little during the night, and a few drops of rain fell, but not enough to prevent Hudgins and Murphy from going out again. I shall stay at camp and write up journal and do some necessary work. I have washed my shirts, handkerchiefs, stockings, etc., and have every day cooked the duck; one of those that I killed I picked. I have never before in my life, that I recollect, picked a duck or washed a shirt. It is amusing to see how we make shifts, and wonderful to observe how readily we adapt ourselves to our situation. I missed a shot to-day, and we have no duck, except what was left in the morning. Hudgins and Murphy returned at half past three, tired and dispirited. The good land has run out. All hands to packing and preparing for a start in the morning. Our examination has been in T 13 R 3 W., on the east of Silver Creek, but a body of very fine land lies between it and the creek; 13-4 is not yet surveyed; of course, not subject to entry. Could the land on the creek be secured, two pretty good sections in 13-3 might be added, but a site on the watercourse is very important, for the double purpose of draining and drinking. It is excellent drinking water. The lands above and below are entered. That on which we now are is owned by Pinckard & Mason.

Wednesday, December 2, 1835.

Fine weather. Up and away by times. We came upon an Indian camp about 11 o'clock. Only three boys at the camp; the men out hunting. One of them brought me a cup of water from the creek. I made him understand what I wanted by signs and words. They had a great deal of deer and bear meat hung around their camp, of which we desired to buy some, but we could not make the boys comprehend us. Showed them the money and pointed to the meat, and spoke in plain

English, but neither we nor our guide, who pretended to have some Indian erudition, could make the boys betray the least understanding of our meaning, so we had to give it up. We had reason to believe afterwards that this was the effect of Indian policy; that they understood us, but were instructed not to betray it, nor to deal with whites. On the way our guide shot a wild turkey with his rifle, which is the first use he has made of it on the excursion. After arriving on our ground and pitching our tent, he returned to the flock and shot two more after night, which is considered a difficult exploit.

Thursday, December 3, 1835.

Fine weather, milder than a few days past. Commenced the examination of our land, which we found of unequal quality. Cane and holly groves on the bayou, extending back an equal distance, and encountering sloughs, too many of them. Nothing remarkable occurred to-day.

Friday, December 4, 1835.

Weather fine. Set out on horseback, down the bayou, to examine the lower section. Hudgins was taken sick, and returned to camp to take physic. I continued the examination, in company with our guide, who to-day has shown himself surly and uncivil. While in a cane brake alone I discovered an Indian mound of considerable dimensions, covered with very stiff, thick cane. Found it hard labor to cut a path from it to the bayou. As well as I could judge, it was twenty feet high, fifty or sixty feet in diameter. Found a corner tree recently cut with an axe, and our guide said he saw men's tracks. On returning to camp was informed by H. that two men had been there who said they were hunting timber to raft out when the water rose. This we did not believe, but set them down for land hunters. Hudgins is better, but still unwell, and as the weather is lowering, concluded to finish the examination to-morrow morning early, and endeavor to reach Hughes' plantation by night.

Saturday, December 5, 1835.

Weather windy all night, cloudy and portending a storm. Hudgins and guide went out early to finish examination, while I cook breakfast and pack. While thus engaged our two timber hunters returned by the camp. At 10 o'clock we mounted and retraced our steps to the haunts of man. Arrived at Hughes' before night, and were again kindly received by Callahan, his overseer. He treated us to venison, which he had just bought from those Indian boys, that would not talk to nor understand us, two of whom we met a short distance from the plantation, on horseback. They brought venison, and received money and pumpkins. Callahan said they spoke good English until the sale of the meat was effected, after which they would not talk, and he had no doubt they understood every word we said to them.

Sunday, December 6, 1835.

Rode over the farm with Callahan. Weather excessively cold. The negroes at work, picking cotton, notwithstanding the day. They say they know no difference between the days of the week in picking cotton time. Callahan receives as overseer only $500 a year. Many of them get $1,000, some $1,200 and $1,500. Opposite to Hughes' is Dr. Lee's estate, and immediately below that is H. Brawner's. These three are the only settlements on Silver Creek, and the nearest to the entry we have made. Dr. Lee has a fine body of cane land next to Hughes, about 1,000 acres, for which he asks $10 per acre.

Left Callahan after 10 o'clock. Took a negro with us to bring the skiff back, after crossing the Panther Creek, Dr.

73

Lee having politely lent the use of it. Arrived at Mr. White's, on Yazoo, before night. He received us with the same kindness as before. He is making great progress in opening his plantation and preparing dwellings for his people. Suppose it will take him three years to put the place in full operation, when he proposes to leave it to his son and nephew to manage, and go himself to Red River! So we go.

Monday, December 7, 1835.

Left White's after breakfast, and crossed the Yazoo at Beale's saw mill, several miles below Manchester. After going a mile, discovered that Hudgins, who charge of the gun to-day, had left it on the other side of the river, and he had to go back for it. I had hitherto been the fool of the party in leaving things and making mistakes, and had consequently been laughed at. This was a heavy item against Hudgins, and placed the balance of account against him.

Lost our way, turned back; could not cross a bayou; had to go round, by which our progress was small to-day. Stopt at a little place on the Yazoo, called Liverpool. Saw but one decent looking man in it, a Mr. Jasper Powlis, who keeps a store there. He treated us very kindly, gave us a nice relish and brandy toddy, and would take no pay. He is a New Yorker, and his wife a Philadelphian. He has been sick, at the point of death, twice this summer, and would probably have died but for his wife's nursing. He will not stay there long. We stopt at night by chance at a little house on the roadside, owned by a man named Haile, who came from Kentucky. Gave us fine fare, good bread, milk, butter, and good, substantial meats. He has been successful, and is vain and boastful. Charged us $1.50 for supper, lodging, breakfast and horse.

Tuesday, December 8, 1835.

Left Haile's after breakfast, and having found the river road hilly and difficult, we regained the ridge road, and after a pretty hard day's ride arrived at Vicksburg just at night. Found an entire new set at the tavern. Prentiss has nearly lost his life by swallowing broken glass with his wine when drinking. It cut his throat and festered. He is now out of danger. H. A. Board dropt a pistol, which went off and shot him in the foot; and another poor fellow had a gun discharged into his arm accidentally. They were handing it out of a boat on the Sun Flower. The gun dropt and went off. He was sent here in a boat, and it was days before the wound was dressed. The arm could not then be saved, and had to be amputated. Received two letters from Mrs. Gray.

Wednesday, December 9, 1835.

Rainy all day. Nothing done.

Thursday, December 10, 1835.

Still rainy, and Hudgins is prevented from going to Clinton to enter our lands. A cotillion party here last night. About forty ladies and as many gentlemen. Hon'l Mr. Jennifer and Col. Legrand, of Maryland, among the gayest of the guests. A very fair assembly, orderly and sober; no noise or disturbance whatever. Wrote to Mrs. Gray.

Friday, December 11, 1835.

Rain having ceased, Hudgins started this morning for Clinton. A number of gents arrived last night from Virginia: Dr. P. Thornton and H. F. Thornton, from Maryland; a Mr. Freeman, Lancaster, two Pyes, Southron, Col. Causin, Dr. Dare, Dr. Edw'd Johnson, Mr. Graham, Mr. Erskine, of Baltimore, and Sam'l P. Carson, also from Baltimore, formerly of Alexandria. Received a letter from my wife of Nov. 20. Wrote to T. G.

Saturday, December 12, 1835.

Great negotiating for land and negroes among the newcomers. Some of them disgusted and disheartened. No sales made to-day. I have been much interested and informed by listening to their calculations and propositions. This has been a fine, clear day. My health uncommonly good, and my spirits buoyant. The operations going on around me excite me, and I cannot help feeling the contagion, and want to be dealing in tens and hundreds of thousands.

Sunday, December 13, 1835.

The negotiations for land and negroes continue with unabated ardor. Went to the Methodist Church. Indifferent sermon from a stranger. Good congregation. In the evening Hudgins returned from Clinton, disappointed and dispirited. All the land he intended entering had been entered while we were examining them. So we go. Better luck next time. Fine weather.

Monday, December 14, 1835.

Fine, clear day; health good, but spirits bad; uncertain how to proceed. Mr. Southron has bought an estate, eight miles from town, 950 acres, 500 opened, sixteen good or bad negroes, fifty hogs, fifty oxen, good dwelling and all other necessary houses, including gin, in good order, $60,000, one-third cash, one-third in one year, one-third in two years. Land estimated at $50 per acre. Considered a good purchase. The Pyes have also bought near him, at $30 per acre; purchase not so good. Dare has also bought, and has already been offered $4,000 for his bargain. Wrote to T. G.

Tuesday, December 15, 1835.

Fine, clear day, health good. Nothing remarkable to-day.

Wednesday, December 16, 1835.

Fine weather, but too warm, writing all day with the window open. Had my hair cut, and caught a bad cold in my head.

Thursday, December 17, 1835.

Fine weather, but too warm. Howard Thornton, Col. Cousin and others returned. Southron dissatisfied with his purchase. Still in Vicksburg. I. A. Parker proposed to me some days ago to accompany him to Texas, and says when he shall have made choice of the port at which he will settle as consul, that I shall have choice of the other ports of Texas, as Vice Consul, if I shall, on examination, think the office worth accepting. The offer appears to proceed from a friendly and confidential feeling, which demands my thanks, and I will consider seriously of it. Inclined to go; think I erred in stopping here so long.

MEMO LAST PAGE VOL. III

Yocknopotopha—ploughed ground.
Nashoba—the wolf.
Tallalioma—black warrior.
Tallalloosa—black rock.
Chockchuma (pronounced Shockshahooma)—red crawfish.
Yalobusha (pronounced Lobo'osha)—tadpole with its tail cut off.
Tala (or *Chala*)—Fox Lake.
Lowish—wasp.

Tuskahoomah—red warrior.
Pearl River was called *Boguehatcha*—Wet, or Swampy Creek.
Yazoo—
Natta—bear.
Nitta—deer.
Tuscaloosa—red rock.

MEMO ON INSIDE BACK COVER

Left with H. Carter to get washed Nov. 16, 1835: Two pocket handkerchiefs, one cotton shirt, two linen shirts, one pair socks, three collars.

VOL. IV

Friday, December 18, 1835.

Weather warm and threatening rain. Received a letter from Mrs. Gray, dated as late as 28th November. Wrote, copied maps, and adjusted accounts. H. F. Thornton, Col. Casis, etc., started for Red River, to go by Plaquemine and Opelousas, etc. My health continues very good, but much in doubt how to proceed in my business. Hudgins equally undecided.

Saturday, December 19, 1835.

Warm and threatening rain; have taken a severe cold in the head. Saw a fellow near getting lynched to-day, and he well deserved it. A Mr. Lindsey had carelessly left on the desk in the bar room a purse containing $70, which Dr. Edw'd Johnson, of Missouri, picked up. This fellow, whose name was Saunders, claimed it, and took it off. The falsehood being discovered, he was pursued, brought back, and, after many falsehoods, finding he was detected, he acknowledged the turpitude of the transaction, and begged forgiveness. He had spent $41 of the money. They made him pledge a gold watch and chain until he raised the money. This he did by borrowing it of his father's merchant; he paid up the whole $70, and was permitted to escape with a whole skin. His father is a wealthy planter of Madison County, and his brother collector of the county. Commenced raining at night. I shall go to Clinton to-morrow.

Sunday, December 20, 1835.

It rained hard all night last night, and all the forenoon today. Parker and Hudgins went off in steamboat to Natchez, to return in a few days. The rain prevents me from going to Clinton. Remained within all day. Wrote to Mrs. Gray. Much talk of the insurrection threatened in the Murrel pamphlet, which was to have occurred about this time. The military have been in training for some time. Patrols are out; arms have been sent to Clinton for a company there, commanded by Capt. House. Robt. Riddle, cashier of the Planter's Bank, has received an anonymous letter, threatening him with the vengeance of the gamblers for the part he took in the revolution of July.

A man by the name of Tunstall, who kept the tavern where I slept two nights when at Princeton, was brought here a day or two ago by the sheriff of Washington County, charged with shooting his assistant. There seems to be no magistrate in Washington County before whom they could take him, and no jail in the county. They took him before Chief Justice Sharkey, who committed him for trial. Said to have been an unprovoked and atrocious murder.

Monday, December 21, 1835.

The weather being clear and cool, I started for Clinton; slept at Bridgeport, on the Big Black. A Mr. * * * from Maryland, a lawyer, who has just come to the State and purchased a farm, was my bed-fellow. Slept badly, much noise, children sick and crying, and house comfortless. Bridgeport is a wretched and sickly place.

Tuesday, December 22, 1835.

Arrived at Clinton in forenoon. Land sales going on; selling low; best lands said to be floated. Rode with an old fellow who lived fourteen years on Deer Creek, who says the situations on the creek in the bottom are more healthy than the Yazoo hills; his name is Armstrong. He wants to buy a quarter section on the Yazoo. A most praiseworthy moderation for a Mississippian.

Found here J. P. Corbin and Dr. W. N. Wellford. Corbin has made an arrangement with a Mr. Davenport for the farm that Morson rented last year. Morson has bought a few miles further from Clinton. I fear Corbin has made a bad arrangement, but he seems much pleased. Poor Dr. Wellford is in distress. He has not purchased, and is in doubt what to do. His negroes are still in camp. He has an unusual responsibility on his shoulders, and has no one at hand capable of advising. I felt much sympathy for him, and endeavored to console and cheer him, while my own feelings almost choked my utterance. We spoke of our prospects, and of our families, and mingled our tears together. We have never been intimate; there is twenty years difference in our ages. I have known him from a child. He now seems to have thrown himself upon me as an old friend, and opened up all his heart. I feel much drawn towards him, and will aid him if I can. Paid twelve and a half cents for a glass of milk at supper.

Wednesday, December 23, 1835.

Fine, cold weather. Ice is seen in the puddles. Attended the land sales. Land went very low, from $1.25 to near $5; average, perhaps $2. Three townships only sold. A. G. McNutt the heaviest purchaser.

Met here Mr. Widgery, who had lived in Fredericksburg some years ago. He now resides in Jackson, is a lawyer and justice of the peace; is well dressed and extremely handsome. Dr. Thornton is also here; has hired out his hands, and not purchased.

Thursday, December 24, 1835.

Wellford having met with some difficulty in his negotiations, on account of the shape his funds are in, determined to go to Vicksburg to try and cash them. I last night gave him a letter to Riddle, but while he was dressing this morning I determined to return to Vicksburg with him. We left Clinton at 8 o'clock a.m., and reached Vicksburg before 6 p.m. Found letters from Hudgins and Parker. They have gone to New Orleans, and I resolved to follow by next boat. Hudgins requested me to sell his horse for $65, and says he will return here and then proceed to Helena.

Friday, December 25, 1835.

Christmas Day. A wet and warm day. A military parade of the Warren troop and the two companies of infantry. Much drinking and rioting. Heard of many egg-nog parties last night, and the landlord treated this morning, but I saw none; of course. drank none. My thoughts have often reverted to home to-day; how differently did I spend this day last year, and how differently are those at home spending it now.

Last night, at a drinking house, two men fought with knives. A third attempted to part them, and got stabbed. One of them is dead, and another in danger. So much for drinking.

Saturday, December 26, 1835.

This morning I saw a horrid spectacle. A man had been shot in the street last night, and was still lying exposed at breakfast time. There was a bullet in the center of his breast, and three buckshot near the heart. He was shot by his cousin, Tom Thatcher, because he would not give up a dirk that he wore, with which Thatcher wished to attack another man. The dirk sheath was still in his bosom, but not the dirk. The coroner's inquest pronounced him murdered by the hands of Tom Thatcher. The proof was ample and clear. The murderer was said to have fled to Louisiana. At 1 o'clock p.m. the steamboat *Chancellor*, Capt. Shallcross, came down, and I embarked on board of her.

Much excitement in Vicksburg to-day. Riddle had presented a Dr. Goderich for cruelty in beating a servant woman unmercifully, and Goderich had threatened to shoot him. A conflict was feared.

Came to at Warrenton, about twelve miles below Vicksburg. While there it was discovered that Thatcher, the murderer, was on board, and young Thompson (son of Mrs. Thompson, of F.,) went into town to get an officer to arrest him, but no magistrate could be found. Some of the citizens came down and said they would arrest him and sent him back to Vicksburg in the North Alabama, then lying at the wharf. He went out with them, but instead of putting him on board the Alabama they walked up into town with him, with no appearance of any disposition to make him a prisoner, and the probability is, he has escaped. I think Capt. Shallcross, of the *Chancellor* very culpable in not arresting him and sending him back to Vicksburg. $1,000 reward is offered for him in Vicksburg.

Found on board Mr. Erskine, of Baltimore, J. H. See and his brother-in-law, Dr. Willis, of Orange, Capt. Bolton and Capt. Perry, of the navy, Mr. Adams (a nephew of J. Q.), of the army, Mr. Thos. D. Carniel, of Cincinnati, etc. Passed Grand Gulph before bed time; from the lights there appeared to be a considerable town; said to be a rising place. The country improves; here and there a plantation of better appearance than those above Vicksburg.

Sunday, December 27, 1835.

Found ourselves this morning lying to at Natchez, 100 miles from Vicksburg. Had only time to run upon the bank and take a peep at the Town on the Hill. A fine town, elegant homes, regular streets, good pavements, etc., public buildings large and in good style, market house full of people as on ordinary days. Passed Fort Adams; saw the famous battleground of the Kempers. Memo. to inquire into their history; they were brothers of Col. Jno. Kemper, of Fauquier. Passed Shreve's cut-off, where the Red River and Atchafalia come in—a remarkable place—also Tunica Bend. Before bed time, passed St. Francesville, and took off passengers; opposite to this is Point Coupee, where Wm. Taylor resides. In the night passed Port Hudson, Baton Rouge, Iberville, Placquemine, etc.

Monday, December 28, 1835.

Found ourselves opposite to Donaldsonville. The whole face and character of the country has changed, the banks of the river on both sides entirely cleared of wood, and thickly settled with large and fine looking plantations, having all the appearance of wealth, elegance and comfort. The savage state has here given way to civilization. Stopt to wood at the plantation of Madame Toureau; went on shore and saw the interior of a sugar house, which was politely shown by young Mr. Toureau; all French; the negroes could only speak French. I asked one old woman how old she was; said she could not tell; was very old; had lived there under the King of Spain. This estate makes this year 158 hogsheads of sugar at $100 per hogshead, and 14,000 gallons of molasses, worth here 35 cents.

150, at $100	$15,000
14,000 at 35c	2,100
	$17,100

Which I should think a small yield, for the apparent size and force. Cotton planting must be more profitable. Each hogshead of sugar produces forty gallons of molasses.

Left Mde. Toureau's at 11 o'clock. Weather mild and genial. The banks verdant with grass; everything wears such a garb as one might expect in mild April weather in Virginia. The negroes look healthy and cheerful. The Creoles look brunette, swarthy and lean, but healthful, cheerful, active; the soft, cheerful, pleasant Creole French meets the ear continually. This looks like a delightful country, where one might live. We shall reach New Orleans before night. The day is so delightful and the country so novel and cheering in its aspect, compared to the dull, monotous, savage aspect of the Upper Mississippi, that I want to be on deck and feast my senses.

Had several conversations with Mr. Carniel about Texas and lands generally. He is interested in Col. Milam's claim in Texas—one-eighth. Does not like the state of things there. Prefers buying United States lands in the States, at government price, to speculating in Texas lands; but says if he was twenty years younger (he is now fifty) he would go to Texas, and with $10,000 he would make as much wealth as he pleased. His plan would be to buy cotton land on the coast, and stock it with negroes from Cuba. He says a plenty of good land may now be bought in Texas for twenty-five cents per acre. My room mate, C. K. Bullard, of New York, thinks he is mistaken; that good lands, in good situations, can't be got under $1.00. Conversed with a Mr. Carson, who lives in Texas, and is just from there—left Mississippi a year ago; he and his family suffered much from sickness in Mississippi; been perfectly healthy in Texas; delighted with the country; does not think the lands more productive than in Mississippi, but climate dry and healthy. He got land from the Empresarios in Zavala's Colony, on Ariet Bayou; the office now closed. Thinks the State will be independent, and then come into our Union. That the leaders are ambitious, and would like to have a separate government, but the people would prefer our Union; that Houston is in bad esteem with the army, and has resigned; the army wants organization and a head; acts mostly in detached parties, captains' commands. (I apprehend he is mistaken about Houston; he is still in command, and appears to be popular.)

Arrived at New Orleans just before dark, and took lodgings at Richardson's Hotel, corner of Camp and Commune Streets. Found here Parker and his brother-in-law Forbes, Raleigh Green, Col. Cousin, Col. Jenifer, etc. Saw also Jere Morton and Geo. A. Smith. Morton's family are here, boarding at Mr. Hagerty's, in Canal Street. After supper, walked out with Parker, and passing Caldwell's new theatre, went in to see it; the play, *Wept of Wishton Wish*. The part of Maranata by the famous *danseuse*, Celeste. The character was interesting and well sustained. After the play Celeste danced, which was the principal attraction of the night. It was a marvelous display of muscular power and of indelicacy. The farce, *Raising the Wind*, a stupid affair; it hardly raised a laugh. The building immense in its dimensions, and splendid in its decorations.

Tuesday, December 29, 1835.

Called to see Arthur H. Wallace, where I found A. D. Kelly, who goes into partnership in the house on 1st of January. A. H. Wallace says he means to live in Louisville. He will leave the business here in charge of his brother, T. H. Wallace, and Kelly. He wishes also to establish a house in Vicksburg, and spoke of trying to get H. H. Wallace, of Fredericksburg, to come out and take charge of it. Called to see Wm. Lambeth; not in. Capt. John Barker is his clerk. The firm is Lambeth & Thompson. Thompson is a son of Jonah Thompson, of Alexandria, D. C. Called and left my card at Dr. E. H. Barton's, whom I afterwards met in the street. Called to see Dr. W. Bird

Powell, who is Professor of Chemistry in the Medical College
here, and invited me to his lecture in the evening. Dined with
Jere. Morton and wife, at Mrs. Hagerty's. At the table saw the
celebrated Clara Fisher, and Miss Philips. Walked with Morton to the Catholic cemetery, a burying place, or rather a city
of splendid palaces for the dead. Had not time to examine
it; ought to devote a day to it. At 5 o'clock walked with Mrs.
Barton and Miss Connoly to hear Dr. Powell's lecture; took
tea with them, and accompanied them to the Lyceum, where
Seth Barton was to deliver an address, and a discussion to be
had on the old question of capital punishments *vel non*. Seth
Barton excused himself from speaking on the score of indisposition. The debaters were Mr. Duncan and Mr. Wharton,
my *quondam* stage companion in crossing the mountains, pro,
and Dr. Powell, con. The Doctor had the best of the argument, but the whole affair, so so.

Wednesday, December 30, 1835.

Jere Morton started today in the steamboat to Vicksburg,
then to cross over through Mississippi and Alabama to Mobile and return here. His wife and child remain here until
his return. Geo. A. Smith went up Red River. Called to see
Robt. Marye, and dined with him. His sister, Mrs. Blackwell,
keeps house for him. They live on upper Levee Street. He
keeps a dry goods store. He has one son, a fine looking youth,
who has just returned from Kenyon College. Mrs. Blackwell
has two boys. There are several Texans lodging here; among
them is Col. A. Houston, who is a member of the provisional
government of Texas, and Quartermaster General of the
army. He is here awaiting the arrival of the Commissioners, Gen'l Austin, Dr. Archer and Col. Wharton. I have had
several conversations with him. He is confident that Texas
will maintain itself against Santa Anna; says a new convention will meet on the first of March; that a full declaration

of independence will then be made. He was in favor of such a declaration in November, and it would have been made but for Gen'l S. Houston, who would not agree to it. Col. Houston offered to sell me a league of land near Sabine Bay for $5,000. It is his own headright. Too high for me. He cautioned me against many of the lands that will be offered, the titles to which are not good. He says if he could sell his land he would immediately buy provisions and return to the army, without waiting for the Commissioners. He is a plain, unpretending man, uncultivated, and of but little information or genius; apparently honest and moderate in his views. Thinks a very large majority of the people wish to come into the Union with Uncle Sam; that all wish it except fugitives from the laws of the States, and a few ambitious men who desire to be leaders.

Also a Mr. David Brown, a surveyor in Texas, and Mr. A. C. Allen, the owner of the armed schooner *Brutus*, now fitting out in this port, about which there is much talk. Some say she is to be a privateer, and wish the United States attorney to stop her sailing. There is a strong monied party here opposed to the revolution in Texas on account of its endangering the trade with Mexico, in which they are largely concerned. The Messrs. Ligardi, Mexican merchants, residing here, said to be worth $15,000,000. Allen, and his brother, Jno. K. Allen, who resides at Nacogdoches, are largely concerned in land speculations in Texas.

Went at night with Col. Cousin, Col. Jenifer and Parker to a masquerade ball. It proved to be a low, vulgar, disgusting exhibition. Met there several gentlemen that I knew, among them Dr. Carter, Mr. Erskine and Mr. Chinn, spectators like ourselves. Looked also into a *Hell*, or gambling house. Jenifer and Cousin put in $5 each, which Jenifer made bets with. In a few minutes their stock in trade was gone, and we retired.

Thursday, December 31, 1835.

Spent the forenoon in visiting different parts of the city, the arcade, cotton presses, etc. Dined by invitation with Dr. Barton. Present, Professor Powell, S. Barton, Geo. French and Shakespeare Caldwell. He said others were invited who sent excuses, among them J. H. Caldwell, who had an engagement out of the city.

Robt. Triplett arrived to-day from Nacogdoches. He had made a conditional purchase of land in Texas of A. C. Allen, dependent on his being satisfied with the title, etc., after having looked into it. His investigations have determined him not to purchase, and he has hastened back, to annul the bargain and receive back his deposit of $15,000. He thinks the titles to lands in Texas are very insecure, have been loosely granted, and the deeds badly preserved. There is no record made of a deed, but the originals are kept in bundles in the office of the Judge of the Primary Court. Brown, the surveyor, says that proprietors may keep certified copies. There is no system in locating grants; the location is left to the grantee and the surveyor; thus several grants, or rights, may be located on the same land, as in Virginia and Kentucky. No right inures without an actual settlement and residence, and compliance with all the requisites of the law. What those requisites are it is difficult to tell, as copies of them cannot be had; and whether they have been complied with or not is still more difficult to ascertain. I do not think quite so well of Texas speculations as I did. Still I will go and look at it.

A fire occurred about 7 o'clock in the upper Fauburg, which burnt several houses before it was extinguished. In returning from it, saw numerous dancing parties of the lower classes, in the little, odd-fashioned Spanish built houses, in the marsh. In one place a large collection were amusing themselves with a riding wheel. Wooden horses were attached in a circle, on the periphery of a wheel, as it were, which was suspended from the top of a pillar, around which it was made to turn with great rapidity. It is New Year's Eve, a period of great relaxation and carousing with these people; yet there is no disorder. Except the firing of crackers by the boys, there is no unusual noise in the central and business part of the town. Indeed, it is generally remarked that New Orleans is a very quiet place at night.

Saw two military companies on drill in a public square, by moonlight. Drill well conducted, companies well trained. Particularly pleased with the rifle drill, firing and loading lying on the ground.

Friday, January 1, 1836.

The Commissioners from Texas, Gen'l Stephen F. Austin, Hon'l Branch T. Archer, and Hon'l Wm. H. Wharton, and several other Texans, have arrived this morning in five days from Brazoria, by water. Introduced to Austin and Archer, who both board here. Wharton does not stop here. They bring particulars of the capture of San Antonio, and are in high spirits about Texas. Archer is particularly excited and vehement. He talks too much and too loud. Austin is more prudent. He appears to be a sensible and unpretending business man. This house is much thronged, many persons are crowding to the bar room to see the Commissioners and hear about Texas. Indeed, we can scarcely hear of anything else. Spent most of the day in conversing with them, and in listening to conversations about that country, its character, condition and prospects.

I went early this morning to see the market, which is very large, and abundantly supplied with fish, flesh and fowl, and the quantity and variety of vegetables exceeds anything I ever saw. From the quantity and excellence of the vegetables, one might suppose it was midsummer instead of midwinter. Indeed, the weather very much resembles May in Virginia.

Returning from market between 7 and 8 o'clock, saw the Cathedral door open and went in. A pretty full congregation was assembled, and most of them were on their knees, some reading their books, some telling beads, and some looking as though their only object was to kneel; certainly there seemed nothing devotional about them but the position. The priest was at the altar, making genuflections, and occasionally a little boy who stood near the altar would ring a little bell, but I could hear not a word spoken. About the portal stood like statues some dozen of miserable, maimed, decrepit and disgusting looking mendicants, who silently held out their open hands to catch the casual alms of the passer-by.

Introduced by Triplett to Geo. Hancock and Col. Woolly, of Louisville, and a Mr. Hawes, of Kentucky. Also introduced to Col. Hotchkiss, of Nacogdoches, agent of the Texas & Galveston Land Co., and Mr. Yates, who is a New Yorker, and a lawyer, but has purchased largely of lands in Texas, and is going to settle a plantation on Galveston Bay. He says he shall go largely into the cattle trade; that he will buy some native Mexicans, who have forfeited their liberty by debt, and use them as herdsmen; that they are the best for that purpose, being well acquainted with herding cattle, and are cheaper than blacks. He showed me a chart of Galveston Bay, which was made under his direction by an old sailor. I have borrowed it to copy. Hotchkiss and Yates both speak Spanish. They have travelled much in Mexico. Hotchkiss says he thinks some old Mexican titles may be bought for $1,000 per league. I am much interested with Yates. He is intelligent and gentlemanly. Raleigh Green has taken passage in the *Brutus*; she has one hundred passengers.

Saturday, January 2, 1836.

Some difficulty has arisen about the sailing of the *Brutus*. She was to have cleared to-day and to sail to-morrow, but a clearance is refused until some investigation takes place, as to her character, it being charged that she is fitting out to cruise as a privateer against Mexican vessels.

Met to-day Mr. L. Pearce and Mr. F. Wharton; the latter has left his pretty wife in Tennessee. Mr. Pearce promised to obtain for me a copy of the laws of Texas, the only one, he says, he believes in New Orleans. No letters from home since 28th of November.

Sunday, January 3, 1836.

The weather, which has been remarkably fine, rather warm, during the past week, has to-day changed to heavy rains. I did not go out all the forenoon, except to inquire for letters, such is my anxiety to hear from home; no letters yet. There is no Episcopal service here; a new church is building, but they have no minister. Wrote to T. Green and Mrs. Gray, letters commenced on board the steamboat and finished to-day. In the evening R. Triplett and myself walked out through the old part of the city and on the quay. The amount of shipping here is immense. In many instances six ships lie alongside of each other, and all having business with the outer one will have to pass over the five others. Jenifer and Cousin left to-day, via Mobile.

Monday, January 4, 1836.

The weather to-day is remarkably fine. A clearer and more delicious atmosphere could not be desired. The weather during all last week was warm, too warm for comfort. Yesterday was a heavy rain, with thunder and lightning. To-day it is clear, pure, balmy and exhilarating, resembling a fine May day in Virginia. The frogs are singing merrily in the ponds.

A meeting of the friends of Texas is called, to be holden at Bishop's Hotel, on Wednesday night. It is announced that the

Commissioners will be in attendance. These Commissioners seem not to know very well how to go about their business. They wish to raise funds to support their army and government on a pledge of the public domain, but have declared no plans, have offered no terms. Triplett and Carniel have been in conference with, and it is understood that they will decide to-day on some propositions that have been made to them. Archer is continually declaiming about the tavern to any and everybody. Austin seems timid and troubled. There is great kindness and affability in his manner, but an expression of anxiety pervades his features.

The sailing of the *Brutus* is stopt, and depositions are being taken before Judge Preval, relative to her armament, destination, etc.

Attended Dr. Barton's lecture at the Medical College, on epidemics. Sensible and interesting lecture. The doctor's manner self-possessed and pretty good, but his articulation bad. He raised voice too high, probably for the benefit of his nephew, Geo. French (one of the students, who is very deaf), and speaks too rapidly, and his enunciation is sometimes thick and indistinct. Class small, only fifteen or sixteen.

Brown, the surveyor, has acquired several leagues of land, which be is desirous of selling. One of them adjoins the league of Col. Houston, near Sabine Bay. Houston's price is $5,000. Brown offers his for 50 cents per acre ($2,214). Says he regards his titles as good as titles in Texas can be, if the requisitions of the law, as to settlement, etc., be complied with, which a purchaser will have to look well to. He hints that some large speculations have been made in Texas, which will not be confirmed by the new government. *Query*—To whom does he allude?

Walked in the evening to the upper cotton press. The buildings owned by a company; very spacious. Called at Rob. Marye's and took tea with them. His son is a fine looking youth, just seventeen. No letters from home.

Tuesday, January 5, 1836.

Weather fine and warm. Went with Mr. Yates to the court to hear the trial of the *Brutus* case. The proceedings are dismissed, and she sailed.

The legislature of Louisiana assembled yesterday. Went today to see them in session. Some of the members speak French and some English. When one speaks in French an interpreter renders it into English for the benefit of the American members, and vice versa. The questions, too, are always put in English and French. This procedure causes much delay. It is altogether very awkward, and must be an unsatisfactory mode of legislating. The building is antique and nowise elegant.

Visited also the basin of the canal, the depot of the Pontchartrain railroad, where I saw a train of cars come in laden heavily with cotton, sugar, salt, etc., and the lower cotton press. In these presses steam power is used. The bales are pressed to one-half the dimensions that they bring from the plantations, and roped anew. The amount of cotton seen at these presses is wonderful and astonishing.

Yates says the practice of the courts in Texas is very simple. All suits, civil or criminal, are first brought before a single magistrate, called Alcalde. The complainant states his cause of action in plain terms, in writing. A summons issues to both parties and to their witnesses to appear before the Alcalde on a certain day to have their cause tried. Two other persons, as arbitrators, or triers, are then associated with the Alcalde. They hear the witnesses and the parties pro and con, and make their decision in writing, giving their reasons. In this way a great majority of the causes of the country are disposed of. But if their decision is not satisfactory, an appeal may be taken to the court above, which is held by what is called the Primary Judge, where the cause is tried by a jury. From the decision here an appeal lies to the Supreme Court, or Court of Appeals, where points of law only are decided the facts

93

having been ascertained before the jury. In this way there is a great deal of business for lawyers, and if I mistake not, there will be much more.

The Constitution of Coahuila and Texas declares that "no body can be born a slave, and the introduction of slaves under any pretext is prohibited." But the law (some law or other) permits persons to bind themselves by contract to serve others for a term of years. In this way negroes have been held in Texas, and I am told a great many are introduced there and held without that formality. There is a general desire to hold slaves, and it is permitted by common consent, no one being willing to prosecute for the violation of the law. It is the opinion of all the *Texanos* with whom I have conversed on the subject that the new government of Texas must sanction the holding of slaves as property.

In Mexico, persons becoming debtors and unable to pay are held to service until the debt be paid, at wages prescribed by law. They are, for a married man, $6 per month. A single man, $4 per month. Boys 10 to 14, $2 per month. Boys 14 to 21, or marriage, $3 per month. Females get $1 per month less in each class. These prices are evidently insufficient for the support of the person; and thus, when one becomes bound to service for debt, he is a hopeless slave for life, as the debt will continually increase. Thus many families become enslaved, and are held by the large proprietors as part of their estate. They are generally bought and sold with the land, sometimes sold individually, by the debtor procuring some one to pay his debt. He then changes masters and serves him who paid for him. Some estates in Mexico are said to have several thousand of these debtor slaves on them, and instead of dying in despair or repining at their lot, they are said to be submissive and content, and much attached to their masters. The practice has obtained but little in Texas.

A heavy fall of rain and a severe thunder storm occurred in the night. Equal to the storms in Virginia in July and August.

On going to bed at 12 o'clock found on my bed a packet, which had been forwarded from Vicksburg, containing two letters from my wife and one from my daughter. The latter and one from Mrs. Gray were dated November 8. They had been sent per Jere Morton, by him carried to Mobile, and then brought back here, sent by Hudgins to Vicksburg, who went up the river as I came down, and now returned by him. The other was dated December 7, 1835.

Wednesday, January 6, 1836.

Fine, clear day, but muddy streets. It is now cool and most delightfully pleasant. Not cool enough to make a greatcoat or fire necessary. The meeting of the friends of Texas took place at 7 o'clock p.m. in the large bar room at the City Hotel. The room was as full as it could hold, but the wealth and respectability of the city was not there. A large portion of the meeting consisted of the lodgers in the hotel. Chairman, Mr. Christy; secretary, J. H. Caldwell.

The Commissioners from Texas, Messrs. Archer, Wharton and Austin, were invited to seats beside the chairman. The chairman first addressed the meeting, then Archer, Wharton, Judge Bledsoe, Austin, and a Mr. Ellis, were successively called upon, and each addressed the meeting in turn. None of the speeches were remarkable for information or eloquence. They all ran in the same circle, the wrongs of the Texans, and their noble resistance of tyranny, etc., and earnest and labored appeals to the feelings and sympathies of the people of the United States. The resolutions were carried by loud and enthusiastic acclamation, and when the noes were demanded not a no was heard, but a person in the crowd sang out yes, which caused the remark that the vote was unanimous and one over.

The gentlemen from Texas are, or pretend to be, highly delighted with the result of this meeting. It certainly is proof of a pretty deep feeling of good will to the cause in the minds of those who attended the meeting; and it may be that the feeling pervades the mass of the community. But it would have been better if the wealth and respectability of the city had given it their countenance. No plan is yet submitted by the Commissioners for raising stock on their lands. Triplett and Carniel are still in conference with them occasionally, and desirous to effect an arrangement by which they may get some of their lands.

Thursday, January 7, 1836.

Fine weather. Called to see Mrs. Barton, who went with me to visit Mrs. Chew. Saw there Miss Connolly, Miss Davidson and Mr. Hancock. Called afterwards to see Mrs. Ker; saw also Dr. Ker. Invited by Pearce, their son-in-law (at whose house they live) to take a family dinner with them to-morrow.

Met in the street J. H. Caldwell, who invited me to dine with him on Sunday.

Took tea, by invitation, with Augustin Slaughter. He called at my lodgings to conduct me to his house. His wife is a pleasant looking woman. They have no children, lost the only two they ever had. His attentions are kind, cordial and unaffected. I feel at home with him. He is in reduced circumstances. Has just come to New Orleans, and opened an office as cotton brokr. Mr. Labuzan is living in Mobile, a commission merchant.

Last night a horrid murder was committed at the Planter's Hotel, a house on the next street to this, by a man named Washington Whitaker, on an unoffending young Irishman, named Owen Murphy. Murphy was barkeeper; Whitaker became drunk, commenced a row, and finally stabbed Murphy with a bowie knife. His brother, Warren Whitaker, and a Mr. Hale, were in the house when the murder was committed, but not present at the murder. They assisted him to escape, and all three took refuge here, at the City Hotel, where they were all apprehended by the *gend'armes*, who surrounded and took possession of the house. It produced a great commotion in the house and in the street. I saw the body this morning. Hale is discharged, Warren Whitaker will be bailed, and the other, it is supposed, hung.

VOL. V

MEMO ON INSIDE FRONT COVER.

Rigaud & Griffin (Mesdames), boarding house.
Alfred Penn, New Orleans.
I. F. Irwin, care of Ker & Byrne, New Orleans.
Archibald Hotchkiss, Empresario.
Augustus Hotchkiss, Judge.
A. J. Yates.
D. H. Vail, Natchitoches.
Col. Hugh Love.
Dr. John Cameron.
John Durst.
Dr. Vincent Alderete, Rio Grande.
Alfred R. Guild, Bejar.
T. Savage, Massachusetts.

Friday, January 8, 1836.

This being the 21st anniversary of the great victory of 1815, the day was distinguished by fetes of various kinds. There was a fine military parade. The Legion of Louisiana are a splendid body of militia. They assembled at the *Principale*, and marched to the State House, where they received the Governor and legislature, and escorted them to the Cathedral. There two orations were delivered, one in English and the other in French, and high mass was celebrated by the priests. While this was going on indoors, the troops in the square commenced a mimic battle, which they kept up for a full hour. The fire was incessant and heavy. About 1,000 men were under arms, and the din was tremendous. About 2 o'clock they ceased firing and dispersed.

Dined at Mr. Pearce's. The company consisted of Mr. Pearce, Dr. and Mrs. Ker, Miss and Master Shields, a Mr. Foster of New York, Mr. Kennedy and Mr. Crawford, of Baltimore, and myself—nine plates. I was invited to a family dinner, and expected a plain family party. Everything was in a style of great elegance, and the party very agreeable. I retired at half past 5 o'clock, having an appointment to meet Byrd Waller, who I met in the street to-day. He did not come, and I walked around to Dr. B.'s office, where I saw Dr. Powell and Seth Barton.

Saturday, January 9, 1836.

The negotiation for the Texas loan is this day concluded, and only waits for the articles to be drawn out in form by a notary. The principal features are, a loan of $200,000 for five years at 8 per cent interest, with the privilege of commuting it into land at 50 cents per acre, the lenders to have priority of choice over all who acquire right to land after this day. We only pay 10 per cent of the loan until it shall be confirmed by the Convention of Texas, and notice given of such confirmation, after which the balance is to be paid in three installments at sixty, ninety and one hundred and twenty days. The lenders to have the privilege of paying no more, if they think proper, than the 10 per cent, in that event to take lands for what they pay; surveys to be made at the expense of Texas. I think it a most advantageous arrangement, and lament my inability to go largely into it. There is but one chance against its being a splendid speculation, that of Santa Anna conquering Texas. Can he do it? I think not.

Saw Byrd Waller; he has lived at Brazoria; came away sick, and is still on regime; says Brazoria is a sickly place, and falling off in population-not more than 500 left; thinks it will never rise. All the river sickly for sixty or eighty miles from the coast; all the coast healthy, also the upper country. Says the lands are fertile, but the salubrity of the country over-rated. (He can hardly be a fair judge; he may view it with a jaundiced eye.) Says the practice of the law is simple and profitable. The provisional government has adopted, ad in-terim, the laws of Louisiana, and the practice of her courts. Gave me the following list of books, as most needful to a practitioner:

Louisiana Revised Code.
C. Code 1825.
C. Practice.
Pattidas, two volumes.
Cooper's *Justinian.*
Pothin on Obligations.
Martiny's *Reps., O. & M.*
S. up to 1825.

There were two more murders committed here last night, one, a sailor cut open by a Spaniard and thrown into the river; the other, a young man, a clerk named Harvey, stabbed by a drayman, on a slight dispute about drayage.

I. P. Corbin, Dabney, Cham. Pollard, Dr. Carter, of Prince Wm., Va., and W. F. Taliaferro, have arrived. Carter is going to Texas.

We have just heard of the massacre by the Indians of Major Dade and his command, except three who escaped badly wounded; loss, eight officers, one hundred and nine men. See newspaper statements.

Had long conversation with A. J. Yates about Texas. Says he thinks Galveston Bay will become the principal commercial depot of Texas. A company of New York capitalists have purchased a league of land on the island, including Lafitte's old fort, on which they design building the city of Galveston. He thinks it the only port on the bay for foreign shipping. Spoke also of the country on the San Antonio; mostly settled by Spaniards. Some old Mexican stations have spacious and substantial buildings. Thinks they may be bought very low. But little wood in the country, and no rain. But all the lands on the river are irrigated from the river with ease. The river flows rapidly but smoothly. A waterfall sufficient for any machinery may be got in every 100 yards. The climate dry and very delightful.

Sunday, January 10, 1836.

Fine day. Wrote to T. Green and to Mrs. Gray. Did not get letters into the office until 12 o'clock. Went then to hear Mr. Clapp, a Unitarian, who has a large church, and a very full congregation. He is said to be much of an orator. He had nearly closed when I went in. The attention of his audience was fixed. What I heard was well expressed, but there appeared too much effort for effect. Went thence to the Presbyterian Church (Parker's), a new and very beautiful edifice, somewhat like that in Fredricksburg, but finished with more splendor and taste. A fine steeple, large organ, seats cushioned with crimson moreen, lighted in a unique manner. A section of a sphere projects from the ceiling, in which is fixed numerous lamps, lighted from above. These shed, as it were, but one ray, diffusing a strong light over all the church. The only other lights are two lamps on the pulpit, and several small ones in remote parts under the galleries. I did not see it lighted, but the effect must be good.

Dined with J. H. Caldwell. The company consisted of Mr. Finn, the actor, Mr. Elliot, the husband of Celeste, Miss Copeland, an actress, Mr. * * *, secretary of the gas works, Mr. * * *, editor of * * *, Shakespeare and myself. The lady well behaved, Finn and the editor sensible, intelligent and agreeable; the secretary an old Hogg; the husband of Celeste, a rowdy, and, by his own account, a bully. Boasted of having beat Count D'Arey in the theater in London for having taken liberties with Celeste on the stage; also flogged Lord Somebody-else. After dinner walked out to the gas works; a noble establishment, built out in the marsh, beyond the hospital. The use of gas becoming general in the city.

H. F. Thornton arrived this evening. He has been sick at Woodville, Miss. Has done nothing in lands. Talks of going to Texas with me.

Had a long conversation to-night with Hotchkiss. He was a student at West Point. Entered the army at the commencement of the late war as a second lieutenant, at the age of nineteen; was in nineteen battles and skirmishes; was at the taking of Fort George. Thinks Dearborn was the best general in the army. He was scientific and prudent, acted slowly, did nothing rashly, but succeeded in what he attempted. The taking of Fort George required much more military talent than any of the battles fought on the frontier. He was in the bloody fight at Bridgewater, and left for dead on the field, where he lay all night with a dead man across him. Rose to a captaincy.

After the war went to Mexico. Contracted to construct a fort at Tampico, which the government failed to do. Was seven years in Mexico. Traveled all over North and South America, in every town on the Atlantic and Pacific, and has acquired the Spanish language. Has latterly acted as agent for the "Galveston & Texas Land Company," and resided at Nacogdoches. He has acquired a good deal of land. Owns the salt springs forty miles from Nacogdoches, which he acquired by buying out the several claimants. Spoke also of the Missions at San Antonio, and the probability of buying out the titles from the Spaniards very low. Says scarcely any of the Spaniards will remain in the country if the Texans sustain the revolution, and that when they determine to go they will sell for what they can get. He wishes to engage in the speculation with some capitalists.

Triplett and he have had some conversation about it. Thinks the new government will authorize the introduction

of slaves into Texas. He and General Houston are not friendly; says Houston is losing popularity, is intemperate, could
not be elected to the Convention at this time. Thinks Texas
has appealed to arms too soon. The event was foreseen as
inevitable, but would have been better postponed until they
were stronger. Austin thought so, too, and Austin might have
averted the event at the time it happened, had he been firm;
but he was induced to consent, and to unite in the revolution against his judgment. Had he said peace, and stood firm,
they would not yet have had war. As it is, thinks there is no
doubt of success.

MEMO. to write T. Green about San Antonio and the salt
springs, and to visit both places, if possible.

Monday, January 11, 1836.

The contract for the loan was executed this morning. We
shall have to wait some days for the signing of the scrip and
printing of the contract. See printed copy.

I have contracted with David Brown, as attorney in fact
for Walter Hughes, for a league of land on Six Mile Creek,
one of the waters of the Sabine, at twenty-five cents per acre,
provided I shall be satisfied with the land when I see it, and
it shall be a good title under the regulations to be adopted by
the legislature of Texas. See contract.

Brown goes up Red River in the *Caspian*. Lives at Robertson's, on the road from Natchitoches to Nacogdoches,
forty-five miles from Fort Jesup, where he invited me to call.

Dr. Barton invited Thornton and myself to a seat in a private box at the theater with him, where I went reluctantly
and spent a dull evening. Play, *Romeo and Juliet*; Juliet by the
celebrated Miss Philips. She does not suit the character, too
majestic, and, to my notion, overacted. The farce, *Bold Dra-
goon*, very tolerable.

Tuesday, January 12, 1836.

Warm and raining. Wrote letters, etc. The loan is much talked of, and the Texans are in high spirits. I feel an increased cordiality in their manner. It has raised their credit, and others are now anxious to come in on the same terms. This they cannot allow. They have offers of credit for supplies, on the faith of the country. I trust the stone, being set agoing, will now go ahead.

Wednesday, January 13, 1836.

Fine day, clear and warm. Hancock left to-day in the *Caspian* for Red River. Memo. to take charge of his scrip, and call for him at Alexandria, send a messenger for him to Judge Johnson's, and he will accompany me up Red River.

Called with Thornton to see Mr. Jones (son of W. S. Jones, of Winchester, Va.), who unhappily killed his fellow-student in Bedford County some years ago. He is now practicing law here. Has traveled in Texas. Speaks highly of what he saw of it, but thinks there is no safety in buying lands.

Chewning and H. Dawson arrived to-day from Vicksburg. No letters for me. Chewning says there were none at Vicksburg. What can be the meaning of this? In a conversation with Dawson he made the following proposition: He and his brother own about 11,000 acres of unimproved land, which they have entered. If I will obtain capital, say $50,000, to invest in negroes, they will put in their land at $2.50 per acre. They will buy negroes in Virginia or elsewhere, and place them in detachments on the land, so as to open several farms at once, and as good sales can be effected, sell land and negroes together. When the lands are sold, the $50,000 to be first returned without interest, and next the price of the land paid to them, and the profit on the operation to be divided equally between the two parties. The two Dawsons to give their exclusive attention to the business, to buy slaves, hire overseers, and see that they do their duty, and make sales, and to make further entries of land, should the capitalist choose to go on in the business. An agent to be established at Vicksburg, to receive and forward the slaves, supplies, etc. This is a good money-making scheme, and is in fact the same plan that I proposed to Green. The Dawsons have acquired a character as land hunters, and are worthy business men. An association with them might be advantageous. H. Dawson says there are a great many good lands to be entered in Louisiana and Arkansaw, and that his brother is going up to look after them. Memo. to write T. Green about it.

Thursday, January 14, 1836.

Dined by invitation with Dr. Barton. Company consisted of H. F. Thornton, Mrs. Morton and daughter, Col. Logan and wife, Judge Chinn, wife and two daughters. Logan is from Kentucky. Lived a short time in Vicksburg; removed to Texas three years ago; is a merchant; resides at Nacogdoches; has acquired large quantity of lands, and is now paymaster general of the Texan army. A handsome, gentlemanly fellow; wife also genteel, but in bad health. They were married very young he nineteen, she fourteen—no children!

Judge Chinn is a sugar planter on the coast. Came from Fauquier, Va. In conversation after dinner we discovered that we had known each other some twenty-seven or twenty-eight years ago in Fredericksburg, at R. Lewis'. He is cousin to Dr. T. T. Withers, Eqr.

Conversed with Logan about Texas. He confirms the statements about San Antonio. Says there are large churches there in the woods, whose turrets rise above the trees, and struck the army with astonishment when they first got there. The Missions are all fortified, with bullet-proof walls (Archer made a similar statement). The river heads a short distance from the town of San Antonio, in numerous bold springs.

When the Texan army was there the Mexican titles might have been bought for a mere trifle. Logan has a league of Gen'l Houston's land for sale (to pay for the General's toggery), on Red River, thirty miles from Pecan Point, best quality $2,500, $1,000 cash, balance one and two years, with interest. Dr. Barton is chaffering with him for that and some city lots.

Mr. Christy is getting out of favor with the Commissioners. He was offensive to them. Capt. Hall has been appointed their purchasing agent, and Mr. Bryan agent for receiving the loan. Cardoza has offered to open an account with them and furnish supplies. He was the first to do it.

Friday, January 15, 1836.

Called to see Beverly Chinn. Found him much altered in appearance. Showed me a splendid map of New Orleans drawn by Bringeir, the surveyor general of the State. In includes Lake Pontchartrain and all the vicinity, with the two canals and railroads. He expatiated on the great increase of New Orleans and the splendid destiny that awaits her. He has lived here forty years. Invited me to a family dinner on Sunday.

Bought *Newman & Barrett's Spanish Dictionary*, $5, and *Jose's Gr.*, $1.50. Hotchkiss says *Cubis' Gr.* is best for learners, and Jose's the next best.

Introduced by Dr. Barton to G. C. Lawhon, one of his students, who lives in Texas, not far from St. Augustine. Promised me a letter to his father-in-law. Recommended me to call on * * * Smith, a surveyor, in Nacogdoches, who has lands on the Neches—a reliable man. Says he knows Brown, but prefers Smith, whose word may be relied on. (*E converso?*) Lawhon wishes to sell one-half league of land on the Sabine, but demands 50 cents per acre. He is a practitioner of medicine. Lived formerly in Mississippi and in Arkansaw. Went to

Texas in bad health, and has recovered. Says the fevers there are milder and more manageable than in Mississippi or Arkansaw. Rheumatisms are scarcely known. Liver complaint and dyspepsia are cured by going there. The Texans ascribe the salubrity of the country to the water, which they think contains some medical virtue.

At Mr. Wharton's request, gave him a letter of introduction to John M. Patton, and received a joint one from the three Commissioners to Governor Smith of Texas. Scrip not yet ready.

Saturday, January 16, 1836.

Fine, warm weather. Taliaferro, Clarkson and Parker left here on the *Homer*, the two former for Virginia, the latter for Vicksburg, and then to return here. Wrote by Taliaferro to my daughter.

The scrip for the Texan loan is at length ready and divided, and there being fractions enough to make four, we drew lots for them. I got one, Triplett two, and Irwin one, which makes my share thirty-two—cost, $1,024. The expenses of notary, printing, etc., was $310, of which my portion was * * *.

MEMO.—It is agreed among the holders that none should be offered for sale until the contract shall be confirmed by the Convention, and that it shall be held at $1.25 until that time.

MEMO.—Mr. A. Penn requested me to write to him should anything interesting occur respecting the scrip.

Wm. F. Ritchie returned from Texas by sea in the * * * eight days from Brazoria. Left there Gen'l Lambert, A. T. Burnley and O. Farish, who intend pursuing their journey still farther. He speaks well of the appearance of the country, but not of the state of things there. Says the provisional assembly was openly insulted and abused by a parcel of citizens (rowdies), who were displeased at Austin not being elected Governor, and that they were only saved from outrage by the interference of Gen'l Houston and a few others who resolved to protect them, and had sufficient influence or force to repress the mob.

Introduced to Dr. Richardson, surgeon general of the Texan army, and Capt. Hawkins, formerly of the Mexican navy, lately in Mexia's expedition, and now in the Texan service. (He is the man who killed Macrae at Key West.)

Went with Triplett and Ritchie to the theatre, the play being for the benefit of Texas. Met the Commissioners and sat with them in the parquet. A poor house; rather a poor performance. Left the house before the performance was over. Wrote till 2 o'clock a.m. Wrote to T. Green.

Understood Yates to say that, by the law of Texas (or Mexico), any person might rescind a bargain after receiving payment, should he desire it, by paying up principal and interest. Can this be so? *Query*.

Sunday, January 17, 1836.

Wrote to T. B. Barton. Received a joint letter of introduction from the three Commissioners to Governor Smith of Texas, also private ones from Austin to Gen'l Houston, and T. F. McKinney, mouth of the Brazos. Gave Austin letter to I. Taliaferro and S. L. Southard. Received letters also from B. Waller to Governor Smith, Edwin Waller, Columbia, and Wm. B. Travis, San Felipe. Employed all the forenoon in writing; did not go to church. Dined at Beverly Chew's; cordially received. Company, Dr. Barton, Dr. Davidson and daughter, H. F. Thornton and self, Mr. and Mrs. Conolly and Miss Conolly. Dinner and wine abundant and excellent. After dinner walked with the gents to see Clayton's ascension in a balloon. He ascended from the State House yard. Went up very finely, and remained in sight some fifteen or twenty minutes. The day was colder and cloudy, threatening rain. His course was northeast or east northeast. Walked to the basin, or head of the new canal. This canal and railroad company is connected with the bank of which Chew is cashier and Arch'd Taylor was first president. It is a great work, and in successful progress. Will add much to the wealth and health of New Orleans.

At night introduced to Major Richard B. Mason, U. S. army. Conversation about Red River and Texas. Says the Red River bears much more to the southwest than is represented on the maps. The Comanches are a deceitful, mischievous, thieving tribe. He has been among them, and saw a great many Spanish prisoners in their nation, a number of boys and girls, whites, that had been stolen by the Indians and raised by them. Thinks the lands high up on Red River not so good as those about the Raft.

Had a long conversation with Dr. Richardson about Texas. He is intelligent, communicative, and unpretending. Corroborates the accounts given by others of San Antonio. No building timber, no rain; the land would be desolate were it not for irrigation, which is easy. One hand will irrigate fifteen acres in a day. The old Spanish buildings are of stone, does not know where it is obtained; none in the country that he saw. The climate is most delightful. The valley, when viewed from the heights, seems covered with a hazy matter, resembling the Indian Summer, but not dense, transparent enough to show the most distant objects, which loom beautifully. The Missions are heavy, strong built places, intended for fortifications as well as dwellings. Says Mexican rights may be bought very low, and they are the best titles. Says contracts are obligatory, not revocable, as far as he knows, in the way stated by Yates. Austin, also, said if there was such a law he did not know it. Wrote a letter to Mrs. Gray.

Monday, January 18, 1836.

Weather warm, and raining. Prepared to go Up Red River in the steamboat *Levant*, which was to have started to-day; but in consequence of the rain, postponed until to-morrow, 10 o'clock. Wrote to J. Taliaferro, and inclosed contract for loan, and letter to T. B. and Mrs. Gray.

Wrote also to J. M. Patton and S. L. Southard, inclosing contracts. (Yesterday received a visit from Dr. McPherson, the husband of Madame Jerome. Promised to call and see Madame on my return.)

Went to see R. Marye; found it a home of mourning. Mrs. Blackwell's youngest son had been buried this afternoon. His complaint was chronic scrofula. He was unwell the last evening that I spent there, but I did not know he was so ill. I was mortified at having been in the city and not knowing the illness and death of the child until after its burial. His name was George Steptoe. Her only other son is William Wyatt, who is at school in Frankfort, Ky. Mrs. Blackwell was sick in bed.

Tuesday, January 19, 1836.

The rain is over and gone, and the wind fresh from north; quite cool. My last care in the city was to call at Wallace's and at the postoffice for letters. None! I have not had a line from Virginia since 7th of December, and there are letters in New Orleans from Fredericksburg as late as 3rd of January. One from Metcalfe to B. Chew informs that I. Smock died on Christmas day. Jere Morton returned to the city last night, and called this morning to see me. He wishes to go into the Texas loan.

Another loan has been made of $50,000 cash—in other respects like the first, only subject to our priority of choice. It was negotiated by Mr. J. P. Irwin (son-in-law of H. Clay). Thornton went in $1,000. Irwin offered them $100,000 for land at fifty cents per acre. This they refused, as they are not authorized to sell lands, nor are they willing to pledge the faith of their government any further on the terms of the first loan.

General Austin, Col. Houston, R. Triplett, Aug. Slaughter and R. L. Marye came on board to see me before starting. Received the following letters: From R. Triplett to P. W. Grayson and Wm. Burley. From Wm. Lambeth to P. W. Grayton; one open, one sealed. From Col. Houston to D. C. Barrett, San Felipe. Coots & Kellogg, San Augustine; Gen'l S. Houston, Washington; A. Hotchkiss, San Augustine, open, and the following sealed, viz.: Gen'l Houston, Mrs. Eliz. Houston, San Augustine; S. Houston (from Norwich, Vt.), A. G. Kellog, Asst. Q. M. Texas army, San Augustine. From J. J. Chewning to Mr. Mills, Brazoria. From W. F. Ritchie to Capt. Vail, Natchitoches, and to Lambert Jones, Burnley and Farish. From Dr. Barton to Col. Thorn, Nacogdoches. From A. C. Allen to Jno. [K.] Allen, Nacogdoches. From J. C. Lawhon to Mrs. Lawhon, San Augustine, sealed, and to Gen'l McFarland, San Augustine, unsealed. Also an official letter from the Commissioners to Governor Smith, open.

The following were committed to me at the moment of starting, by Gen'l Austin, sealed—

To Thos. F. McKinney, Quintana, mouth of Brazos.

To Gail Borden, Jr., 8an Felipe.

To Col. Phil. Soublett, or Frost Thorn, San Augustine, or Nacogdoches.

To Col. Thos. J. Rusk, San Augustine.

To P. W. Grayson, Columbia.

To D. C. Barrett, Washington.

The boat did not leave the levee until 1 o'clock p.m. The day is fine, and the plantations look lovely. They are burning off the old cane, and ploughing the ground for a new crop. The gardens are rich with green vegetables and full blown roses and other flowers, like ours in May.

The boat is crowded with passengers. The captain says 350 souls on board, many settlers for Red River and Texas, with women and children. Very few that I know; among them Mr. J. F. Irwin, of Cincinnati, Mr. Chenoweth, of Louisville, with whom I went down in the *Chancellor*. Introduced to Mr. Beeman, of Red River, Mr. Trotter, of Kentucky, a lawyer, who is seeking a new home. J. G. Bryce is also on board. He lives at Alexandria.

Wednesday, January 20, 1836.

Much disturbed last night by the gentlemen gambling. They kept it up until a late hour, some, I believe, all night. We stopt for two hours in the night at Donaldsonville. Mr. Chenoweth has left us. His object is to buy the sugar crop of some planters on the river. Gave me his card— "T. L. Chenoweth & Co.," Wholesale Grocers, etc., Louisville, Ky.

This morning passed Placquemine, a poor, decaying place, * * * miles from New Orleans. Stopt to wood in the Parish of West Baton Rouge; went ashore and saw cabbages and turnips in bloom and going to seed. At 11 o'clock passed the town of Baton Rouge, on the east side of the river, * * * miles from New Orleans; a beautiful situation, and apparently a regularly built town, but as the boat did not touch, had no opportunity of going on shore. An armory and barracks for United States troops prettily built on the shore. We have a bugler on board who plays well, and he saluted the barracks with his best tunes as we passed. In the afternoon passed close to Point Coupee, the residence of Wm. Taylor. Had a fine view of the house and plantation. House two stories, painted white, with verandas, or galleries, as they are called here. Taylor wishes to sell the place. It has not been profitable. Said to be too far north for sugar, and too far south for cotton. Immediately opposite is the little town of Bayou Sara, so called from the stream of that name, at whose mouth it is built. It is the landing place for the town of St. Francisville, which stands a mile or two back, on high land. Stopt again to wood on the estate of Col. Morgan. Saw a negro with a Buffaloe fish that he had just caught with a hand net in the river. It would weigh twenty or twenty-five pounds.

Thursday, January 21, 1836.

A heavy storm of thunder, lightning and rain ushered in the day. The boat had laid by at the mouth of the Atchafalia when the storm came on, and resumed her voyage at daylight. When I arose we were entering Red River. The gambling was kept up last night, as before. When I arose a party was still sitting around a table with cards in their hands and a candle burning. I was unconscious both of storm and gamblers, for I had been wearied with loss of sleep, and last night slept soundly. It continued to rain heavily until about 11 o'clock. It then ceased, and cleared up. At that hour the steamboat *Caspian* passed us on her way down, laden so heavily with cotton that her bends are under water. She left New Orleans last Wednesday. She, too, has a bugler, and he and ours played at each other as long as they could be heard.

The river presents a most forbidding aspect. The color, from which it takes its name, is a dusky, dirty mud, of a brick dust tinge, but not so bright, resembling the muddy water in which bricklayers dip their facing brick. Its average width, I suppose, is from 150 to 200 yards. On both sides swamp, over which the water is now flowing, as the river is pretty full. It is the dreariest region I have ever seen, worse even than the Mississippi. 3 o'clock p.m. The banks begin to show themselves a little above water. 4 o'clock; stopt at a place called Groton's Landing, in the Parish of Avoyelles. Here is the first human habitation I have seen since we entered the river. The banks here are some four feet above the water, but I am told 100 or 150 from the shore they fall off into impenetrable swamps.

A Mr. Beeman, to whom I was introduced in New Orleans, who emigrated from Middlesex, Va., in 1812, and acted as an overseer here for a number of years, has now become a wealthy planter, and lives on Bayou * * *, was very civil in introducing me to several gentlemen on board. A Judge Miller, formerly of this State, now of Cincinnati; a Mr. Carey, a brother of the one of that name who was killed in the celebrated Bowie fight near Natchez. The widow, who is a daughter of Judge Miller, is now on board, and her little son. A Gen'l Thomas, a lawyer, living near Alexandria, formerly a [member of Congress] from Tennessee. A Dr. Burr, who came from New York, near Troy, says he landed at Alexandria about two years ago with his wife and two small children, and not more than $6 in his pocket. By the practice of medicine and planting, which he commenced on credit, he is now worth $24,000. Says it is his design to return to the North; he has health, but his family is unhealthy, and it is impossible to raise children morally here. Although he has had health in his family (having only lost one child, and that by scarlet fever), yet of thirteen other men who came from New York with him, only one remains. He ascribes the mortality of the country to intemperance. The inordinate use of ardent spirits and of coffee, of which the people here drink a great deal, and he thinks it injurious to the nervous system. Says the climate relaxes the system very much, and the settlers suppose it necessary to raise it by the use of intoxicants, than which nothing can be more erroneous. That the moderate use of the ordinary wholesome food is all the stimulus needed; that the use of strong meats should be sparingly indulged in. The best diet is bread and milk, and the free use of vegetables. He lives on Bayou Boeuf.

Beeman says the best lands in this part of the State are on Bayou Bceuf, Bayou Rapides, Bayou Robert and Bayou Puffbower. This latter is said to derive its name from a man, who, traveling through this country many years ago, got swamped in that bayou with his horse, and was near perishing. The lands on the bayous are higher than those on the river, and never overflow. They are thickly settled, and form fine neighborhoods.

Gen'l Thomas mentioned what I had before heard from Major Mason, that six or seven hundred miles above the Kiomitia, the Red River runs through a sterile desert for a great distance, where it is perfectly clear, beyond which little or nothing is known of it. Its upper waters are strongly impregnated with mineral substances; their prevalence, even here, is said to be the reason that the water of this river is not good to drink. Even after it settles and becomes clear its taste is offensive, hence the water generally drank in this country is preserved in cisterns. The Pawnee fork of Red River, which is the great North fork, is very salt, and is said to run over immense rocks of salt. The Indians sometimes bring in large lumps of pure salt, said to be taken from those rocks. Major Mason was shown by the Indians large masses of salt, hanging like immense icicles from the rocks on the mountain sides. He did not go to examine them, but he saw them on the march, and the Indians told him they were salt, and from what he saw in their possession he did not doubt the fact. Fort Towson is at the mouth of the Kiomitia, and is north of the 44th deg. N. Above that the Red River bears away to the south, much more than is represented on the maps. Its waters interlock with those of the Brazos.

Friday, January 22, 1836.

Found ourselves this morning lying at Alexandria, 329 miles from New Orleans, 104 from mouth of the river. An old and decaying looking place, about 1,000 population. A good looking brick court house, a wretched market, some large and well assorted stores. Here we put off some passengers, and a good deal of freight, which detained us until noon. On the shore I found a servant of Judge Johnson, who had come into town to market. Gave him a note to Geo. Hancock, who was at the Judge's, and came in and joined us. Saw William Dunbar, who looks very well, and Robert Mackay, who is keeping a drug and bookstore, also well. Saw also Geo. Duncan, the yellow barber from Fredericksburg, who has erected a pole here. Called on Mr. Satterfield, and delivered to him his hat, which had been inadvertently landed at Helena in October from the *Algonquin*, and which I have had charge of ever since.

Introduced by Hancock to his brother-in-law, Dr. Davidson, of Alexandria (Hancock married Doctor's sister), who is the son of the elder Dr. Davidson, of New Orleans, with whom I dined at Chew's, and married a daughter of Dr. Ker; also to Mr. J. Cable, of Natchitoches, who has a map of the Raft and the intermediate country from that to the Sabine. MEMO.— try to get a copy. (Jared Cable.) Left Alexandria at 1 o'clock p.m. At 8:30 entered the Bon Dieu.

The day has been very cold; the morning was drizzling and raw, and the wind has been keen from the north all day; very like snow, and I doubt not snow is now falling at the North.

Saturday, January 23, 1836.

Daylight found us fifteen miles from Natchitoches, where we had stopt to wood; arrived at Natchitoches about 8 o'clock, while at breakfast. Learned on inquiry that J. F. Scott, of Hempstead County, Arkansas, had been here several days, and left it yesterday morning on the *Privateer* for New Orleans—unfortunate. Saw here the Mexican Governor of Coahuila and Texas, Viesca, and the political chief of Nacogdoches, Rueg, and several other Mexicans, on their way to New Orleans. Saw Capt. Vail, to whom I delivered Wm. Ritchie's letter; his trunk had been sent to San Augustine. The *Levant* returned down the river this evening. Irvine and Hancock returned in her. Endeavored to get a horse, but could not find a decent one in the place for sale.

Got acquainted on board the *Levant* with a Col. Horton, from Alabama, who is going to Texas with his slaves, to settle a plantation on the Colorado. Also a Major Wm. Fortson, who is going to settle on public land, near the Grand Cave, * * * miles from Natchitoches; says he travelled with Scott & Burnley last summer; and a Mr. Mays, who is also going to settle on public land, sixty miles above the Raft. He has his wife along, and a family of fine children.

D. H. Vail lent me a newspaper printed at Nacogdoches, called the *Texan and Emigrant's Guide*, No. 7, January 9. It commences a publication of the colonization laws of the Mexican United States. By this paper I learn that emigrants may now go into that country and take lands according to their colonization laws. See the report of the select committee, J. D. Clements and James Power, December 30, 1835.

The wind has continued all day from northeast; cloudy, raw and cold, threatening snow.

Sunday, January 24, 1836.

It has rained during the night, and the trees are all covered with sleet. It is still drizzling and cold, wind northeast. No church here but the Roman Catholic, and that very little respected. Called in for a few minutes to hear the priests chanting masses in Latin; about thirty persons present, black and white, men, women and children. Stores all open, and every kind of business going on as on any other day. Continued my efforts to buy a horse all day, which I could not effect without submitting to great imposition, until the afternoon, when I got a very good one of a Creole, on a plantation across the river, for $100. He is to bring him over at 8 o'clock to-morrow morning.

Fell in with a Scotch family, Wm. Sturrock, with his wife and two sons, lads, his son-in-law, Robert Galletly, wife, and several fine, hearty looking children. They emigrated from Scotland to New York two years ago, tried Canada, found it too cold, lived one year in the interior of New York; at length got some scrip from the "Galveston Bay and Texas Land Co.," in New York, for which they paid ten cents per acre. They have wended their way this far towards Texas, and are waiting here until the spring opens, when they mean to go over. Sturrock is a carpenter, Galletly a farmer. They have gone to housekeeping and working at the carpenter's trade. The old man says he and his boys are now earning $3 per day. They are very decent people; belong to the Kirk of Scotland; have some good books; among them saw *Henry's Commentary*. They will make valuable citizens of any country.

Introduced by landlord (* * * Cooke) to * * * Chapman, formerly of Madison County, Virginia, now sheriff of Natchitoches Parish; living here seven years; married. Said he remembered buying books of me when he was a boy.

Monday, January 25, 1836.

Purchased a horse of Ramie Poipot, a French overseer, who could not read nor write, for $100. Had to get him shod, which, with the procuring of equipments, kept me too late to reach Fort Jackson to-day, and as Mr. Thompson is going there tomorrow, waited for him.

Introduced to * * * Carter, of Albemarle, Va., who settled a plantation in Madison County, Miss., a few years ago, and sold out last spring. He is just returned from an exploring trip above the Raft. Says there are some fine lands in Claiborne Parish, which have just been surveyed, and some that have not been surveyed. They are in small parcels, on high land, equal to the best Mississippi upland. They are not thought of by speculators. Carter is going back to Virginia, there to remain.

Tuesday, January 26, 1836.

Left Natchitoches at 12 o'clock, in company with Lieutenant Blanchard, of the army, and his brother-in-law, Mr. Thompson. Road very bad. Passed in the route the Rio Hondo, somewhat famous in the history of this country as having once been considered the boundary line between the United States and Spain. It is a narrow, insignificant stream. Settlements on the road few and paltry. Reached Fort Jessup at 7 o'clock. Found Larkin Smith well, who got me a good supper, one of the items of which was milk and hominy, a feast that I had not enjoyed since leaving Virginia. Visited by Capt. Walker, Capt. Thos. J. Harrison, Lt. McLeod, Lt, Eaton, Lt. Macrae.

Wednesday, January 27, 1836.

Remained all day at the garrison, a very pleasant place. It is situated on the highest land between the Red River and Sabine. Soil sandy and dry; growth pine, with hickory, oak, etc. Very healthy. Everything appears to be conducted in good order in and about the place. The gardens are very fine, abundance of fine vegetables, flowers now in bloom, peach trees in bloom; the vine grows well; fig trees very large, mulberries, etc.; each company has a garden. Force consists of six companies, not now full; eight or ten of the officers are married. Dined with Major Nelson, a son of Roger Nelson, of Maryland; married a Widow Dexter, of Pennsylvania; has a step-daughter, Miss Dexter, very pretty, but has lost an eye. Company: Mrs. Irving, the sister of Mrs. Nelson; Mr. and Mrs. Vail, of Natchitoches; Lt. Smith and self. Miss Vail, a niece of Mr. Vail, is sick in the house. Paid a visit to Capt. Walker and Lt. Macrae. In the evening went to a social party at Lt. Macrae's, where they played cards and backgammon. Lt. Macrae is from P. Wm. Co., Virginia, and brother of the late Capt. Jno. Macrae. Introduced to Lt. Bonnell and wife, Lt. Alexander, of P. Wm., and Capt. Lewis. The regiment has an excellent band of music, which gives much life to the parades. Lt. McLeod has sent up his resignation, and only waits its acknowledgment so that he may join the Texan army.

The lands in this part of the State are generally poor, but some of the officers are about to make investments and go to farming. Capt. Harrison and Lt. Smith are about to buy a piece in partnership. Clear and cold; thermometer 28.

Thursday, January 28, 1836.

The weather this morning clear and cold; a fine white frost; ice on the puddles. Thermometer 14. Left the garrison at 10 o'clock, in company with Capt. Sherman, of the Newport, Ky., Volunteers, on his way to Texas. He has been sick at Natchitoches two weeks, and his company has gone on before him. We missed our way, and lost nearly an hour in regaining it. While endeavoring to do so, encountered a family in the woods who had removed from the Brazos, on account of the unhealthfulness of that country, and were taking up a residence here on Uncle Sam's waste land. After a pleasant ride (bating muddy roads), arrived at dusk on the banks of the Sabine, at Gaines' Ferry. Found two gents waiting to get across the ferry, Dr. Leon Jones and Mr. * * *, of Natchitoches. There was a swell of water in the river from recent rains, and the ferry was consequently half a mile across, through swamp and woods; the river, not 100 yards wide. The gentlemen had been waiting and hallooing some time for the boat, which was on the Texas side, and out of sight. There was a horn suspended to a bush, to be blown as a signal, but neither of them could blow it. I gave a few blasts on it, and in a little while the boat was brought over. We, were now joined by Col. Horton and Mr. Bullard, with two others of their party, making, in all, eight horses and their riders. The boat, fortunately, was a large flat, and took us all over at once.

The ferry and tavern are owned and kept by Capt. Jas. Gaines, who emigrated nearly thirty years ago from Culpeper., Va. He has seen much of Texas, and appears to be well versed in its history; is much of a politician, and a candidate for the new convention, the election for which takes place next Monday. Gaines says he fixed himself at this place in * * *, believing that Texas belonged to the United States, Mr. Adams having proved that it did, and he still hopes that it will. He goes for the independence of Texas, and then, to unite with Uncle Sam, if he will.

Found at the tavern a number of travelers, among them Col. Frost Thorn, of Nacogdoches, to whom I had letters, which I delivered. He, too, is a candidate for the Convention, and for Independence.

Friday, January 29, 1836.

The morning was lowering, and threatened rain. Left Gaines' at 9 o'clock. Soon after starting, rain began to fall, and it continued to rain all day. Stopt at the house of a Frenchman, named Maximilian, who said he had been living there forty years; that the King of Spain had made a grant of four leagues of land at that place to his uncle, who surveyed it and settled on it, and, dying, left it to the present occupant; that various persons had since intruded on his grant with their surveys, so that he now had only about three-fourths of a league left to him; that he had never sued them for his land, and was averse to contention, and was desirous of moving away, if he could sell. He offers his whole claim for $4,000, and it is likely he would take less. This is the first instance we have met of Texas justice, a sample of what I expect to see in their land operations.

About 4 o'clock we reached Roberts' where we found Mr. David Brown, whom I had met in New Orleans, and as it continued to rain, and we had yet four or five miles to make to San Augustine, concluded to stop here all night. Roberts has been here about eight years. This is a good farm, but the house, stables and everything about the establishment are rude and comfortless in the extreme. Brown is a candidate for the Convention.

Saturday, January 30, 1836.

It continued to rain heavily all the forenoon, and we remained within doors. The rain having ceased, after an early dinner we started. Brown accompanied us as far as San Augustine. Delivered letters to Coote and Kellog, and Mr. Houston. Judge Hotchkiss was at Nacogdoches, also Col. Rusk. San Augustine is a new place, not two years since the first house was built. Has now about a dozen finished and going up. Laid out in the woods, on red land. Rode on to Gen'l McFarland's, about six miles. Found the General at Dr. Lawhon's, his son-in-law. Kindly received and treated with marked attention after I had delivered my letters from Dr. Lawhon and he found out who we were; but the house being small and unfinished, we had to take a bed on the floor, and the General rolled in with us, in his clothes. Mrs. Lawhon occupied the only other room in the house. The General's two sons, living on an adjoining place, came in to supper. The elder one had been in the campaign on the San Antonio. He is also a surveyor, and says that in his surveying he has discovered many indications of minerals. In one place he found so many crystals that he could have filled a half bushel with them. Made a great secret of it. General McFarland thinks the lands between the Bays of Sabine and Galveston, near the coast, are the finest in Texas. He entered a league headright there for Dr. Lawhon, the deed for which he had sent to him in New Orleans, to sell a part to pay his winter's expenses. He supposes the doctor will have to give it away for about fifty cents per acre, and it is worth twenty dollars.

Sunday, January 31, 1836.

A fine, clear, frosty morning, with a cold northwest wind. Left Dr. Lawhon's at half past nine o'clock. Were soon overtaken by Lt. Col. Hy. Millard, of the First Regiment, Texan Infantry, who rode with us into Nacogdoches. Passed over a diversified country, much sand, and pine growth, some strips of red land and some black land on the bayous. Passed the Ayish Bayou, Attoyac, Morel, etc.; growth, pine, black jack and scrub hickory. General appearance not promising.

Very much like the uplands in Hinds and Madison Counties, Miss., except in the color of the land.

Col. Millard had been a merchant in Natchez, then in New Orleans, and now in Texas. Came to this country last July; had a store on the Neches, kept by his brother, some years before. Has operated in lands. Was a member of the Convention in November, 1835, and also of the Provisional Council, which he left, some weeks ago, after getting his appointment in the army. Thinks the new Convention must declare for independence; if they do not the army will. He is now superintending the recruiting service.

Arrived at Nacogdoches before night. Saw Col. Edwards and Mr. J. [K.] Allen, to whom I delivered my letters. Was invited by the former to his house, along with Capt. Sherman, where we took lodgings, with an old Virginia welcome.

Col. Haden Edwards is a native of Stafford County, Virginia, born near Aquia Church, whence he removed with his father in 1779, he being then but eight years old. Has experienced various fortunes since. Been a lawyer and a merchant, lived in several States of the United States, and in Mexico; got a grant of lands, which has not been confirmed so as to be available to him. He is now sixty-five years old; lives with his son-in-law, Col. Frost Thorn, who is a merchant in Nacogdoches.

Monday, February 1, 1836.

This is the day designated by the Provisional Council for a general election of members of the new Convention. There are a large number of candidates. This place is much divided on the questions of adhering to the Mexican Constitution of 1824, or declaring for absolute and immediate independence. Much excitement prevailed. The constitutional party have enlisted on their side all the Mexicans, or native Texans, who are a swarthy, dirty looking people, much resembling our mulattos, some of them nearly black, but having straight hair. The company of Newport, Ky., Volunteers, has been detained here to vote; they are on the independence side. Several of the candidates addressed the people, and among them the famous Robert Potter, of North Carolina, who has been here some months. On the volunteers offering to vote they were refused by the judges, which caused an angry excitement. The company was drawn up with loaded rifles, and the First Lieutenant, Woods, swore that the men should vote, or he would riddle the door of the Stone House, where the election was held, with rifle balls. The Captain, who had only arrived the night before, had not yet resumed the command of the company, and determined not to interfere, but to let the company and the judges fight it out. The citizens were then called on to decide by a count of heads whether the volunteers should vote or not, and on being polled the Constitutionalists outvoted the Independents some thirty votes. On this the Mexicans sent up a shout of triumph, which enraged the volunteers, and it was feared they would fire on the citizens. Judge Hotchkiss and myself interfered to restrain them. I addressed them publicly, and attempted to convince them that by the law of the country and the ordinance under which the Convention was held, they had not the right to vote—or that it was at least a questionable right; that it was unbecoming in them, coming into the country as soldiers, to be stickling at the threshold for political rights; that it was derogatory to their character to be mingling in the political and personal squabbles of the country, contrary to all the principles of republicanism, and destructive of the freedom of election; for soldiers with arms in their hands to interfere in elections; exhorted them to abstain from violence, reserve their weapons for the enemies of the country, etc. I think the address was effective, although Mr. Potter attempted to neutralize it by a short reply, *ad captandum*, appealing to the passions of the men, and exhorting them to perseverance in their determination to vote, etc. They were also addressed by Col. Rusk, one of the candidates, who stated that the judges were reconsidering the subject, and would announce their determination after dinner. Mr. J. K. Allen also said a few words, exculpating Lt. Woods from some charges that had been raised against him. After dinner it was announced that the volunteers might vote if they chose. They had in the meantime consulted, and unanimously resolved that they would not vote, at which I was much gratified. I was more gratified at hearing it said by a citizen that I had been the means of preventing bloodshed. But the volunteers, with the waywardness of children, reconsidered their determination, and subsequently all voted. They were all day under arms, and frequently marched to and fro, with drum and fife, before the door of the Hustings—a shameful spectacle, which I never before witnessed. But, notwithstanding all, the Constitutionalists carried the day by a considerable majority. The polls, however, are to be opened again to-morrow.

Tuesday, February 2, 1836.

The polls have been open all day, and 401 votes have been taken in the two days. Inasmuch as the volunteers, and all other "free white males" have been permitted to vote, and I was desirous of becoming a citizen as soon as possible, I went forward and tendered my vote, which was cheerfully received, and I am now considered as identified with the interests of the country, and entitled to all the rights of citizenship! This day has gone off quietly. The angry feelings excited yesterday are hushed, if not extinguished. The foremost candidates are Th. J. Rusk, 247; C. P. Taylor, 221; Jno. S. Roberts, 203; Jno. K. Allen, 200. These four are supposed to be elected, but there are other election precincts in the municipality, the returns from which may vary the result. The next highest were Robert Potter, 157; Col. Haden Edwards. 133.

The weather for the two last days has been very fine, cool, but clear, dry and elastic, like fine autumn weather in Virginia. I wear no overcoat.

Wednesday, February 3, 1836.

Another fine day, but warmer than yesterday; three white frosts and then a rain is the rule here, so we may expect rain to-morrow.

Subscribed for the *Texan and Emigrant's Guide*, a paper published weekly, at $5. Sent then also to Enquirer and Arena, and requested exchange. It contains an abstract of the colonization laws. Gave some New Orleans papers to the editor, D. E. Lawhon, the brother of Dr. Lawhon. Took a survey of the town and suburbs. The town is prettily situated on a sandy plain, between two fine, clear streams—the Banito (Little Bath), on the west, and the Nana (Mother), on the east—each of them of sufficient volume and fall for mills or machinery, and amply sufficient for a large canal, which might be easily constructed to their junction with the Angelina, which has boat navigation to within eight miles of this place. There are several mounds on the north side of the town, where the Roman Catholic (or Mexican) burying ground is located; that of the Protestants or Anglo-Americans is several hundred yards from it, on the east side of the town. The town is old, and once contained four or five thousand souls, now scarce as many hundreds; the buildings, with one or two exceptions, miserable, shabby, old Mexican jacals, constructed by inserting pickets in the ground and fastening them on the top by a plate, and daubing the interstices with red mud, some built of logs, covering, clap boards, chimneys of mud. They are scarcely equal in appearance to the negro houses in the suburbs of Fredericksburg. The appearance is shabby in the extreme; not a decent tavern in the place. But there is a tolerably good society in a few families of Anglo-Americans. There is no social intercourse between them and the Mexicans. The latter much resemble our mulattos in appearance and manners. Yet there are among them some intelligent and respectable people, and their character generally is that of a quiet, orderly, cheerful people, fond of dancing and gambling, unthrifty and unambitious.

The horses belonging to the baggage wagon of the volunteers escaped from the stable lot on Monday night, and have not yet been found. The company was marched off this morning under command of the Second Lieutenant, and left their baggage to go on when the horses shall be found. The citizens were drawn up in a line to salute them as they departed. They were treated with liquor, and some gents drank toasts in the street. Mr. J. K. Allen's toast gave offense to Mr. Potter, who resented it. Some sharp words were exchanged, and a fracas was about to ensue, which was prevented by the prompt interference of Col. Rusk, who rebuked and silenced them. It is manifest that much ill blood exists in this little community. Potter is regarded as a disorganizer, and his coming among them is greatly deprecated by the intelligent and well disposed. He is courting popular favor with all his art, and is succeeding to a wonderful degree. He can only float in troubled water.

VOL. VI

Wednesday, February 3, 1836 (continued).

Rode out in the evening with some ladies a few miles up the Pecan Point road, north; a beautiful carriage road, over sand and red land, leading up the Banito. Was informed by Col. Raguet that the lands around the town for three miles from the Principal or Plaza, in all directions, belongs to the town for public use. If so, and the Trustees or Corporation of the Town could sell or lease them, the town of Nacogdoches might be made very rich, have beautiful squares and walks, and other valuable improvements. What mighty things might here be done under a good government, with wise laws and a little public spirit among the people. Here might flourish a populous city, distinguished for opulence, learning, arts, sciences, trade, health and all the blessings and comforts of civilized life. Weather warm and cloudy, threatening rain.

Thursday, February 4, 1836.

I had arranged to leave Nacogdoches to-day, in company with Mr. T. Savage, an intelligent gentleman of Massachusetts, who has lived some years in Mexico, and who is now going to Galveston Bay to see some lands. But I could not obtain, in time to start with him, some documents that were promised me, and was compelled to let him depart alone, which I regretted, as he would have been a valuable traveling companion. He is the gentleman who was imprisoned at * * * in * * *, on account of some copper Mexican coin shipped to him from the United States, contrary to the Mexican laws. See the newspapers of that period.

I have here become acquainted with Henry C. McNiel (brother of Major Alexander McN., of Miss., and cousin to Angus McN.); Dr. John Cameron, whose name figures on the maps as an Empresario (a shrewd Scot); Judge Augustus Hotchkiss, Col. Love, John K. Allen, all of whom are intelligent gentlemen, and in several conversations with them I have learned much of the history and present condition of Texas. Cameron is particularly well informed and interesting. He has suffered imprisonment by the Mexicans. Was at the capture of Bejar in December, acted as interpreter, and his name is signed to the Articles of Capitulation. McNiel has traveled much in Texas and in the interior. Love was at Bejar immediately after its fall. Allen has been to Monclova. They all concur in representing the Southwest as the finest part of Texas—not to say of the world; indeed, one of them called it the Garden Spot of the World.

Col. Love is a native of the County of Brunswick, Virginia, but his parents removed to Georgia. He now hails from Columbus, Georgia. Has been a trader among the Indians; is fond of the Indian life; says he never drank a drop of spirituous liquor, wine or beer, smoked a cigar, or chewed tobacco! He is a strange but interesting character. He traveled from Columbus, Georgia, via Natchitoches and Nacogdoches, to Bejar, in thirty days, in hopes of being at the capture of the place—arrived a few hours too late!—chagrined. He is now acting under the orders of the Texan government, going among the Indians in the northeastern part of Texas, the Creeks, Delawares, etc., to embody them to act against the Western Indians, who are in Mexican interest and are becoming troublesome. He is in fine spirits, and appears to be in his element. He thinks it practicable to remove all the Indians from this part of the State and place them on the head waters of the Brazos, Colorado, etc., on the east side of the mountain, which forms the western boundary of Texas, and thus make them a barrier against the Comanches and other thievish and hostile tribes who inhabit the western side of the mountain. This would be a most valuable step for this part of the country. The Indians have settlements above and below Nacogdoches. Those above commence within five or six miles of the town, and they occupy nearly all the country between this and the Red River. They bring in skins, venison, pecan nuts, etc., and their trade is valuable to the merchants, but they are unpleasant neighbors, and retard the settlement of the country by whites. There have been many of them in town all this week, men, women and children, fantastically dressed, and exhibiting disgusting scenes of drunkenness and bestiality.

I attended a ball at Brown's Tavern, given by the Anglo-Americans, to which I had a ticket of invitation. It rained hard from noon until midnight; there are no carriages in the place, but this did not prevent the ladies from attending. They trudged to it on foot through rain and mud, to the number of about twenty; the gents were more numerous. I was really surprised to find that so shabby a looking place could assemble so many good looking, well dressed and well behaved women. The ball room was shabby and uncomfortable, and the entertainment coarse, but there was better dancing and more decorum than I have often seen at parties in Fredericksburg. They dispersed about 1 o'clock; all sober, and in good humor. The music consisted of two violins and a triangle, tolerably well played. It was, on the whole, a favorable specimen of Texan society.

There was last night a Mexican ball, or fandango, at the other end of the town, of which I was not apprised until today, which I much regret, as I am desirous of seeing life in Texas in all its varieties. The Mexicans hold their fandangoes at the Monte, or gambling house, of Miguel Cortenoz.

Friday, February 5, 1836.

It continued wet and cold all the forenoon. Held a long conversation with Major George Anthony Nixon, or Don Jorge Antonio Nixon, the Commissioner for giving land titles. He professes great disinterestedness and candor. I rather suspect he has neither. Showed me the arrangement of his office. The deeds to land are merely folded up, labeled and laid in numerical order in the pigeonhole of a wooden box, in the garret of an old wooden building, perfectly combustible. A spark would consume the fabric in a few minutes. There are no secure fastenings to the windows. I could enter it any night and bear off the whole of the titles. And these are the originals, and the only record that is kept—no book in which the deeds are recorded, as with us. The plan is to leave the original in the office and give the grantee a certified copy, which has the validity of the original. When another sale is made a similar deposit is made and a new copy issued. If the copy is lost a duplicate may issue, or a triplicate. The whole proceeding seems to be loose and insufficient, and opens the door for fraud, much of which has been practiced. The operations of this office are now suspended, and some hundreds of deeds are now lying here incomplete, waiting for some formalities and the payment of fees. Nixon expected to be removed or to have his duties superseded, and he has had the shrewdness to certify all the incomplete deeds, prior to a certain date, so that when the purchaser comes for his deed he will find it ready as far as the Commissioner can make it so. He showed me titles to a large quantity of land in his name, which he said he wished to sell in a body; he offered the whole at sixty-two and one-half cents per acre. Of course, in his opinion, it was worth a great deal more, twenty or thirty dollars per acre. The impression, on the whole, was unfavorable to the manner of giving and securing land titles and to the Commissioner.

I was desirous of obtaining from Major Nixon copies of the late laws passed by the Congress, respecting lands, but he would not give me a sight of them. Mr. W. S. Allen very kindly lent me a book containing all the colonization laws, constitutions, etc., and many other documents, which I am to return when we meet again. He came here as agent for the New York Company, but finding his vocation gone, he is about to return.

Mr. Jno. K. Allen showed me a charter for a bank in Spanish, which was read to me in English by Dr. Cameron. The charter was obtained at Monclova last February 7. The principal provisions were: Capital, * * * million; a mother bank and a branch; 10 per cent to be paid in on subscribing, and the balance secured on real estate, loans for six months, to be made at 8 per cent, for a longer period at 10 per cent. Each office to be under the management of * * * directors;

shares, one hundred dollars; five shares to give a vote; no stockholder to have more than fifty votes. He offered, as a favor, to let me in for a share of the stock, if I would advance the 10 per cent. required for the first payment on 350 shares. Chartered for * * * years.

Introduced to Judge Underwood, of Kentucky, who has been on the Brazos, near the Falls, and bought lands; he is now returning home for his hands to settle them. A pleasant intelligent gentleman. Wrote by him to T. Green, to be put into the office at New Orleans.

Capt. Archibald Hotchkiss arrived this evening, and with him Dr. Edwin Herndon, who is on his way to see the Surgeon General, with the intention of joining the Texan army. He has arrived opportunely to accompany me.

Visited, in company with Herndon and Judge Hotchkiss, a gambling house, kept by Miguel Cortinez; Mexican women and men, and some Americans, were playing at monte, roulet, faro, etc.; a dirty and mean looking place.

J. K. Allen thinks the Texan loan a capital investment. Says he will put 400,000 acres of land in with the $200,000, and take a joint interest with the lenders.

Saturday, February 6, 1836.

Dr. Herndon had foundered his horse, and left him at San Augustine, and borrowed one of Col. A. Houston, the back of which he hurt coming to this place. He did not succeed in buying one until dinner time, and we concluded not to start until to-morrow.

Introduced to Col. Bean, a gentleman of Texas, who owns an estate beyond the Angelina. He holds the command of Colonel in the Mexican army. Saw also Judge Raguet, the brother of the political chief of Nacogdoches. They are Swiss. Introduced to Judge Forbes, the Alcalde at this time, and to Major Arthur Henry, the Surveyor General, Postmaster, etc.

Dined at Col. Raguet's, in company with J. K. Allen, H. C. McNiel, Capt. Sherman. Saw Almonte's account of Texas, in Spanish. Miss Anna Raguet has translated the part relating to the Department of Nacogdoches, which she obligingly lent me to copy.

Judge Hotchkiss has made the following proposition to me: He will put sixty leagues of land, in the Colonies of Zavala, Aihlein and Burnett—all good titles, at 35 cents per acre; he will divide it into six parts, and will retain one part himself; he will give me one part, for selling, in the United States or elsewhere, the other four undivided parts.

Sixty leagues, *4428* acres, is English acres	265,680
At 35 cents, is	$92,988
Divided into six shares, one share is	$15,498
Four shares is	61,992 [acres]
Commission, one share for selling	15,498 [acres]
	$92,988

I could not close with him now, and he declines holding himself bound by the offer, at any future time. MEMO. to keep it in view. David Brown had made a similar proposition, and would put his land at thirty-three cents.

Capt. Sherman's horses were returned this evening, and his wagon will be got off to-morrow.

Col. Edwards has determined to go to the United States and solicit donations from the ladies, to raise a regiment for the defense of Texas. Gave him letters to Mrs. Gray, and Browne, Barton and Botts, Green, Triplett and Peyton, and C. H. Smith.

Wrote to J. M. Patton, Mrs. Gray, Dr. Barton, Wm. Bryan (N .O.).

In conversation to-day, offered myself to the members-elect as the secretary to their Convention, in which I am much encouraged by them. My main object in doing so is to become acquainted with the leading men of Texas, with its history, politics, resources, etc. The office of secretary to the Convention will, perhaps, accomplish all that better than any other position I can hold. It may be a stepping stone to something better. Wrote to Major James Gaines, to Gen'l McFarland, and to Col. Houston, on the subject, also to the delegates-elect from San Augustine. MEMO. to learn as soon as possible the names of the members-elect, and apprise them of my intention.

Sunday, February 7, 1836.

I shall here record a remarkable occurrence, which illustrates the manners and customs of the native Mexicans, a part of which I witnessed. A little child, daughter of Miguel Cortenoz, died yesterday. She had had the measles, was recovering, went out in cold, damp weather, took cold, and died suddenly. The family lived opposite to Colonel Edwards. The poor mother made loud and heart rending lamentations, which were heard from time to time all the evening, in which she lavished on the departed child all the endearing epithets in which the Spanish language is remarkably rich, and called upon the Virgin and all saints in the Roman calendar. The child was laid out in a room opening on the street in full view. During the evening the neighbors began to assemble, a violin was obtained, and the musician played all his liveliest airs for their amusement. No grief was manifested by anyone but the bereaved mother, and the contrast between her wailing and the lively tones of the violin was horrid. About 12 o'clock at night the corpse was moved from the dwelling house to the Monte house, kept by the father, accompanied by the violin and all the company. There it was laid out in form, and the company danced to the violin all night. This morning tickets of invitation were issued to the citizens to attend the funeral. M. Cortenoz is popular with the American population for the part he lately took in some Indian affairs, and many of the Americans attended the funeral, which is an unusual mark of respect with them.

The poor, unconscious infant was sumptuously arrayed in costly apparel, a full dress, even to shoes, a nosegay in its clasped hands, and its head and other parts decorated with numerous artificial flowers and gaudy ribbons, which were made up and adjusted by the Mexican women, in public, while they chatted and laughed with as much glee as if it had been a country quilting. A silver crucifix dagger was placed in the bosom of the corpse, and it was carried to the grave by six young females in a recumbent and almost upright position. There was no priest, but a Sacristan officiated and chaunted the service. The procession was accompanied by a drum, fife and two violins, playing lively tunes. A crucifix was carried before the corpse; the persons in the procession were all uncovered. Some of them, twenty or thirty, carried spermaceti candles in their hands, all burning, and others of the Mexicans carried guns, which they fired off from time to time during the procession to the grave. Amidst all the preparation, merriment and noise, the wailing, screaming, howling of the mother was heard from time to time; until the procession left the house; she remained behind. In the interior, I am told by Dr. Cameron, rockets are discharged during the procession, instead of the firing of guns. It is indeed considered by them an especial occasion for every demonstration of rejoicing, as they think the deceased has gone to Heaven. The mother alone permits the animal affections to predominate over her religious faith, and she seems to feel bound to make all possible demonstrations of outrageous grief. The following day, I am told, she goes about her business, or dances like other women, and shows no signs of mourning. Such are some of the inconsistencies and vagaries which poor human nature exhibits, under perverted religious influences, and deprived of proper mental and moral culture.

Left Nacogdoches about noon, in company with Dr. Herndon. Rode to Col. John Durst's, on the Angelina, eighteen miles, before sunset. This is a beautiful farm, and the best house that I have yet seen in Texas. Col. Durst is a native Texan. His parents came from Louisiana, but were of Scotch origin. He speaks French and Spanish better than English. Has a small library, some good books, mostly relating to Mexican and Texas history, laws, etc., and nearly all in Spanish. The honeysuckles, which clustered about the pillars of the piazza or gallery, were just blooming. Found here Don Vincente Alderete, a man somewhat conspicuous in the history of Texas of late years. He is a Mexican, and now hails from Bejar. Does not speak English. About 8 o'clock Dr. Cameron came in, and expressed much surprise that some gentlemen who had left Nacogdoches before him had not arrived. He, Durst and Alderete had much conversation in Spanish. The gentlemen expected were Mr. Guild, Mr. Newland and Capt. Sherman. They did not arrive.

Monday, February 8, 1836.

Capt. Sherman and Mr. Newland arrived to breakfast, also a number of travelers from Tennessee, etc., seeking for land and a home in Texas, among them Col. Geo. Reed, John B. Reed, J. W. Stamps, Jas. Beatty, Iredel Redding; they all started before us. Guild, it seems, had gone back to Nacogdoches, and Newland stops here. He is a young Scotchman, and it would seem there is some secret business on foot, in which he, Cameron, Durst, Alderete and Guild are concerned, and probably some gentlemen in Nacogdoches. They are all of the Constitutional party, and are very solicitous to sustain the election of the four delegates from Nacogdoches who are of that party. Forbes, the Alcalde, speaks of setting it aside for some informalities, at which they are indignant. We are in the midst of a revolution. Many intrigues are doubtless on foot—*nous verrons.*

Durst has acquired possession of a great deal of land, and is, or pretends to be, alarmed at the state of things, and anxious to sell. He says he has upwards of 40,000 acres in the tract on which he lives, which is part of an old Spanish grant, and will sell it for less than fifty cents per acre, including the beautiful improvements, a mill, and the ferry across the Angelina. It could not fail to be a good speculation.

Durst was in the last Congress that sat at Monclova. Austin and Sam'l Williams were also elected, but when the Congress sat Austin was imprisoned in Mexico, and never took his seat.

Durst and Williams were the only two who represented Texas. It was that Congress that authorized the Governor Viesca to sell 400 leagues of land, and it is said Durst got 100 of them. The country is now ringing with charges of fraud and corruption, and Durst is out of favor with the sovereign people, who say that the revolutionary government must set the sale aside. Durst explained the thing to me thus: By the Constitution, or the laws, the government is authorized to sell portions of the public land when the exigencies of the country require it. The last Congress resolved that the exigencies of the country then required it, and authorized the sale of 400 leagues, for the same price that colonists pay to the Empresarios. The colonists, however, have a credit of four, five and six years on their purchases, and are allowed six years to make a settlement in. The purchasers of the 400 leagues pay the whole purchase down at once, and stipulate to settle them in six years, in the same way that the colonists do. If this be a true statement of the case, I do not see that there is any good ground for the clamor that is raised against the speculation, and I suspect the clamor is principally raised by those who are disappointed in a participation in the speculation. A good speculation it certainly is, and, by the showing of Durst, a fair one.

Left Durst's after breakfast, Capt. Sherman in company, going on to overtake his men. Crossed the Angelina (pronounced here Anchleen), two miles; eight miles further on came to the estate (haciendo) of Col. Peter Ellis Bean, a Colonel in the Mexican service, to whom I had been introduced at Col. Edwards'. Stopt to see him; found him sick in bed; had been very sick, but was recovering.

Near Bradshaw's, a few miles west of the Neches, met Major General Samuel Houston, accompanied by his aids, Major Geo. W. Hockley and Major Alex. Horton, and a Capt. Lawrence, of the Tennessee Troop, and * * *. Delivered our letters. He dismounted, and, sitting down on the ground, wrote a number of memoranda with his pencil on them, addressed them to Governor Smith, and returned them to us. Found on examination that his memoranda were highly flattering. He said he was going to hold a treaty with the Indians settled in Texas, north of Nacogdoches, Cherokees, Shawnees, etc, and that he would be back at Washington by the first of March. Spoke highly of Governor Smith; said he was as honest a man as ever lived; that the Council, with which the Governor disagreed, was bribed, etc.

Crossed the River Neches, or Snow River, ten miles from Bean's. The Neches and Angelina are about the same size, about thirty or forty yards wide at the ferry, which is crossed in a flat. Arrived after dark at McLean's, a small house on the road near the San Pedro, which enters into the Neches. Here we found our Tennessee friends who left us in the morning. Supper coarse but good, bed excellent; some had to sleep on the floor. My age stood me in good service, both at supper and bedtime.

The country for the last two days has been improving. The color of the land is becoming darker, and the pines scarcer. The surface is rolling, and in some places presents fine views, but the soil does not appear rich, except on the watercourses. The high lands are sand ridges. The ground is dotted with innumerable little sand hillocks, resembling ant hills (which I suppose them to be), the sizes of which are from a peck to a half bushel. Roads very fine. Weather * * *. Fare at Durst's, $1. Ferriage at Angelina, 25 cents; ditto at Neches, 25 cents.

Tuesday, February 9, 1836.

Left McLean's early, and rode to Jacob Master's, twelve miles, to breakfast, where we again overtook our Tennessee friends, who had again got the start of us in the morning. Here is a store kept by Major Wm. Lewis, from Tennessee, who weighs 248 pounds. I weighed without any coat on 153; I had, however, just eaten breakfast, and had on thick over-shoes, which I suppose equal to the odd three pounds, 150 being my maximum. Four miles further on crossed Hurri-cane Bayou, a small stream with very steep banks. Six miles further brought us to Henry Master's, where our Tennessee friends parted from us. They went to the right, to examine the lands on the Trinity. Ten miles further arrived at Colin Aldridge's, on the Salado, or Saline, called also Caney Creek. Aldridge was not at home, and a Machanick named Little, who occupied a cabin close by, told us all the family was sick with measles, but he could accommodate us, and we could get nothing further on the road for our horses. For their sake we stopt, and had them well fed with Aldridge's fodder and corn. Little's whole establishment consisted of a miserable hut about sixteen feet square, which was kitchen, parlor, chamber, meat house, etc. There were two beds, and he had a wife and four children, the youngest sick with measles. Yet here he was to lodge us. He gave us a supper of very coarse fried bacon and pork, six boiled eggs, tolerable coffee, but no cream or milk, Indian pone, with so much grease in it that I could not eat it. I asked for cold bread, which fortunately they had, without shortening. I ate heartily but unhappily, gave of-fense, as I afterwards learned, by criticising the boiling of the eggs. In the meantime Aldridge came home, came over, and invited us to his house, which also consisted of but one room, but a large one. There were here only two beds, which were occupied by himself and wife, another woman, and several children, all sick with measles. A comfortable bed was spread for us on the floor, where I should have rested well but for the crying of the poor children, who were very restless. A stout negro fellow also slept on the floor near us, sick with measles. The house was so open that I could see the stars through the apertures.

Supper and lodging and horse at McLean's, 75 cents; breakfast and horse at J. Master's, 50 cents.

The lands to-day have been improving in appearance; their beauty is such as to call forth continual exclamations from our party. We begin to see a good deal of prairie, and about noon to-day enjoyed the sight of a prairie on fire. It was not extensive, but driven by a strong south wind through the dry prairie grass it was not without sublimity, and enabled us to form a clear idea of what the same phenomena would be on a large scale.

The settlers regularly burn both prairies and woods at this season. Their object is to clear the surface of any dry grass, to enable the cattle the sooner to get at the young grass, which immediately springs up. It is now very green on those parts which have been some days burnt. Some of the prairies exhibit the appearance of the most extensive and beautiful wheat fields. Herds of cattle and some sheep begin to appear.

The practice of annually burning the woods. I have no doubt, is, in part at least, the cause of the scarcity of timber. Almost all the woods we have passed through being stunted and scraggy black jack and hickory, very sparse, and little or no undergrowth. Some few oaks and pines grow to a large size, but generally the trees on the uplands have the appearance of disease. Many of them have the hard, irony appearance mentioned by Irving as characterizing the cross timbers. *Query*, may not these be the running out of the cross timbers? They cross the Red River about the south of the False Washita, and run on southward about in this longitude. May not the causes which produced them extend partially this far south?

Wednesday, February 10, 1836.

Rose early, intending to give our horses a good feed, take an early breakfast and make a good start. But the rascal who had in a manner cheated us into his house last night to supper, it seems, took offense at our not lodging with him, and now refused to give us breakfast, on the plea of the sickness of his wife and child. All a flam. After a while Aldridge had breakfast got for us, but his family were really sick, and it delayed our departure until almost 9 o'clock. Supper, 25 cents; mending great-coat, 25 cents; lodging, horse and breakfast, 75 cents. Aldridge rode with us a few miles, and was very civil. He is a Yankee; had been a settler at Fort Towson for some years. Came here and took the place he lives on as a headright. Intends planting and improving his place.

We were also joined at Aldridge's by a Mr. Whitely, who is going to Washington to attend the court which is to sit there on the fifteenth. He has business in A* * *. He, too, is a Yankee, and came to this country with Aldridge. Took one-fourth league for his headright, he being a bachelor, and has bought more. Bought a league from a Mexican for $400, which he showed as we rode through it. It is pretty looking land; offers it for 50 cents per acre.

Leaving Aldridge's, in about three miles we passed the Mustang Prairie, the largest yet seen, being about * * * miles across, and very beautiful, extending up the country as far as could be seen. About 2 o'clock we crossed the Trinity, which we approached through a boggy, miry, nasty prairie, or rather marsh, of several miles extent, which is subject to overflow when the river is high. The Trinity is here about fifty yards wide, and runs rapidly between steep banks, some twenty or twenty-five feet above the present stage of the river, which is somewhat up. Crossed in a flat. The ferry is owned by a Mr. Robbins, who lives on the west bank, and has got a town laid off there. A large number of towns are projected in various parts of the country, one about * * * miles lower down the Trinity, called Bath. (Ferry at Trinity, 25 cents.)

Leaving the Trinity, we passed through a most beautiful prairie of several miles extent, presenting all the appearance of cultivation. Soil black, and in many places a great many marine shells are observable on the surface. There is evidently a great deal of lime in the soil here, for it is taking the hair from my horse's legs, as though they had been limed for the purpose.

The weather for several days has been very warm, and indicating rain. On Sunday I killed a black snake which was crossing my path. The frogs are singing on every side, and butterflies are occasionally seen. Numerous little flowers begin to spring up. Before leaving the prairie we were met by a storm of thunder, lightning and rain. The thunder was heavy, and the storm in all respects equal to what we have in Virginia in July and August.

Nine miles from Trinity we came to a cabin kept by a man named Larrison. We had intended to reach Sims', sixteen miles further on, but the rain brought us to a halt, and with some difficulty we prevailed upon the man to take us in and give our horses some corn. We found our fellow traveler, Whitely, a valuable negotiator in the matter. The house was about twenty feet square, only one room; family consisted of two women, five children. There were three beds. Captain Sherman and myself had one, the family the other two. The Doctor and old Whitely took a pallet on the floor, and covered with our blankets. The supper consisted of fried pork, coffee, coarse but good cornbread and milk. I ate heartily.

Thursday, February 11, 1836.

Rose early and saddle for a start by sunrise, intending to reach Sims' to breakfast, sixteen miles. Crossed a watercourse called Bidais (pronounced Beedeyes, and so written by many of the illiterate country people); the rain of yesterday had swollen it very much. Arriving at the cabin of Eduardo Ariola, a Mexican, was informed that it was so full that we should have to swim. Met here Dr. Field, who left Nacogdoches on Saturday, returning, who said he could not cross. But we prevailed on a young Mexican, who called his own name Dolores Ariola, to show us the ford, which he readily undertook. Coming to a creek which had flowed out beyond its banks upwards of 100 yards, he manfully waded in and sounded the bottom to point out to us a safe path. We took our saddle bags on our shoulders and followed him, our Texan fellow traveler, Whitely, first, and I next. It took the poor Mexican up to his arms. He was dressed only in shirt and cotton trousers and shoes, and I got over with only one foot a little wet; the water came over my boot and ran down, which would not have happened had I not lent my leggings to the Captain, who improvidently had taken the road in his best military pants, without leggings. About one-half a mile further on we came to another branch of the same watercourse, within steep, narrow banks. Our young Mexican friend ran on with us in his wet clothes, to show us across that, and on the way very obligingly instructed me in the Spanish vocabulary, as far as there was time to make inquiries. The second stream presented greater difficulties than the first. We stripped our horses and carried our saddles and baggage across on a log, which was felled across the stream a short distance from the road. The difficulty then was to get our horses over. We attempted to drive them, but they bolted, and were with difficulty caught and brought back. The Mexican then stript and mounted Dr. H.'s mare, which he swam across; the others were then driven in and followed, but Capt. Sherman's mare went too low down the stream, and striking a steep bank, among drift wood, was near drowning before she could be got over. The obliging alacrity of the young Mexican in serving us, and the exposure he underwent, called for our commendation and liberal reward, with which he seemed much gratified.

The delay in crossing these streams prevented our reaching Sims' until 11 o'clock. We found the house kept by a Mexican named Antonio Rios, a native of Nacogdoches, who spoke the English language well, and gave his name as Rivers, but his Gipsy-like visage betrayed his origin. He is a smart, obliging fellow, who has rented the place of Sims, a rude house of two rooms and an open passage: the common style. Here we found a company of eleven men from Tennessee, going to join the army. Having to wait for them to be served, and to rest our horses, we did not leave Rios' until 2 o'clock, designing to reach the Widow Anderson's, twelve miles. We did not reach the widow's until dark, and then found the house to consist of one small room, and no food of any kind for the horses. We got a good supper of the coarse kind usually found on the road, but no sugar for the coffee.

Soon after our arrival a foot traveler, a young man from Georgia, who is going to join a volunteer company from that State now in Texas, came in and partook of our supper. He left Nacogdoches about the time we did, and has kept up with us, generally sleeping and eating with us. His baggage consists of a surtout coat and saddle bags. These we occasionally relieve him of by carrying for him. He stops for nothing, but pushes right ahead, through rain, mud and watercourses. Today he swam the stream that our horses waded. He did not know the ford that the Mexican showed us. He will make a fine soldier if he lives to reach the army. (Fare and lodging at Larrison's, 75 cents; dinner and horse feed at Rios', 75 cents; paid the Mexican 50 cents.) We gave the only spare bed the widow had to the foot passenger, who complained of a little fever, and we all slept on the floor. Our poor horses were tied in the woods.

Friday, February 12, 1836.

Rose at daylight, wishing to reach Boatwright's to breakfast, fourteen miles, the only place where we could get food for our horses. A gloomy, drizzling morning, threatening rain. Five miles from Mr. Anderson's, reached the *Uagalote,* or Turkey Creek, which was so much swollen as to be past fording. We found a log by which we could cross, but our horses must swim. While preparing to do this, a very heavy storm of thunder and rain came on, which wet all our baggage and clothes. We passed our baggage over with difficulty in the midst of the storm. The foot traveler came up at the instant and assisted us. The log was difficult, and we took stations on it, and passed the baggage from one to the other. In driving the horses over one of my overshoes was pulled off by the mud, but for which I should have preserved dry feet. Reached Boatwright's at 11 o'clock, where we breakfasted, and got corn for our horses. At half past 12 remounted and set out, but found the Caney Creek so much swollen that it could not be passed without swimming. The log was under water, and to cross we could not avoid getting wet, and no chance of entertainment short of Washington, seventeen miles. So we resolved to return and wait for the creek to subside, which we were assured would be the case by morning, if it did not rain again. In the evening another heavy thunder cloud came up. Whitely to-day informed me that he knew a salt spring, about six miles from the Trinity, and thirty miles above Robbins' ferry, which he says is better than Hotchkiss' salines. It was surveyed for a headright by a man named Anderson, who died without making a settlement. Whitely says he is a creditor, and means to take out administration on Anderson's estate, he having no relations in Texas, and if the title has not been cleared out, he will clear it out as administrator, or I may clear it out, and he will convey me one-half, and he will hold the other half for the heirs of Anderson, should they ever come forward. *Query,* can he do so? This must be looked to.

Saturday, February 13, 1836.

The Caney Creek did not subside sufficiently to ford until 10 o'clock, when we ventured. I got both of my overshoes full of water, which made my feet damp and uncomfortable. The day was very cold and raw. We stopt once to warm at a cabin, where they complained bitterly of the conduct of a troop of horse that passed through here last November; they not only took what was necessary, but turned their horses into the field and destroyed nearly all their crop. They are now obliged to go off to a great distance and buy corn at * * * per barrel of ears. The country through which we passed yesterday and to-day consisted of high, black prairie and black mud swamps alternately. The soil has generally a mixture of sand, and bears evident marks of richness. Very few settlements visible. Fine herds of cattle grazing, and occasionally deer, started by the appearance of travelers, would gaze at us for a moment, then show the white flag and bound away, visible for miles on the open prairie. As we approached the Brazos, the road descended into a marsh of several miles extent, all subject to overflow. The soil being red alluvium, like the soil of the Red River counties, and the trees showing the marks twenty and thirty feet high. The Navisot, or Navasota, as it is written on the maps, lay on our right, and enters the Brazos opposite to the new town of Washington, which stands on the south bank. Arriving at the ferry we saw Capt. Sherman's company on the opposite bank, drawn up in order, and a crowd of citizens, drawn up to receive them in military style, resembling in a striking degree Falstaff's famous corps.

We stopt at a house, called a tavern, kept by a man named Lot, which was the only place in the city at which we could get fodder for our horses. It was a frame house, consisting of only one room, about forty by twenty feet, with a large fire place at each end, a shed at the back, in which the table was spread. It was a frame house, covered with clapboards, a wretchedly made establishment, and a blackguard, rowdy set lounging about. The host's wife and children, and about thirty lodgers, all slept in the same apartment, some in beds, some on cots, but the greater part on the floor. The supper consisted of fried pork and coarse corn bread and miserable coffee. I was fortunately lodged on a good cot with a decent Tennessean named Kimball, who is looking for land, but says the state of anarchy is such that he is afraid to buy, and is waiting to see the course of things after the meeting of the Convention.

Was introduced to Dr. Goodrich, a physician of the place, and a member-elect of the new Convention, a strenuous Independence man.

Itinerary of the road from Nacogdoches to Washington, given by Mr. Whitely:

From Nacogdoches	Miles
To Loco (or Crazy) Creek	10
To John Durst's	8
To Angelina River	2
To Col. Bean's	8
To Neches (or Snow) River	10
To McLean's	6
To John Master's	12
To Hurricane Bayou	4
To Henry Master's	6
To Aldridge's, near the Salado Creek	10
To Mustang Prairie	3
To Strother's Place	6
To Trinity River	6
To Larriston's	9
To Sims' (Antonio Rios)	16
To Widow Anderson's	12
To Whittaker's	6

To Boatwright's	10
To Arnold's	8
Washington	8
[Total]	160

Sunday, February 14, 1836.

A clear and cold morning. Rose early, took a wretched breakfast of the same coarse and dirty materials that we had last night.

Found that Governor Smith was in San Felipe, and none of the government here. Resolved to go directly on to San Felipe. Our fellow traveler, Whitely, appointed to meet me at Tinoxticlan on Friday or Saturday, and accompany me to the Falls of Brazos. The foot passenger who has accompanied us for the last six days, whose name is James Pinchback, this morning enlisted in Sherman's company of volunteers—for the war.

The following are the members-elect of the Convention from the municipality of Washington: Dr. B. B. Goodrich, Dr. S. Barnett, Capt. G. B. Swisher, Jesse Grymes, Esq.

The following are the members from San Felipe: Dr. C. B. Stewart, Thomas Barnett, Randall Jones.

Dr. Goodrich gave me a letter of introduction to Dr. Stewart.

Left Washington at 10 o'clock. Glad to get out of so disgusting a place. It is laid out in the woods; about a dozen wretched cabins or shanties constitute the city; not one decent house in it, and only one well defined street, which consists of an opening cut out of the woods. The stumps still standing. A rare place to hold a national convention in. They will have to leave it promptly to avoid starvation.

We intended to reach the home of Col. Edwards, thirty miles from Washington, but my horse became lame, and we were obliged to stop at the house of one Lakey, a wretched open log cabin. Family rude and uncourteous; fare, fried pork and bad corn bread; coffee made of corn without sugar; but our horses were well provided. Lodged in the kitchen, an open and filthy place. There were two beds. One was occupied by the overseer and a neighbor. I was allowed the other, which was of straw, with dirty and few clothing.

Monday, February 15, 1836.

We were awakened before day by the negroes cooking breakfast, which they said must be ready by sunrise. We, however, did not get it until near 7 o'clock. It consisted of boiled * * *, fried fat pork, coarse corn bread, corn coffee, without sugar, and boiled eggs, alum salt and pepper, in a tea cup, all coarse and filthy.

While breakfast was preparing, saw a yoke of oxen of extraordinary size. One of them was fifteen and a half hands high. Another had horns that spread to the width of five feet, and the ends had been cut off, two inches each, which made their natural width five feet four inches!

Left Lakey's at 8 o'clock. Arrived at Col. Edward's about 11 o'clock, where we found Mr. Childers, of Milam, to whom I had a letter from Mr. Kimbal. Childers informed me that himself and Mr. Robinson, the Empresario, were elected from Milam. Had an argument with him on the tariff question.

Arrived at Cumming's at half past 1 o'clock; took dinner and had our horses fed. While there the Post came in, with his mail completely wet, he having just swam Mill Creek, and got overset in the midst of it. He had the mail in a pair of saddle bags, which he opened, and spread the wet packages out in the porch to dry. Some travelers also came up, who had crossed the creek on a log, below the ford, and swam over the horses. They brought a hand bill issued by the Provisional Council, announcing the approach of Santa Anna with an army, and calling upon the Texans *en masse* to take the field. A great pother is now to be made, and if the population of the country can be raised, and an armed force sufficient to keep them in arms should be on the frontier, the Council may perhaps escape a part of the execration and disgrace that seems to await them. In less than a fortnight their brief authority expires, and they will have an awful reckoning to make to the people.

We rode to-day over wide and beautiful rolling prairies. The country everywhere presents the appearance of a cultivated region, only wanting a few good farm houses on the beautiful eminences that everywhere present themselves to form a splendid picture of rural beauty and fertility. Immense flocks of geese and cranes were feeding on the prairies, and some ducks in the ponds; herds of cattle were grazing, and now and then a fewer, larks and blackbirds in great numbers. The prairie consists mostly of the stiff, black soil, with some sand. On the top flats a great deal of water lies. The surface is ridged and furrowed, very much resembling the ridges left in an old cornfield. They excited our surprise and appeared unaccountable, but Mr. Cummings explained them thus: those appearances are only met with on the black prairies, which are of a stiff soil, which bakes very much, and when it bakes it cracks open to a considerable depth. When hard rains come the water sinks into these cracks, the edges crumble and wash off, and fall into the crevices, and thus make the vicinity of a crack lower than the surrounding surface, while the space between two neighboring cracks becomes comparatively elevated. When the ground dries again the water lies longest on the low part; or furrow, which again becomes hard baked, and again cracks, and thus each successive season increases the phenomenon, until the whole extent of that kind of soil becomes furrowed, as if by the hand of man.

We left Cummings' at 4 o'clock, intending to reach San Felipe, but mistook the crossing place, and after going down

Mile Creek some two miles found our error and returned. It being then near sunset, we resolved to remain till morning.

Sat up until 12 o'clock writing and listening to Cummings talk, who, although illiterate, is a shrewd man, who has seen much of life, and observed things attentively. He first came to Texas in 1806, in Burr's army. He afterwards visited it a-trading, and has been settled here since 1824. Owns his own headright, those of his mother and two brothers, and a hacienda of five leagues, where he now resides; is a bachelor, and his house is kept by a maiden sister, now some thirty odd years old, who keeps it well; everything is in plenty and of good kind. He values the place where he lives at $1 per acre, and his headright on the San Bernard at $2 per acre. Says the prairie lands over which we have passed will produce a bale of cotton to the acre, and thirty to forty bushels of corn; thinks the lands nearer the coast more fertile, which, together with their greater facilities of transportation to market, makes them doubly valuable. His observations on Texas affairs, and his delineation of the prominent men and parties of the State, were shrewd and interesting; thinks well of Austin; execrates the capitulation of Bexar; is in favor of independence; condemns the provisional government; says Wharton and Austin are the heads of opposing parties; thinks Wharton ambitious and selfish; says he openly abused Austin before they went to the United States, and he is much pleased to find them acting amicably together.

Tuesday, February 16, 1836.

Left Cummings' at 9 o'clock; crossed Mill Creek on a log, and drove the horses through the stream, which was still too high to ford. The road was wet and miry; did not reach San Felipe until 12 o'clock. Waited on Governor Smith immediately. Was very courteously received. Sherman reported his company and received his command. Dr. Herndon found that Doctor Richardson had resigned the office of Surgeon General, and he resolved to return to the United States again immediately—that is, to Mississippi. So he and Sherman returned forthwith to Cummings', in company with a Mr. Phillips, from Mobile, who has been buying land here, and is now returning to the United States, but who will return to Texas in a month. I am now left alone in this far-away land, and cannot help feeling lonesome.

Spent an hour or two with Governor Smith, who expatiated very freely on Texan affairs, and particularly on the state of parties. Abused Austin; said he is Mexican in his principles and policy, and that he ought to be hung! Thinks Austin was opposed to the meeting of the consultative convention, and that the expedition versus Bexar was got up in order to defeat it, and attributes the foolish or wicked terms of the capitulation to his policy. Blames Austin for the dissensions which have arisen between him (Smith) and the Provisional Council. In short, Austin is, with him, the evil spirit which has instigated all the mischief which afflicts the country, and is to be made the scapegoat of all others' faults. Archer he thinks honest, but too philanthropic; he wishes to carry the war to the walls of Mexico. Wharton he thinks is "About right," "Are you there, old truepenny?" (My impression of Governor Smith is, that he is a strongly prejudiced party man. Too illiterate; too little informed, and not of the right calibre for the station he has been placed in. Organs of self esteem and combativeness large; perceptive faculty good; intellectual, small; little reflection or imagination; no reverence.)

Waited on Mr. John R. Jones, the Postmaster General. Invited to take tea with him. An excellent supper. His wife a plain, good looking woman; has lived here five years, and she is very much pleased with Texas; came from Missouri. Introduced by him to a Squire Thompson, a member of the Council. A plain, illiterate, farmer looking man; very illy qualified, I should judge, for the business of government. Like most of the Texans that I have met with he has a Munchausen-like idea of Texan prowess and of Mexican imbecility and insignificance. I fear it will prove a fatal error.

San Felipe is a wretched, decaying looking place. Five stores of small assortments, two mean taverns, and twenty or thirty scattering and mean looking houses, very little paint visible. No appearance of industry, of thrift or improvement of any kind. On the west side of the Brazos, which is here about * * * yards wide, and on a prairie of great extent. The opposite side of the river is low, and overflowed flats extend a great way, which causes the place to be unhealthy.

Wednesday, February 17, 1836.

Delivered letters this morning to D. C. Barrett, Esq., one of the Council; he is from Western Pennsylvania; and to Col. Jack, of Columbia. Introduced to Governor Robinson and to Thomas J. Chambers. This gentleman is a native of Orange County, Virginia, which he left very young. A spirit of adventure carried him to Texas, and thence to Mexico, where he resided three years. He was, before the Revolution, appointed Chief Justice of Coahuila and Texas, and resided at Monclova. He is an interesting man, and said to be a fine lawyer. He told me he was going to the United States to try and get men sent on to fight the battles of Texas. He expects to unite Felix Huston's project with his own. I also became acquainted with a Mr. Ira P. Lewis, of Matagorda, a lawyer, who informed me that Lambert had purchased one-half a league on the Colorado, six miles above League's Ferry. Mr. L. arranged the purchase for him. The title is taken in the name of Peter W. Grayson. Lambert returned to the United States in the schooner *Brutus*. So did Raleigh Green. Mr. Lewis urged me to visit Matagorda before I settled in Texas. He thinks it will be a great commercial place, and a fine field for the practice of the law. Very fertile lands, and a pleasant climate.

With Governor Robinson I was not much struck. He board-ed with his wife in the tavern where I am staying. She is an ordinary looking woman. The Council have all taken their departure to-day for Washington. Nearly all the strangers who yesterday thronged the tavern have departed, and the place to-morrow will be quite deserted.

Went out to the land office at Gail Borden's, about a mile from town. Dr. Peebles, the Commissioner, was from home, and did not return until night. Stayed to supper. Entered on the books of the office as a colonist, to take a league of land, the selection to be made at my leisure. Went to the printing office and subscribed to the *Telegraph*, in which the decrees, etc., of the provisional government are published. Also pro-cured there a copy of Austin's publication of the laws, etc., of Texas. *Telegraph*, $5; pamphlet, $1. Also purchased to-day a Spanish grammar and dictionary, $4.

Arranged to start to-morrow up to the Falls with Colonel Chambers and Mr. Lewis, it has come on to rain hard, and I fear I shall be again disappointed.

Introduced to-day to Major Rob. M. Williamson, of the Rangers, who seems to be an intrepid Indian fighter. Has a wooden leg. Also to a Mr. Simms, a surveyor, who lives at Milam; and delivered my letter to Dr. C. B. Stewart, who is the secretary to Governor Smith.

Thursday, February 18, 1836.

It rained hard last night, but this morning, like yesterday, was very foggy. Cleared off about 9 o'clock. Prepared to leave town after breakfast, intending to go to Milam with Cham-bers and Lewis, but my horse was missing. Not being able to get any corn for him to eat, I had placed him under the care of a Mexican named *Ignotis*, who undertook to pasture him, but had lost sight of him. He borrowed a horse to go in quest of him. About 12 o'clock a black fellow, the servant of Major Lewis, told me he had seen my horse not far off, and for a promised reward he went and brought him in a half hour. The old Mexican, all this while, had not reported himself, so I left him without his reward. It is a common trick with them to secret horses until a reward is offered, after which they are easily found.

Introduced to Asa Brigham, a delegate from Columbia. He is called here a cornstalk lawyer, which is explained to be equal to a quack among physicians; also to Mr. Moody, the auditor of public accounts.

Had some interesting conversation with Chambers. He has very little confidence in the land titles that are given out at this time. He says the government with which the Empresarios made their contracts is destroyed, and the Convention of Texas ordered the offices to be closed. Titles given under such circumstances he thinks would not stand in law, though it is possible and probable that, in the present deranged state of things, they may be permitted to stand. Thinks the titles given in Milam's Colony are not good; that Milam's grant for colonizing was forfeited, and renewed under false pretenses. Williamson claims to be Milam's agent, and to have authority to act under an irrevocable power, although Milam is dead. This Chambers says is not good. He thinks the civil law, as a rule for property and for practice better than the common law; that the civil law being that under which all the titles in Texas are held, it should continue to be the law of the land.

While my horse was standing at the door, Major Williamson offered me half a league of land in Milam's Colony for him; but not having confidence in the title, not knowing what confidence to place in the man, he not having the title here, nor indeed in himself yet, and not having it in my power to procure another horse, and he being a little lame, I declined the trade.

Went again to the land office, and finding the surveys of three leagues on the River Navidad not taken, I entered one as my headright.

Paid Commissioner's fees	$15.00
Clerk's fees	10.00
Stamps	2.00
Recording	2.00
Surveyor's fee	48.00
	$77.00

The government dues, which will be some thirty or forty dollars more, are to be paid in three installments or four, five and six years. Dr. Peebles is to bring me the deed to Washington by 1st of March.

Left the land office at 4 o'clock, intending to reach Cummins' before dark. This I should have done, but missed the road on the prairie, and went six or seven miles out of my way, so I did not reach Cummins' until after 7 o'clock. It was quite dark, and the latter part of the road very bad. In crossing Mill Creek I got wet up to the knees, both boots full of water. Arrived safe, found a warm fire, good supper and comfortable lodging. Washed my feet, put on dry socks and did not take cold.

Friday, February 19, 1836.

After breakfast rode as far as Col. Edwards', where I found Mr. Childers. Waited until after dinner, expecting Chambers and Lewis. They did not come. After night Chambers arrived, in company with a Dr. Motley, a delegate to the Convention from Goliad. Found that Chambers had abandoned his trip to the Falls, and would proceed directly to the United States after waiting to-morrow for Lewis. They also persuaded me not to attempt to go to the Falls alone, as the Indians were troublesome, and it might be dangerous. Wrote to my wife. An express was received at San Felipe last night which brings intelligence of the approach of the Mexican army; 1,000 men have passed the Rio Grande; as many more are on the opposite side, and they are passing over wagons, pack mules, etc. It is not known where Santa Anna is, but this is supposed to be the advance of the grand invading army. He has sworn to win Texas or lose Mexico. The Texans say if he crosses the Rio Grande he will never return alive, and if he sustains a defeat or a check here it will be the signal for revolt in Mexico.

Saturday, February 20, 1836.

Determined to stay here to-day and recruit my horse and write letters, to go to Virginia by General Chambers. Wrote to T. Green and gave Chambers letters of introduction to Patton, Jenifer, T. Green, Dr. Barton, and T. B. B.

General Chambers has a command from the provisional government of Texas to proceed to the United States and raise a brigade of * * * men, to be called the army of reserve for the defense of Texas. He makes a donation of $10,000 to be expended in that object, and the faith of the country is pledged for the payment of the expenses of the corps, etc. He has blank commissions, and is authorized to appoint all the officers of the Brigade.

Had much interesting conversation with Chambers on Texan affairs, and received much information. He explained the speculation of the 400 leagues differently from John Durst. Says that Gen'l Mason obtained the first sale of 300 leagues. Mason attempted to get more, but was defeated by Chambers. Sam'l Williams was the principal actor in the second sale. He openly pronounces it to have been obtained by fraud. The objections to it are, that it was authorized by eight members of Congress, which was not a quorum, there being thirteen and two-thirds necessary for a quorum. The sale was made before the decree was published, so there could be no competition. It was made to themselves—Durst got 100 leagues, Williams 100 leagues, and several others smaller portions. It was sold for a small sum, when there were many persons there in Monclova willing to buy at a much larger price, but there was no chance allowed them. The government of Mexico denounced the transaction as illegal. He says the Austin party, of which Williams is the master spirit, caused him to be arrested for treason, and would have had him hanged if they could; that he has been the especial object of their persecution. Thinks Austin a man of no moral firmness, but more to be pitied than blamed. He is a child in the hands of his party, who act upon his credulity and weakness, and use him for their purposes.

Chambers was appointed the Superior Judge of Coahuila and Texas, and resided at Monclova. He has with him as a protege a young Mexican, a native of Santa Rosa, whom he has raised, and he intends taking him to the United States and putting him to school. He is an interesting youth, named Manuel Valdes.

Sunday, February 21, 1836.

Left Col. Edwards' at half past 8 o'clock, in company with Dr. Motley, a member of the Convention from Goliad, who is going to Washington. Bill, $2. Three miles on the road discovered that I had left my pistols. Returned to get them, and Motley rode on, so I lost his company. Determined to reach Col. Coles', thirty miles, but stopping to avoid a shower, I was delayed too long, and could not reach it before night. Was informed by a Mr. James Stevens that Gideon Walker and William Townsend had each a league of land that they wished cleaned out on shares. Called to see Walker, and found that he had already made an agreement with a Mr. Elijah Allcorn to clear out his land, and that Townsend had also made an agreement with a Mr. Richardson. He informed me that his brother-in-law, Mr. Gary, wished to get a league cleared out for himself.

I met Allcorn on the road to-day, and he was very desirous to sell me land. He has a league on Cypress Bayou, which was the headright of a Dr. Wright, which he is willing to sell for 50 cents per acre; also the league which he himself drew, east side of the Brazos, and west of Stafford's league, and running across Oyster Bayou; adjoining it he has bought some, making one and one-fourth leagues and 200 acres. Price, $3 per acre.

Stevens also has land for sale, one-third of a league on Caney Creek, which he offers at $1 per acre, and 757 acres within three-fourths mile from Washington for which he demands $3.

Went to see Gary and found the house open but nobody at home. It consists of a cabin of one room, two doors and no window. There was only one door hung, the other was open, and two or three chains laid before it. In a little while Garey returned, having left his wife with her mother, who was sick. Got corn for my horse, and took lodging for the night. Supped on fried sausage, bread and milk; made a bargain with him to take a league of land in Austin's Colony, to clear it out for him, and take half myself.

Harry Davis Garey married the daughter of James Walker, who gave him the land on which he lives. Has three children, and his wife's nephew, a youth of thirteen, lives with him. Yet all sleep in one room, and that a rough log house, open in every direction, and one door never closed. A heavy storm of rain came on in the night, which beat on me where I slept.

VOL. VII

DEFINITIONS ON INSIDE FRONT COVER.

Matagorda—the great plant.
Alamo—Cottonwood.
Nana—Mother.
Banito—Little Bath.
La Bahia—The Bay.
Yegua—Mare.
Colorado, Roxo—Red.
Brazos—Arms.
Nueces—Walnuts.
Neches—Snow.
La Vaca—Cow.
Hondo—Deep.
Papalote—Kite.
Sance—Willow.
Cibolo—Mexican Buffalo.
Tordillo—Grey.
Atascosa—Boggy.
Cuchillo—Knife.
Tortuga—Turtle.
Tehocate—A fruit resembling a quince.

Monday, February 22, 1836.

The morning was clear and beautiful, the air mild, and all nature looks sweet and inviting. Having bargained with Gary to clean out his league of land for half, I started to go to the Falls. Gary was to go to San Felipe and make the entry of the land against my return. About two miles from his house, in attempting to cross New Year Creek, being ignorant of the ford, I got very wet, coat pockets, boots and saddle bags all full of water. With some difficulty I got the horse out and returned to Gary's. Fortunately, his wife and children were from home, and did not return until evening, so I had the freedom of the whole house. It took me all day to dry my wet articles, clothes, books and papers. I was now assured that it would be impossible to make the trip to the Falls before the Convention, as the Yegua would also be up, and that is a much more considerable stream than the New Year's Creek, so I gave it up, and remained with Gary another night.

Tuesday, February 23, 1836.

Rode over in the morning to Gideon Walker's, and contracted with his son, Sanders Walker, to clean out a league of land for him, being his settlement right. Thence to old James Walker's, who told me he was from Orange County, Va. Contracted with his son, John M. Walker, to clear out a league of land for him, as a settlement right, he having been twelve years in the country. While at Walker's Judge Chambers and Major Lewis rode up, accompanied by young Manuel Valdes. They were seeking a ford across the New Year's Creek, on their way to the United States. Rode with them to Washington, which we did not reach till after night. Had much interesting conversation with Chambers and Lewis on Texan affairs. Found Sherman and his company still at Washington. Dr. Herndon returned to the United States without making any stop here.

Wednesday, February 24, 1836.

Started about noon for San Felipe, with the intention of clearing out the land for Gary, Walker, etc., in company with a man named Fitch, who had brought an express, and was on his return to Gonzales. Learned from him that he had been a soldier in the United States army eighteen years, and had been eight times tried by court martial. He is now a lieutenant in the Texan army. His person, manners, conversation, etc., were such as might be expected from such an education. Arrived after night at the home of a Mr. Foster, a venerable old man, a native of King and Queen County, Virginia, and his wife, of Spottsylvania County. Her name was Waller, and she is a cousin of Absalom, Aylette and Curtis Waller. They appear to be an amiable, worthy and pious couple. Here, for the first time in Texas, I heard a blessing asked for our meal at supper. Found Mrs. Childers here. Had a good supper, plenty of corn and fodder for our horses, and a good night's rest; $1.

Thursday, February 25, 18:36.

Started early and rode to Col. Edwards' to breakfast (sixty-two and a half cents). At Cummins' found Mill Creek very high, but he having recovered his perogue, passed us over dry, and we swam our horses (twelve and a half cents). Reached the land office about 2 o'clock, and found they had stopt business, and Dr. Peebles, the Commissioner, had gone to his farm. Rode into town to buy powder for a young man at Col. Edwards', but could get none. Saw Mr. Townsend, the partner of J. R. Jones, to whom I had borne a letter. Learned that Col. J. A. Wharton was in town, but could not see him, nor Governor Smith. Returned to Borden's at the land office, purchased half a bushel ears of corn in the neighborhood for seventy-five cents, fed at Borden's stable, and took my supper and lodgings with him.

I ought to have mentioned a splendid sight that I saw last night before reaching Foster's. It was the prairie on fire, after dark! A similar object seen by day a few days since was striking; this was beautiful, not to say sublime. It extended upwards of one-half mile in one unbroken, steady blaze, and almost on a level line.

Yesterday the weather was warm and cloudy, indicating rain. All the forenoon to-day we were met by a strong south breeze, blowing a drizzling rain in our faces. About noon the drizzle ceased, and it was so warm that I rode in my shirt sleeves. It was summer heat. At night the wind chopped suddenly round to the north, and there commenced what is familiarly called in this country a norther, by which is always understood a hard and cold blow from the north. It generally lasts for two or three days, and is sometimes so excessively cold that persons have been known to freeze to death in crossing the plains. Long observation has taught them to expect a norther between the 20th of February and 1st of March, and that generally closes the winter.

Friday, February 26, 1836.

This morning it was excessively cold for this southern region; yesterday it was summer heat. I put the thermometer out in the porch and it fell to thirty-five degrees. It being so cold, I did not start until near noon. Last night an express was received from Lieut. Col. Wm. B. Travis, at Bexar, February 23, stating that 1,000 of the enemy were in sight of that place. He had but 150 men, and was short of provisions and ammunition, but determined to defend the place to the last, and calling for assistance. The people now begin to think the wolf has actually come at last, and are preparing for a march. Mr. Gail Borden is packing up the papers of the land office, in order to remove them eastward should the enemy approach.

Not being able to get my land business arranged, left Borden's at noon. Dined at Cummins' (thirty-seven and a half cents), and rode down on the Brazos to the plantation of Dr. Peebles, who had walked to a neighbor's. I met him, and conversed a few minutes, then rode on to Col. Edwards', where I met Capt. Swisher and Dr. Barnett, two of the delegates from Milam, and a Mr. Bartlett, a surveyor. $1.50.

Saturday, February 27, 1836.

The wind yesterday and to-day blew hard from the north, right in my face; a most uncomfortable ride. Left Edwards' after breakfast; stopt at Mrs. Panky's to feed my horse, where I got an excellent dinner of bacon, turnip tops, boiled eggs, coffee and milk, with fine corn bread. I relished it more than any meal I have eaten in Texas. Arrived at Washington after dark. Met Capt. Sherman's baggage wagon going out, the men having marched on ahead. A considerable excitement prevailing at Washington, owing to the news from Bexar. Found that the express to the east and north had not yet gone, owing to the want of funds or energy on the part of those in authority. Dinner and room fifty-six cents.

Sunday, February 28, 1836.

Cold and drizzling. Some of the citizens raised a collection, to which I contributed $1, to send the express on to the eastward. The Acting Governor, Robinson, with a fragment of the Council, is here. He is treated coldly and really seems of little consequence. The only members of the Council now here are McMullen, an Irishman, Patillo, and Thompson. McMullen is he whose name appears on the maps as an Empresario. Powers, another Empresario, and an Irishman, is also here. He is a shrewd man; married a Mexican woman, and speaks the Spanish well.

Another express is received from Travis, dated the 24th, stating that Santa Anna, with his army, were in Bexar, and had bombarded the Alamo for twenty-four hours. An unconditional surrender had been demanded, which he had answered by a cannon shot. He was determined to defend the place to the last, and called earnestly for assistance. Some are going, but the vile rabble here cannot be moved.

This evening a number of members arrived, among them Lorenzo de Zavala, the most interesting man in Texas. He is a native of Yucatan; was Governor of the State of Mexico five years, minister of the fiscal department and Ambassador to France from the Republic of Mexico, which post he renounced when Santa Anna proved recreant to the liberal cause, and he then resided for some time in the United States. He now lives on his estate on Buffalo Bayou, near Galveston Bay. He is a fine writer and a Republican; a fine statesman, although by some accused of inordinate ambition. Has published a volume of travels in the United States, printed in Paris in the Spanish language. MEMO. to procure a copy.

Monday, February 29, 1836.

A warm day, threatening rain from the south. Many other members are coming in, and it is now evident that a quorum will be formed to-morrow. Gen'l Houston's arrival has created more sensation than that of any other man. He is evidently the people's man, and seems to take pains to ingratiate himself with everybody. He is much broken in appearance, but has still a fine person and courtly manners; will be forty-three years old on the 3rd of March–looks older (born 3rd of March, 1793). He is a native of Virginia, I think of Augusta County; entered the service of the United States as a private; was wounded at the battle of Horseshoe, and commissioned for his gallantry; was a favorite of Gen'l Jackson; was a lawyer; became member of Congress in * * *; served * * * years; was made Major General and then Governor of Tennessee. An unhappy passage in his domestic relations induced him to resign and go to live with the Indians. Has been * * * in Texas.

Tuesday, March 1, 1836.

Yesterday was a warm day, and at bed time I found it necessary to throw off some clothes. In the night the wind sprung up from the north and blew a gale, accompanied by lightning thunder, rain and hail, and it became very cold. In the morning the thermometer was down to 33 degrees, and everybody shivering and exclaiming against the cold. This is the second regular norther that I have experienced.

Notwithstanding the cold, the members of the Convention, to the number of * * *, met to-day in an unfinished house, without doors or windows. In lieu of glass, cotton cloth was stretched across the windows, which partially excluded the cold wind.

The Convention was called to order by Mr. Childers, of Milam. Mr. Collinsworth, of Brazoria, was called to the chair pro tem., and Mr. Farris appointed Secretary pro tem. A committee on elections was then appointed, to whom the credentials of members were to be submitted, and the Convention adjourned until half past 1 o'clock.

At half past 1 the Convention met, and the committee reported forty-one members present who were duly elected, and some about which there was contest or difficulty, on which they wished the action of the house.

MEMBERS-ELECT OF THE NEW CONVENTION

Nacogdoches: Thomas J. Rusk, Ga.; Jno. S. Roberts, C. S. Taylor, England; R. Potter, North Carolina.

San Augustine: Martin Parmer, E. O. Legrand, S. B. Blount, South Carolina.

Sabine: James Gaines, Va.; William Clark.

Washington: Dr. B. B. Goodrich, Virginia, via Tennessee and Alabama; Capt. G. B. Swisher, Tennessee; Dr. S. Barnett, Tennessee; Jesse Grymes.

San Felipe: Dr. C. B. Stewart, Thomas Barnett, Randall Jones.

Milam: Geo. C. Childers, Tennessee; S. C. Robertson, Tennessee.

Columbia: Edwin Waller, Virginia; J. S. D. Byron, James Collingsworth, Tennessee; Asa Brigham.

Matagorda: Bailey Hardeman, S. Rhoades Fisher.

Mina: Rob. M. Coleman, Dr. Thos. J. Gazley, J. W. Bunton.

Goliad or La Bahia: Dr. Wm. Motley, Virginia, via Kentucky; Incarnation Bascus, Mexico.

Jefferson: Claiborne West, Wm. B. Scates.

Colorado: Wm. Menifee, Tenn.; W. D. Lacy.

Harrisburg: Lorenzo de Zavala, A. Briscoe.

Liberty: M. B. Menard, A. B. Hardin.

Bexar: Juan Seguin, Antonio Navarro, Col. Francisco Ruis, Miguel Arciniega. (Jesse B. Badgett, Sam'l A. Maverick, elected by the Volunteers at Bexar.)

Jackson: James Kerr, Elijah Stapp.

Refugio: Gen'l S. Houston, James Powers, by citizens; Edw'd Conrad, Penn; David Thomas, by Volunteers.

Gonzales: M. Caldwell, J. Fisher.

Jasper: S. H. Everett, G. W. Smith.

Shelby: S. O. Pennington, Wm. C. Crawford.

San Patricio: John Turner, * * * Bowers.

Pecan Point: Rob. Hamilton, Rich'd Ellis, Collin McKenna, Albert H. Latimer, Sam'l P. Carson.

Victoria: * * * Carbejal, * * * Lynn.

The house was then organized by the appointment of Judge Richard Ellis, President, and Herbert S. Kimble, Secretary. On motion of Mr. Geo. C. Childers, a committee consisting of Childers, Colin McKenna, Edward Conrad, Jas. Gaines and Bailey Hardeman was appointed to prepare and report a declaration of independence, with directions to report as speedily as practicable. A motion was then made to wait on Governor H. Smith and inform him that the Convention is organized, and ready to receive any communication he may have to make. This led to a discussion in which some excitement was manifested. The quarrel between the Governor and Council was spoken of in unmeasured terms of reprobation. It was finally amended so as to include the Governor, Lieutenant Governor and Council, in order, as was avowed by members in debate, to take no cognizance of the private quarrels or private griefs of either party, but to call on each for whatever official information concerning the common weal they may have to communicate.

The house then adjourned until to-morrow morning at 9 o'clock.

Wednesday, March 2, 1836.

The morning clear and cold, but the cold somewhat moderated. The Convention met pursuant to adjournment. Mr. Childers, from the committee, reported a *Declaration of Independence*, which he read in his place. It was received by the house, committed to a committee of the whole, reported without amendment, and unanimously adopted, in less than one hour from its first and only reading. It underwent no discipline, and no attempt was made to amend it. The only speech made upon it was a somewhat declamatory address in committee of the whole by General Houston.

Assistant clerks were appointed, and, there being no printing press at Washington, various copies of the Declaration were ordered to be made and sent by express to various points and to the United States, for publication; 1,000 copies ordered to be printed at for circulation. A committee was appointed to procure and attend to the dispatching of expresses. Additional members attended, three from Nacogdoches, Rusk, Taylor and Roberts; Brigham from Columbia, Menard from Liberty.

A motion was made by Mr. Scoty that the members of the Convention should arm themselves and wear their arms during the session of the Convention. It was scouted at and withdrawn. A committee of one member from each municipality was appointed to draft a Constitution. They subdivided themselves into three committees, on the executive, legislative and judicial branches; Zavala chairman on the executive.

A copy of the Declaration having been made in a fair hand, an attempt was made to read it, preparatory to signing it, but it was found so full of errors that it was recommitted to the committee that reported it for correction and engrossment.

An express was this evening received from Col. Travis, stating that on the 25th a demonstration was made on the Alamo by a party of Mexicans of about 300, who, under cover of some old houses, approached to within eighty yards of the fort, while a cannonade was kept up from the city. They were beaten off with some loss, and amidst the engagement some Texan soldiers set fire to and destroyed the old houses. Only three Texans were wounded, none killed. Col. Fannin was on the march from Goliad with 350 men for the aid of Travis. This, with the other forces known to be on the way, will by this time make the number in the fort some six or seven hundred. It is believed the Alamo is safe.

Thursday, March 3, 1836.

Morning clear and cold, but became more moderate as the day advanced. Wrote to T. G. and W. M. B., to go by express to Natchitoches.

The Convention met at 9 o'clock. Some new members appeared and took their seats; some contested elections were decided. The engrossed Declaration was read and signed by all the members present. Roberts and Taylor, from Nacogdoches, at first expressed some difficulty about signing, but finally yielded and added their names. It was forthwith dispatched by express in various directions, and the Convention adjourned to give time to the committees to sit on the subjects referred to them.

The Convention has so far got on harmoniously. The only exciting subject seen ahead is the delicate subject of the schism between the Governor and Council, and the doings of the latter body.

Wrote by the express to T. G. and W. M. B.

Friday, March 4, 1836.

To-day several important committees have been appointed, on the Constitution, on finance, on the army, on the organization of the militia, etc., and the Convention adjourned until Monday, to give time for the committees to act. No business of any importance transacted.

Committee for Organizing the Militia: Rusk, Barnett, Collingsworth, Badgett, Lacy, Caldwell, Mottley, Zavala, Smyth, Stapp, Scates, Hardin, Bunton, Robertson, Hardeman, Latimer, Thomas, Blount, Clark, Pennington, Turner and Swisher were appointed a committee to draft an act to organize the militia. Houston appointed Commander in Chief.

Saturday, March 5, 1836.

Took my lodging in a carpenter's shop, and changed my boarding house. Paid Lott $7.50. Entered as a boarder at Mrs. Mann's at $1.25 per day. My horse has been out on the prairie.

While writing a letter to my wife, I was agreeably surprised by the approach of Albert Burnley, who had just arrived from the West, in company with Peter W. Grayson, to whom I had letters of introduction. From him I learned that Lambert had returned to New Orleans from the coast; that Farish had gone to join the army at Bexar, and that he, Burnley, had purchased some $15,000 worth of land on the Guadalupe, LaBaca, etc. They are conveyed to P. W. Grayson.

This evening two Mexican prisoners were brought here from Goliad, charged with improper communications with the enemy, and pointing out to them a place to build a bridge over the San Antonio. One of them is an old priest, named Jose Antonio Valdez, a miserable, meagre, squalid looking creature, who is said to be a very immoral character, and yet a man of considerable property. The other is a young man named Eugenio Hernandez, a lieutenant in the late army of Cos, and on parole. They were brought under the care of Capt. Wm. G. Cooke, late of Fredericksburg, Va., who now commands the New Orleans Greys, and stands high in the army of Texas. Poor Cooke was very badly off for a wardrobe, and Waller and myself were happy in supplying him with such of ours as we could spare, which he received with thanks and without any false shame.

Burnley gave me the following MEMO. Raymond Musquis, who lives at Bejar, owns five and one-half leagues on the LaBacca, about Demitt's Point, including the town of LaBacca. Lynn says they may be bought for $10,000.

Lynn owns land—ten leagues of which A.T. B. offered $15,000 for. A. T. B. has bought one and a half leagues from McCoy, who lives ten miles from Gonzales; bargain not finally closed.

Sunday, March 6, 1836.

This morning, while at breakfast, a dispatch was received from Travis, dated Alamo, March 3. The members of the Convention and the citizens all crowded to the Convention room to hear it read, after which Mr. Potter moved that the Convention organize a provisional government and adjourn and take the field. An interesting debate arose (for an account of which see my letter to Blackford), but they adjourned without any action, the motion being lost.

A great many persons are starting and preparing to start to the seat of war. In the afternoon Houston left, accompanied by his staff, Capt. Cooke, Capt. Tarleton, etc. The town has been all day in a bustle, but is now quiet enough. Wrote letters to Mrs. Gray, to W. M. B. and to T. G., to go by Burnley, who starts early in the morning. Grayson goes with him, for the purpose of trying to raise men and money for the aid of the country.

Monday, March 7, 1836.

Burnley and Grayson started early.

The Convention proceeded to work on the *Constitution.* It is reported in part only. Mr. Thomas is the chairman, or organ of the committee who reported it. It is awkwardly framed, arrangement and phraseology both bad; general features much like that of United States. It is too close a copy, for some features of the *Constitution of the United States* which they are attempting to introduce here are not applicable.

To-day the communication of Governor Smith was at length made, not in the usual official form, addressed to the President by letter, but handed to Mr. Potter, and by him introduced to the house. The letter of the Governor only was read. It spoke of the loan for $200,000, the contract for which was communicated, but that, with the other documents, was referred to Messrs. Collingsworth, Gazley, Hamilton, Childers and Goodrich. Thus the subject was smuggled out of sight of the house, a course seemingly inauspicious to the confirmation of the loan. Indeed, I learn there will be serious opposition to it, arising from the wretched selfishness of members, who regard the terms of the loan as too favorable to the lenders, the land being too low, in their opinion. To national faith and credit they are insensible. I begin to find myself uncomfortably situated here. I am told I am regarded as a spy in the camp, and viewed with jealousy. I have fancied I perceived less cordiality towards me than was at first manifested. I must therefore be guarded. I have shown the contract to Zavala. He thinks the interest low, and that we have given too much for the land.

The Constitution was first committed on the 2nd to the following: Potter, Stewart, Waller, Grymes, Coleman, Fisher, Bunton, Palmer, Gaines, Zavala, Everett, Hardeman, Stapp, Crawford, West, Powers, Navarro, McKinney, Menefee, Mottley, Menard. Others have since taken a hand in it, and it will have to undergo much alteration and revision to make it respectable in language and arrangement.

Tuesday, March 8, 1836.

Fine weather. The Convention are diligent in their meetings, but get on slowly with business. Too much talk. The manner in which Gov'r Smith's communication was yesterday introduced was thus: Potter inquired if the committee appointed to wait on the officers of the late provisional government had acted. The chairman replied that notice had been given to them. In the course of the remarks that arose the loan was alluded to by Collingsworth as a matter that required action, and which was not before the house. He said it was doubted whether it would be confirmed by the house or by the lenders. Potter suggested that the documents in possession of the executive would give all the necessary information. Governor Smith was behind the bar, and said in a low voice to Potter that he had had no opportunity of making a communication. He then (on Potter's offer to present them) gave his papers to Potter, who presented them to the house. Ordered to be read. Potter undertook it, but could not get through. Dr. Stewart, the late secretary of the Governor, read them. The letter of the Governor only ordered to be printed. The rest laid on the table—referred.

Collingsworth to-day reported on the loan favorably, Indian treaty, etc. No action on the loan. (See my pencil memo. of the proceedings.)

Mr. Conrad to-day introduced a resolution directing the closing of land offices, collecting records, appointing a Commissioner, etc., which lays on table.

What with the advance of the Mexicans on one side and the Indians on the other, and the organization of a new government, this Convention would seem to have enough on their hands to do. Yet they get on slowly. The evil spirit of electioneering is among them for the high offices in prospect. And the land quest also requires much log rolling, to make it suit the existing interests or selfish views of members. The Constitution gets on slowly.

A document read to-day stated that the officers of the army amount to 128; navy, 1 captain, 2 lieutenants, 1 surgeon.

Wednesday, March 9, 1836.

Weather warm and fine. I have made a bargain with Heath, the carpenter, for his shop. He is to put a good floor in it, and rent it for $25 until 1st of April. Zavala, Navarro, Ruis, Badgett and myself are to occupy it and divide the cost equally. We shall then be retired, and comparatively comfortable, and I shall enjoy the benefit of an intercourse with Zavala, whose character and attainments interest me. He has kindly offered to give me lessons in Spanish, and I have already received several. He is obliging, kind and very polite. So are Ruis and Navarro. They seem much gratified at my efforts to learn Spanish; they and the servants all help me, correct my mistakes, and praise my diligence. They, however, do not speak English as Zavala does. They are a kind people, but indolent. My industry in writing and studying surprises them.

Dr. Everett, a member of the Convention, to-day asked me if the lenders of the $200,000 loan would not be satisfied with having the amount paid returned with interest. I told him I could only speak for myself, and asked him if he was prepared to return it. He said yes, there were some gentlemen who would advance the money. I told him they had better take all they could get, for that they would want all that could be got beside the loan. He observed that the Commissioners had transcended their powers, had made hard terms, and must have been asleep, plainly intimating that they had been overreached. I find from various circumstances that a great hostility exists in the Convention against the loan, and that it will probably not be ratified, and, what is unfortunate, I feel that the hostility to the loan extends in some degree to me. I do not experience so much cordiality as I did at first.

The business of the Convention drags. There are some questions that they seem afraid to approach. They are sure to produce excitement, come up when they may. The land question is one, and the loan they are unwilling or afraid to ratify. Such miserable narrow-mindedness is astonishing. There is a great want of political philosophy and practical political knowledge in the body.

Thursday, March 10, 1836.

Fine weather, and we have got comfortably fixed in our new lodging. The eating at our house is becoming sorry, no butter, no milk, no sugar, little or no vegetables, and not much meat except pork.

Navarro to-day showed me a deed for five leagues of land below the San Antonio road, and on the head waters of the * * *, which he offers for $1,500 per league. It is an old Mexican title which he bought.

Ruis also has four leagues of land, a military grant, in Robertson's Colony, which he wishes to sell.

Zavala has an eleven-league grant, located about the Trinity in various places, which he offers for thirty-seven and a half cents per acre. MEMO. to endeavor to make some arrangement with him.

The business of the Convention moves slowly. The Constitution is on the tapis every day. It is a good one, on the whole, but clumsily put together, indifferent in arrangement, and worse in grammar.

No news yet from the Alamo, and much anxiety is felt for the fate of the brave men there. It is obvious that they must be surrounded and all communication with them cut off.

This evening Dr. Neblett, from Virginia, and several other gentlemen arrived here. Sam'l P. Carson, a member of the Convention from Red River, also arrived and took his seat. He informed me Robert Triplett is on the road.

Received letters from Mrs. Gray, dated January 23, February 1, brought by Captain Briscoe.

Friday, March 11, 1836.

This morning Triplett arrived, accompanied by a Mr. Hies, from Tennessee. Capt. Briscoe, who brought my letter from Nacogdoches, took his seat as a member of the Convention.

Nothing of particular interest to-day, in Convention. Intrigues for the high offices of State are said to be going on, and much log rolling on the land question. A great hostility exists against the large grants made by Coahuila and Texas to certain large land operators. It is made a stalking horse by the demagogues of the house, and they are endeavoring to sweep away all titles to lands in Texas except headrights. It is a most iniquitous attempt, and I trust there will be virtue enough left to defeat it.

No action yet on the loan, nor does any great measure approach maturity.

Mr. Carson has at once taken a prominent part in the business of the house. He has made a good impression, and much is expected of him. He is not yet forty years of age, but is in bad health, and looks much older. He and Potter are the only two members of the body who have ever been in Congress (except Gen. Houston, who is now with the army), and their experience in public business gives them an ascendency over the rest of the body. The President is losing ground. He made a good impression at first, but by his partiality and weakness and great conceit he has forfeited the respect of the body, and a laxity of order begins to be apparent.

Among the persons here who are attracted by the Convention is David G. Burnett, one of the Empresarios of this country, who is spoken of as the President. He is said to be an honest, good man, but I doubt his ability for such a station.

Saturday, March 12, 1836.

Weather warm and pleasant. No intelligence yet from the Alamo, nor from Houston. The Constitution has been gone over by sections, and much altered and amended; but it is still so imperfect that it has been recommitted to another committee to amend the phraseology and arrangement—as the President expresses it, to correct the verbiage.

Sunday, March 13, 1836.

The Convention continued their business as usual, without regard to the day. Indeed I have seen little or no observance of the day in Texas. They are a most ungodly people.

To-day a very pretty debate arose on the subject of imprisonment for debt. It arose on a motion of Rusk, which went to prohibit imprisonment for debt, except in cases of fraud. Motion to amend made by Potter. Childress moved: "No person shall ever be imprisoned for debt, on any pretense whatever."

It was advocated by Childress, Carson, Parmer and Potter; opposed by Rusk, Collingsworth and Thomas. (See the article in the Constitution.)

No intelligence yet from the Alamo. The anxiety begins to be intense. Mr. Badgett and Dr. Goodrich, members of the Convention, have brothers there, and Mr. Grimes, another member, has a son there.

Zavala expresses the belief that in twelve months he will be in Mexico. He thinks that Santa Anna's race is nearly run; that a revolution will take place in Mexico, and the liberal party will be in the ascendency; that he is the most popular man of that party, and he thinks that he will be called to head it. The seeds of ambition are not yet extinct in him, and vanity is his weak side.

Monday, March 14, 1836.

No intelligence yet from the Alamo. The weather is gloomy and warm, indicating rain. The wind is from the south, and the wild geese are mustering for the North. Large flocks are seen flying over, but in very militia-like style. They have not yet got drilled into a regular echelon form of march.

Conrad to-day introduced a series of resolutions, giving large land bounties to the volunteers. (See the document itself.) It will doubtless succeed in some shape, for the military interest has a great ascendancy in this body. It is necessary to conciliate the military, and scarcely anything that they can ask will be refused. They know the country will have to be defended by volunteers from the United States, and they therefore will bid high for them.

Tuesday, March 15, 1836.

This morning Lieuts. Teal and Snell, with between thirty and forty men, recruited at Nacogdoches, arrived on their march to the army. They were drawn up before the Convention house. Collingsworth, as chairman of the Military Committee, addressed them, and welcomed them to the capital. They were also addressed by Carson and Rusk, in warm and animated terms, and the celebrated * * * Norton, who, some years ago, gave rise to the term *Nortonized*, in connection with a postoffice appointment, addressed them in a bombastic style. He is figuring here as a Texan patriot, but has not much consideration. Lieut. Teal was, by resolution of the Convention, appointed a Captain, and he and Snell both invited to a seat in the Convention.

In the afternoon, while the Convention was sitting, a Mr. Ainsworth, from Columbia, arrived and brought news that an express had arrived below, with the intelligence that an attack had been made on the Alamo, which was repulsed with great loss to the enemy. The rumour was doubted, on account of the circuitous route by which it came. All hoped it true, but many feared the worst. In half an hour after an express was received from General Houston, bringing the sad intelligence of the fall of the Alamo, on the morning of the 6th. His letters were dated on the 11th and 13th, and a letter from John Seguin, at Gonzales, to Ruis and Navarro, brought the same account. Still some did, or affected to, disbelieve it. (For a detailed account, see letter to Blackford.)

The Convention adjourned until to-morrow at 9 o'clock, but met again after supper, spontaneously, and went earnestly to work on the Constitution. A motion was made to organize a provisional government, which was laid over till to-morrow.

Wrote to W. M. B.

Wednesday, March 16, 1836.

A Dr. Southerland arrived this morning from Gonzales, who puts the intelligence of the fall of the Alamo beyond a doubt.

The land question came up in Convention this morning, and created much excitement. The late disastrous intelligence and the perils which are approaching made members impatient of debate. The land question has been much modified since its first introduction, and now goes only to declare null and void the three large grants, and to set aside the location of eleven league grants within twenty miles of the United States line, which may have been located contrary to the laws of Mexico. (See the shape it shall pass in ultimately.)

Some members are going home. Col. Parmer, Mr. Waller and Mr. Gazley have obtained leave of absence. Col. Parmer was authorized by resolution to press wagons, horses, etc., and to take possession of the public arms at Nacogdoches, etc. Express and dispatches were sent off in different directions, and authority given to move and provide for some defenseless families from the Colorado.

The President went out of his way this afternoon to give the loan a blow. He distinctly pronounced it a bad bargain, said it should be confirmed in order to preserve the public faith, but hoped no more such would be made. Collingsworth has become disgusted, got drunk, and speaks with much asperity of the conduct of the Convention. Says he has reported all the business before his committee, and been discharged, and he intends to do no more; that he has no rights, and shall perform no duties.

Great confusion and irregularity prevailed in the Convention to-day. The President has lost all dignity and all authority. The house adjourned until to-morrow, 9 o'clock.

At supper a printed hand-bill was received by express from San Felipe (which see). The house met spontaneously, and after having the express publicly read, proceeded to business. The Constitution not being quite ready, they adjourned to 10 o'clock. They met at that hour, and went to work. At 12 o'clock the Constitution was finally adopted. (See the document.) An ordinance organizing a provisional government was then adopted, consisting of President, Vice-President, four Secretaries, and an Attorney General, with most of the powers conferred by the Constitution on the President and Congress. (See the document.) Authorized to contract for a loan of $1,000,000, and to pledge the public faith and the proceeds of the public land. An election was held forthwith. David G. Burnett and Samuel P. Carson were nominated for President. Burnett was elected by a majority of seven. Lorenzo de Zavala was then nominated for Vice-President by Potter; no opposition. He was elected by a unanimous vote. Carson was elected Secretary of State, Hardiman Secretary of Treasury, Rusk Secretary of War, and Potter Secretary of Navy, David Thomas Attorney General. The new officers were sworn in at 4 o'clock in the morning, and the Convention adjourned until to-morrow, 9 o'clock.

Frequent alarms were brought in during the night. Spies and patrols were ordered out; much excitement prevailed. No action yet on the loan. The proceedings of the house to-night were disorderly in the extreme, and boyish. Nearly all the members were sometimes on the floor at once, some calling "question," some laughing and clapping, etc. The President, by his manifest partiality, egotism and alarm, has lost the respect of the house. He frequently argues questions from the chair. Proposed to adjourn the Convention to near Nacogdoches!

Thursday, March 17, 1836.

Fine, mild weather.

The Convention met after breakfast, earlier than would have been expected, after the late work of last night. The subject of the loan was at length brought up. The Alamo has now fallen, and the state of the country is becoming every day more and more gloomy. In fact, they begin now to feel that they are hourly exposed to attack and capture, and, as on the approach of death, they begin to lay aside their selfish schemes, and to think of futurity. An invaded, unarmed, unprovisioned country, without an army to oppose the invaders, and without money to raise one, now presents itself to their hitherto besotted and blinded minds, and the awful cry has been heard from the midst of their assembly, "What shall we do to be saved?" They now see their folly in regard to the loan, and the necessity of doing something to repair it. They were thrown into much agitation by a report spread by a person, unknown, who passed through the town to the eastward, without stopping, but stated in his transit that the enemy's cavalry were passing the Colorado at Bastrop, about sixty miles from Washington. The contract for the loan, made by the Commissioners in New Orleans, and the letters of the Commissioners in relation thereto, had been communicated to the Convention by Governor Smith, and referred to a committee. The committee had reported favorably, but up to this time neither the contract nor the other documents had been read in Convention, and it was now too late to consider them. Triplett was called upon to explain to the Convention the nature of the loan, and the circumstances under which it was negotiated. He being the largest lender, was supposed to speak by authority, or at least to represent the interests of the others. He, however, disclaimed it, and said he acted for himself alone, but supposed the others would concur in what he might do. He stated that he had learned that a strong opposition to the loan existed in the Convention, and gave an outline of a different arrangement which he would be willing to accede to, and proposed to leave it to the new executive to arrange with the lenders. This was promptly acceded to, and a resolution passed authorizing the executive to do what they thought best. They now see the need they have, not only for this money, but for more, and they are willing to get it on the best terms they can, but are not disposed to take the responsibility on themselves. They have blinked the question. They have not actually rejected the loan, but have not confirmed it, as the contract required they should do, and it is, in no point of view, obligatory on the lenders to pay up the balance. Three days ago there was a decided hostility to the loan, and had the question been taken before the fall of the Alamo was known, it would have been rejected. I am warranted in this conclusion by what was told me by some members, and others who had opportunities of knowing, both before that event was known, and since the adjournment.

Soon after the passage of the resolution on the loan, the Convention adjourned, *sine die*, without any vote of thanks to the President. One member wittily said he thought the friends of the President ought to give him a vote of thanks for his partiality.

The members are now dispersing in all directions, with haste and in confusion. A general panic seems to have seized them. Their families are exposed and defenseless, and thousands are moving off to the east. A constant stream of women and children, and some men, with wagons, cars and pack mules, are rushing across the Brazos night and day. The families of this place, and storekeepers, are packing up and moving. I had sent some clothes to be washed by a woman who occupied a shed at the end of the town. I went this morning to get them, and found the place deserted. The pots, pans, crockeryware, etc., and some bedding, were left, and only the articles more easily moved were taken. But in their haste and panic they had not forgot to be honest. My clothes were washed and neatly tied up, and placed in an adjoining office, whence I got them. The name of this worthy family was Blair; where they had gone I could not learn.

The new executives have determined to go to Harrisburg, on the Buffalo Bayou, as a place of more safety than this, and of easy communication with the seaboard, New Orleans, etc.

My Mexican friends are packing up, with the intention of crossing the Brazos to-night. Zavala has politely invited me to his house, which I shall accept.

I crossed the ferry after dinner, expecting to reach Groce's, where Triplett and Dr. Neblett had gone, but waiting too long at the river for company, I found it impracticable. Mr. Menard and Mr. Hardin, two members of the Convention, coming across, I joined them, and went as far as the edge of the prairie, four miles across the Brazos bottoms, to the house of a Mr. Whiteside. The establishment consisted of a log house of one room, and two or three little outhouses. The houses and grounds around were fully occupied by a number of families, moving from the other side of the Brazos, who had encamped here, or rather bivouaced here. Among them was the wife of the late Lieutenant Governor Robinson, who made loud complaints against Col. Parmer, who had pressed into the public service her horse, which her husband, who was gone to the army, had left for her to retreat upon. She was now afoot, and in her indignation she said she would be durned if she did not take the first horse she could find.

Here we got corn for our horses to eat, which they had not tasted for several days before. My horse had actually eaten nothing, since the day before, when he was brought in from the prairie. Having fed him I had him hobbled and turned him out on the prairie. We got a good supper, fried bacon, good corn bread, coffee, and a cup of milk. Menard and Hardin slept on the ground in the open air, by a fire. I took my rest in an open wagon, where our baggage was, and slept pretty well. Another person slept under the wagon. It rained a little in the night, but not enough to wet me.

Friday, March 18, 1836.

This morning was cloudy and drizzly. Many persons, moving eastward to escape the anticipated storm of war, came along with their families, some in wagons, some in carts, and some on foot, with mules and horses, packed with their moveables. Menard went on to Nacogdoches, in company with Taylor. Hardin returned to Washington, to see after the family of a friend of his. I determined to wait for some one going on towards the bay, with whom I might keep company, and in the meantime employed myself in writing to the United States. The poor Mexican prisoners, the old priest and the young officer, came by on foot, going to Nacogdoches. They are alone and unguarded—very little like prisoners. About 10 o'clock Zavala, Ruis and Navarro, with their attendants and caviard (cabellards) of horses and pack mules, came by on their way to Groce's, where they are to stay to-night. Zavala rode a little mule. I was soon after joined by Pyle and Badgett; also by Ikin, the English capitalist, who, it was said, was to lend Texas $5,000,000. He was on foot, and as we all were going the same road, we agreed to take dinner with Mrs. Whiteside and go on to Groce's to-night.

Before we started Pennington came by, with a proclamation from the President designed to lull the panic and stop the flight of the people toward the eastern frontier. (See proclamation.) Intelligence was received contradicting the report of the approach of the enemy by Bastrop, and stating that General Houston had not crossed the Colorado, and was receiving reinforcements. We also learned that they were making a breastwork of cotton bags at the Brazos ferry, in case the enemy should come that way. After dinner we all started. At Walker's, about half way to Groce's, we encountered Zavala and his Mexican friends, encamped in the woods. They would go no further to-night. We went on, and arrived at Groce's at half past 7 o'clock. Found there Triplett, Hise, Carson, Kimble, Ellis, Hamilton, Everett, Blount, McKinney, etc.

The country over which we have passed to-day is beautifully diversified with wood and prairie. It is prettier than the west side of the river. Groce's is prettily situated. Houses numerous, but small, and much crowded. I slept on the floor with Badgett and Kimble.

Had the misfortune to lose one of my pistols to-day. It must have broken loose from the belt.

Saturday, March 19, 1836.

Remained at Groce's all day. Nothing yet done with the loan. Dr. Southerland arrived, and reported Zavala sick at Walker's. Several gentlemen arrived here to-day, among them Capt. Morehouse, of the company of Lancers, lately arrived from New York. He said that Capt. Stanley, whom I had seen showing off at Washington, did not belong to the Lancers, but is an Englishman, who had gone there to endeavor to get the command of them conferred on him by the government.

President Burnett, Secretary Rusk and Attorney General Thomas are here, having arrived during the night. Pyle and Ikin left here in the afternoon, for the bay. Pyle is disgusted, and urged me to go with him, saying he disliked to leave me in such company.

A Mr. Green, from Florida, arrived last night, and has obtained a brigadier general's command and authority to raise men and provisions, etc., in the United States, on the faith of the government.

Sunday, March 20, 1836.

This morning Messrs. Zavala, Ruis and Navarro arrived. The cabinet are now all here, except Hardiman. The servant of the late lamented Travis, Joe, a black boy of about twenty-one or twenty-two years of age, is now here. He was in the Alamo when the fatal attack was made. He is the only male, of all who were in the fort, who escaped death, and he, according to his own account, escaped narrowly. I heard him interrogated in presence of the cabinet and others. He related the affair with much modesty, apparent candor, and remarkably distinctly for one of his class. The following is, as near as I can recollect, the substance of it:

The garrison was much exhausted by incessant watching and hard labor. They had all worked until a late hour on Saturday night, and when the attack was made sentinels and all were asleep, except one man, Capt. * * *, who gave the alarm. There were three picket guards without the fort, but they, too, it is supposed, were asleep, and were run upon and bayonetted, for they gave no alarm. Joe was sleeping in the room with his master when the alarm was given. Travis sprang up, seized his rifle and sword, and called to Joe to follow him. Joe took his gun and followed. Travis ran across the Alamo and mounted the wall, and called out to his men, "Come on, boys, the Mexicans are upon us, and we'll give them Hell." He discharged his gun; so did Joe. In an instant Travis was shot down. He fell within the wall, on the sloping ground, and sat up. The enemy twice applied their scaling ladders to the walls, and were twice beaten back. But this Joe did not well understand, for when his master fell he ran and ensconced himself in a house, from which he says he fired on them several times, after they got in. On the third attempt they succeeded in mounting the walls, and then poured over like sheep. The battle then became a melee. Every man fought for his own hand, as he best might, with butts of guns, pistols, knives, etc. As Travis sat wounded on the ground General Mora, who was passing him, made a blow at him with his sword, which Travis struck up, and ran his assailant through the body, and both died on the same spot. This was poor Travis' last effort. The handful of Americans retreated to such covers as they had, and continued the battle until one man was left, a little, weakly man named Warner, who asked for quarter. He was spared by the soldiery, but on being conducted to Santa Anna, he ordered him to be shot, and it was done. Bowie is said to have fired through the door of his room, from his sick bed. He was found dead and mutilated where he lay. Crockett and a few of his friends were found together, with twenty-four of the enemy dead around them. The negroes, for there were several negroes and women in the fort, were spared. Only one woman was killed, and Joe supposes she was shot accidentally, while attempting to cross the Alamo. She was found lying between two guns. The officers came around, after the massacre, and called out to know if there were any negroes there. Joe stepped out and said, "Yes, here is one." Immediately two soldiers attempted to kill him, one by discharging his piece at him, the other with a thrust of the bayonet. Only one buckshot took effect in his side, not dangerously, and the point of the bayonet scratched him on the other. He was saved by Capt. Baragan. Besides the negroes, there were in the fort several Mexican women, among them the wife of a Dr. * * * and her sister, Miss Navarro, who were spared and restored to their father, D. Angel Navarro, of Bejar. Mrs. Dickenson, wife of Lieut. Dickenson, and child, were also spared, and have been sent back into Texas. After the fight was over, the Mexicans were formed in hollow square, and Santa Anna addressed them in a very animated manner. They filled the air with loud shouts. Joe describes him as a slender man, rather tall, dressed very plainly-somewhat "like a Methodist preacher," to use the negro's own words. Joe was taken into Bejar, and detained several days; was shown a grand review of the army after the battle, which he was told, or supposes, was 8,000 strong. Those acquainted with the ground on which he says they formed think that not more than half that number could form there. Santa Anna questioned Joe about Texas, and the state of its army. Asked if there were many soldiers from the United States in the army, and if more were expected, and said he had men enough to march to the city of Washington. The American dead were collected in a pile and burnt.

A list of those who fell in the Alamo, March 6, 1836, as far as they are known:

David Crockett, Tennessee.
Col. Wm. B. Travis.
Col. Bowman.
Col. James Bowie, Tennessee.
G. Washington, Drum Major.
Adjt. I. Baugh, Virginia, New Orleans Greys.
Capt. S. C. Blair, Artillery, Ireland.
Capt. Carey, Ireland.
Capt. Baker, Mississippi.
Capt. Wm. Blazeby, New Orleans Greys.
Capt. Harrison, Tennessee.
Capt. Forsyth, New York.
Lt. John Jones, New Orleans Greys.
Lt. Kimble, Gonzales.
Lt. Dickenson, wife and child.
Lt. Robt. Evans, Master of Ordnance, England.
Lt. Williamson, Sergt. Major, Philadelphia.
Dr. Mitchison, Civil Engineer.
Dr. Pollard, Surgeon.
Dr. Thompson, Tennessee.
Charles Despalier, Aide to Travis.
Elliot Melton, Quartermaster.
* * * Anderson, Quartermaster.
Major G. B. Jamison, Kentucky.
Col. J.B. Bonham, Alabama.
* * * Robinson, Scotland.
* * * Nelson, Charleston, S. C.
* * * Nelson, Austin's clerk.
Wm. Smith, Nacogdoches.
Lewis Johnson, Mina.
E. P. Mitchell, Georgia.
* * * Thurston.* * * Moor, Mississippi.
Christopher Parker, Mississippi.

* * * Hieskell, Nacogdoches.
* * * Rowe, Nacogdoches.
John M. Hays, Tennessee.
* * * Stewart.
James Blair, Nacogdoches.
William Simpson.
Albert Martin, Gonzales.
David Wilson, Nacogdoches.
Wm. Howell, New Orleans Greys.
Charles Smith, Bastrop.
J. McGregor, Scotland.
* * * Rusk.
Col. * * * Hawkins, Louisiana.
Samuel Holloway, Texas.
* * * Browne, Travis' Company.
* * * Smith, Travis' Company.
* * * Browne, Philadelphia.
* * * Henderson.
Wm. Wells, Tennessee.
Wm. Cumming, Pennsylvania.
* * * Battentine, Pennsylvania.
R. W. Valantine, Pennsylvania.
R. Cockran, Boston.
Capt. Robt. White.
Sergt. Isaac White, Harris, Ky.
* * * Sterne.
* * * Jackson, Ireland.
* * * McAfferty.
Wm. D. Southerland, Navidad.
Three Taylors, Trinity.
* * * Taylor, Little River, Texas.
R. M. Kinney, Bastrop.
S. B. Evans, Tennessee.
Tom R. Miller, Gonzales.
Wm. R. King, Gonzales.

J. Kane, Gonzales.
Wm. Durduff, Gonzales.
Geo. Tomlinson, Gonzales.
Dan'l Jackson, Sailor.
John C. Goodrich, Tennessee.
Wm. Marshall, New Orleans Greys, Arkansas.
Jon'a Lindley, Tennessee.
Micajah Autry, Tennessee.
Jas. Sewall, Nacogdoches.
John Wilson, Nacogdoches.
A. C. Grimes, Alabama.
Jas. C. Day, Nacogdoches.
Tapley Holland.
James George, Gonzales.
* * * Bailey, Logan County, Kentucky.
* * * Cloud, Logan County, Kentucky.
* * * Lewis, Philadelphia.
* * * Stockton, Virginia.
* * * Thomas, Tennessee.
* * * Bowen, Tennessee.
* * * Bailiss, Tennessee.
* * * Crawford, Kentucky.
* * * Devault, Missouri, Plasterer.
* * * Dewell, Blacksmith.
Jas. Kinney.
* * * Warner.
John Garvin, Missouri.
* * * Wornell.
Capt. * * * Gilmore, Tennessee.
* * * Smith, Tennessee.
Spain Summerlin, Tennessee.
* * * Thompson, Tennessee.
* * * Pollard.
* * * Nelson, New Orleans Greys.
* * * Butler, New Orleans Greys.

Wm. Ellis.
Jos. Shead.
Sam'l Holloway, New Orleans Greys.
* * * Ballard.
* * * Spratt.
Jacob Dust, Gonzales.
Christopher Parker, Mississippi.
* * * Robbins, Kentucky.
John Flanders.
Isaac Ryan, Opelousas.
David Murphy, Tennessee.
Jon'a Lindley, Illinois.
Jas. Ewing.
Jas. Stewart, Nacogdoches.
Robt. Cunningham.
Francis Desooks, Storekeeper.
* * * Lynn, Drum Major.
John Balone.
* * * Burns, Ireland.
John Burnell.
Geo. Neggin.
F. Desanque, Philadelphia.
John (clerk in Desanque's store).
Robt. Musselman, New Orleans.
Robt. Crossman, New Orleans.
Richard Starr, England.
J. G. Ganett, New Orleans.
J. G. Dinkin, England.
Rob. B. Moore, New Orleans.
Wm. Lynn, Boston.
* * * Hutchinson.
Wm. Johnson, Philadelphia.
Dan'l Bourne, England.
* * * Ingram, England.
Charles Lanco, Denmark.

Capt. A. Dickerson, Gonzales.
Geo. C. Kimble, Gonzales.
Dolphin Floyd, Gonzales.
Thos. Jackson, Gonzales.
Geo. W. Cottle, Gonzales.
Andrew Kent, Gonzlaes.
Isaac Baker, Gonzales.
Jesse McCoy, Gonzales.
Claiborne Wright, Gonzales.
Wm. Fishback, Gonzales.
* * * Millsap, Gonzales.
Galby Fuqua, Gonzales.
John Davis, Gonzales.

DEFINITIONS ON INSIDE BACK COVER.

Tahuacanas—An Indian Tribe.
Bidais—An Indian Tribe.
Zuichais—An Indian Tribe.
Haacos—An Indian Tribe.
Sabine, *Sabinas*—The name of a tree, called cypress in United States.
Potranca—A small mare.
Salado—Adjective, salt.
Bosque—Woody, or Forest.
Loco—Mad or Crazy.
Garapatos—Ticks.
Piedernales—Flint.
Calaberas—Death's Head.
Matamoros—The place of the death of the Moors, or massacre of the Moors.
Garcitas—Little Cranes.
Garza—Crane.

VOL. VIII

Monday, March 21, 1836.

The cabinet this morning left Groce's for Harrisburg. The following gents accompany them: Triplett; Hise, Kimble, Gray, Dr. Southerland, Sage, Farris, McCloud, Hill and Hizer. The following also departed in different directions: Navarro and Ruis for San Felipe; Blount, Brigham, etc.

Some gents had expressed an unwillingness to remain at Groce's, because they thought it imposing on the hospitality of a gentleman too much. This delicacy was cured when, on starting, he presented each with a bill for $3 per day, man and horse. My bill was $8 from Friday night to Monday, morning.

Our journey was without interest, but over a beautiful prairie country. As accommodations were very scarce on the road, and the President gave a broad hint that he wished the Cabinet to keep together and be freed from the presence of the untitled and unofficial part of the cavalcade, *We the People* stopt at the house of * * * McEarly, and the Cabinet wabbled on to Roberts', three miles further. Discovered that I had left my umbrella and inkholder at Groce's. Wrote a note to him, to be sent back by some traveller, desiring him to send them to me at Harrisburg.

On attempting to go to rest, found my blankets were missing, and with all my exertion could only raise one of them, which was obtained from the camp of a small party of soldiery who were encamped a short distance from the house. Their captain, whose name was Henderson, a little, conceited and insignificant whippersnapper, was well lodged in the house, and although it was obvious his men had stolen my blankets, he would not use his authority to compel restitution, so I had to put up with one blanket, and rather cold lodging. This Captain Henderson is a Tennesseean, and is hanging on to the government with his little party of about ten or twelve as a kind of bodyguard, under the pretense of being an express corps. What a government! What an army! *"Sing Ditton and Whitton,"* etc.

A flying report was received at Roberts' that Fannin had left Goliad and blown up the fort; that Houston did not know where the enemy was, etc.

Tuesday, March 22, 1836.

I this morning recovered my blankets from the camp of the valiant soldiers, who have thus shown the materials of which they are composed.

Left McEarly's at 7 o'clock—bill, $1.50. Overtook the government at Roberts' and all proceeded together. Stopt at Mrs. Burnett's, a widow woman, who keeps the only house on the road between Roberts' and Harrisburg, a distance of forty miles, at 11 o'clock. Got a feed of corn for our horses, and an excellent snack of broiled beef, butter, milk and good cornbread for ourselves. She is a poor widow, with several young children, yet she would receive nothing for what we ate. She charged twenty-five cents only for the feed for each horse, and for that she made the apology that corn was scarce, and when what she had was gone she would have to buy more. She had a plenty of meat and milk, and we were welcome to it. What a contrast between the kindheartedness of this poor widow and the fleecing disposition of the rich Mr. Groce! This is the second instance of the kind that I have met with in Texas. Mrs. Whiteside was the first. She would have nothing, not even for horse feed. Such instances should be recorded as redeeming circumstances.

Had a long and tiresome ride over uninteresting prairie. The Brazos bottom lay far away to the west, sometimes out of sight, when the horizon over the prairie had all the appearance of a water view. The beautiful woods of the San Jacinto lay eastward to our left, and near enough to distinguish the deep green of the cedar and pine which abound there. Zavala pointed out to me some of his possessions there. He has five leagues on the San Jacinto, three of which he designs for his oldest son.

Arrived at Harrisburg after dark. Approached the town by crossing Buffalo Bayou, on which it is situated, in a flat, which would only admit of the passage of four horses at a time. Zavala escaped in the first boat with me, and I was struck with the cordial and affectionate manner in which he was greeted wherever recognized. Stopt at the house of Mrs. Harris, widow of the founder of the town. No corn or other food to be got for our horses. Had to turn them loose to graze. The house is crowded and lodging indifferent. I slept on the floor under the same blanket with the Secretary of War. The Secretary of the Navy and Attorney-General also slept on the floor. The President, Vice-President and Secretary of State were accommodated with beds.

I found here Pyle and Ikin; they had arrived only a short time before us, and had got their suppers; but finding a crowd coming in they crossed the bayou and lodged on the other side.

Weather lowering.

Wednesday, March 23, 1836.

The President and Vice President being now about fifteen miles from their homes, both went home to-day to see their families. Being invited by Zavala to go with him, I resolved to do so, but being detained, let him start first, expecting to overtake him. Started in company with Pyle and a young man named Lyon, from Georgia, on his return to the United States. Overtook Ikin at the bayou. As he was on foot and I in a hurry, we soon parted company. Lyon and I rode on together. At Earle's met with Dr. Neblett and Mr. Nat. I. Dobie, of Harrisburg, on their return from the bay. Detained some time in conversation. (MEMO. * * * Earl wishes to sell his land. Has a salt spring on it.) A few miles further on passed a vacant house, which by inquiry I learn belongs to a widow who has left the country and resides in Cincinnati or Boston, named Wilson. There are three labors attached to it. She gave $350 for it. Pretty place, good spring; keep it in view. Stopt at the house of * * * Atkins, an English farmer; wife a spruce and kindly woman. Asked her for a drink of water and she gave me a bowl of fine milk. He rents the place of Dr. Patrick for $100 per annum. Says Patrick has no deed to it, but expects to get one of Austin. A pretty place. The lands all along the Buffalo Bayou are beautiful and fertile.

Arrived at Zavala's before 2 o'clock. Was ferried over by an old Frenchman; horse swam the bayou, which is here as wide as the Rappahannock at Fredericksburg. Received a cordial and kind reception. They had dined, but the table was still in the floor. Young Zavala came down to the shore to meet me and conduct me to the house. Zavala only owns one labor of land here, which he bought for the sake of the situation and the buildings. It is beautifully situated on a point at the junction of Buffalo Bayou and Old San Jacinto, the present San Jacinto running some distance off. The house is small, one large room, three small bed closets and a porch, kitchen, etc. Mrs. Zavala is a fine, beautiful woman, of tall, dignified person and ladylike manners, black eyes, twenty-seven years old, a native of the State of New York; maiden name West. She is the second wife of the Vice-President; the first was a lady of Yucatan, and the mother of young Lorenzo, who is now * * * years of age. The Vice-President is forty-seven. They have three little children, Augustus, Emelie and Ricardo, the youngest just beginning to crawl; sweet children, mild, gentle, well bred. Oh, how they made me think of my own dear ones! Mrs. Zavala spent one year in the City of Mexico after her marriage, and speaks the Spanish language fluently. She and her husband always converse in Spanish when alone. She was also in Paris with her husband when he was minister of the Mexican Republic at that court. She has but one house servant, an Irish girl, the same that accompanied her to Paris, who is chambermaid and nurse, one black woman in the kitchen, who is cook, etc. There are two or three Frenchmen about the establishment, who do all the outwork, attend the horses, cows, garden, etc. The plantation is small. They only took possession of it last fall, and have all the improvements yet to make. When the foreign taste and skill of the proprietor and his servants shall have had time to make an impression on the face of nature, we may expect to see the desert smile.

Young Zavala is preparing to join the army. He goes as a volunteer in the cavalry, to be accompanied by Joseph, a young French valet. He is a fine, sprightly youth, small stature, black eyes, good teeth, a light, active person, Mexican in appearance and manners; good education, speaks Spanish, French and English; a native of Yucatan; mother's name Carrea. His name, according to Spanish custom, would be Lorenzo Zavala de Carrea, but he follows the American style and writes it Lorenzo Zavala, Jr.

This afternoon the clouds, which had been lowering for some days, poured down a heavy rain. The wind from northeast blew a regular equinoctial storm, and being near the Bay of Galveston, it came up heavy and cold. Mr. Baradere, a Frenchman, who is living at Lynchburg, had come up directly after dinner to see Mr. Zavala, and notwithstanding the wind and rain, he refused a pressing invitation to stay all night, and rowed himself back in an open boat, about one mile. Mr. Zavala spoke of him as a scholar, and one that wishes to establish a seminary in this country. He showed great deference to Zavala, who called him *"Mon cher ami,"* and treated him affectionately.

The bed rooms of the little house being fully occupied by the family, a bed was spread for me on the floor of the sitting room, where, after some reflection on the circumstances in which I found myself and the vicissitudes of human affairs, which had placed me under the roof of this remarkable man, in this remote region, far away from my family, I slept soundly.

Thursday, March 24, 1836.

The rain has abated, but the wind is still strong from the northeast; cold and cloudy. Went a short distance in the woods. Vegetation very forward, trees in leaf, and a profusion of wild flowers blown. Saw the mulberry in abundance, and the Sabinas, the tree from which the Sabine River takes its name—a species of cedar, or cypress.

After breakfast went in a boat with Mr. Zavala and son to Lynchburg, about a mile distant. Young Zavala rowed. Lynchburg was laid out for a town some years ago, but it will never be a town, one or two houses and a saw mill, built by President Burnet, but which was not profitable, and is not now worked. Burnet told me he sunk $8,000 by that mill. It is just below the junction of the San Jacinto and Buffalo Bayou, on the road that goes by Liberty, on the Trinidad, Tevis' Ferry on the Neches, and * * * Ferry, on the Sabine, and on to Opelousasa road much travelled.

Before dinner President Burnet arrived in a boat, and after dinner he and Zavala went off to Harrisburg in an open boat. I took my leave of the amiable family and recrossed the bayou. Stopt again at Atkins' to chat with him and his wife. He has contracted with Dr. Patrick to clear out his league of land, but he says there are two young men now in the army, John Cheevers and John Barker, who have not got their land. He promised to write to them by young Zavala, and engage the clearing out of their land for me.

Arrived just at night at Earle's, by whom and his family I was kindly received and hospitably entertained. They are

Irish, and a large family of daughters, two sons in the army. Has been himself in the army. His wife makes the best butter that I have tasted in Texas. He told me that Mr. Wilson, who owns the vacant house below him, bought the place of his son-in-law, Moor, who now lives down on the other side of the bayou.

Got acquainted here with an odd fish named Capt. * * * Hunnings, formerly of North Carolina, and who was a privateersman during the war with Great Britain. He is now building a steamboat on the bayou, and makes Earle's partly his home. I suspect he is courting one of Earle's daughters.

Talked with him and Earle on the politics of the country and the leading men of this district particularly. There is no man of distinction in the district that is at all popular; Burnet decidedly the reverse; Zavala, Earle says, becoming less popular since the arrival of his wife. Unfortunate woman; she is too refined a lady for this sphere. Morgan, rich, but unpopular. Moore, a stupid man, and never had any popularity. Briscoe gone to the army. In short, Earle said they would elect me to Congress if I would serve! That they wanted some smart, sensible man, and had none such in the district! Here's a chance for distinction.

Friday, March 25, 1836.

Earle this morning showed me his salt spring. He took a spade himself and dug a well about seven or eight feet deep, and got a spring of very salt water. Mrs. Earle says she has frequently salted butter with it. He asked $8 an acre for 500 acres, including the salines, or $2 per acre for the league. He will rather sell two-thirds or three-fourths of the league than the whole. He wants to buy laborers.

He has staying with him four young African negroes, two males, two females. They were brought here from the West Indies by a Mr. Monroe Edwards. (See proceedings of the

199

Convention, and Fisher's Report.) They are evidently native Africans, for they can speak not a word of English, French or Spanish. They look mild, gentle, docile, and have never been used to labor. They are delicately formed; the females in particular have straight, slender figures, and delicate arms and hands. They have the thick lips and negro features, and although understanding not a word of English, are quick of apprehension; have good ears, and repeat words that are spoken to them with remarkable accuracy. I wrote down the names by which they called some things to which I drew their attention. (See the vocabulary.) Their habits are beastly.

While at Earle's, Captain Henderson and three other persons came by on horseback, on their way to the United States, having abandoned Texas. Captain Henderson has given up his military prospects and returns to the dull pursuits of civil life in Tennessee. They reported that Houston was falling back, and the enemy had marched, but they did not know where. Fannin's position not known.

Left Earle's after dinner. He would receive pay only for my horse feed, $1; said he regarded me as a friend, and should always be glad to see me; family all civil, but coarse.

Stopt at Wm. Vince's, where I met a man with a harelip, named Merry, who said he was a native of Orange County, Virginia. Remembered my father-in-law, Mr. Stone, and Mr. D. Triplett. Vince has one and a half leagues of land, extending to within half a mile of Harrisburg. Price, $2 and $1.

At the bayou near Harrisburg met Hise, Kimble, and Colonel Hill, of Tennessee, all on their return to the United States, disgusted with Texas. They were accompanied by Mr. Ritson Morris, of Galveston Bay, a native of Virginia, of the Hanover family, called here Jawbone Morris. They had met with much difficulty in crossing the bayou with their horses. Hill was upset in the middle of the bayou by a horse attempting to jump into the perogue, and had to swim ashore. Parted with them reluctantly.

On arriving at Harrisburg found Triplett in high spirits. He had agreed on satisfactory terms for the arrangement of the loan contract to be consummated to-morrow.

No decisive movement of the army yet.

Col. Wm. T. Austin has just come up from Velasco, and says he read a letter written by * * * Fisher, of New Orleans, to T. F. McKinney, which states that a revolution had broken out in Mexico; two parties have united to put down centralism; that the person who had furnished Santa Anna with funds had been discovered, and measures were taken to prevent any more from going to him; that Santa Anna had returned to Mexico, etc. The report is believed here, probably because they wish it true. Zavala thinks it probable.

Saturday, March 26, 1836.

This morning Mr. Thomas is found to be opposed to the terms agreed on yesterday about the loan, and further negotiations have to be entered into. Potter goes to the coast, to take a view of the ports, and arrange for fortifications, etc. This is unfortunate, for he is the most liberal and conciliatory member of the executive board, and I fear the negotiations will get on badly in his absence.

Had conversation with Scates about a league of land in Zavala's Colony. Headright not entered; he gave $250 for the settlement right; on the Opelousas road, called Buxton league. Dr. Neblett has offered him $250; wants $500; offer him $300 and $100 each for the right of clearing out two leagues for other persons.

Stanley, McLaughlin and others arrived with five Mexican prisoners from the army, one of them a person well known, and believed to have been a spy, named * * *.

Houston's army is on the east side of the Colorado, near Beason's, and the enemy is on the other side, in sight; no fight yet. Fannin's fate not known. It is reported he has had a fight. A person has arrived at headquarters, who stated that he was one of an advanced guard, who, seeing an attack making on Fannin's party, and finding it impossible to join him, they had pushed on. They heard firing until 10 o'clock at night, and next morning heard two guns, but did not know the result. The worst is feared.

Sunday, March 27, 1836.

Negotiations for the loan still continue, but appear to be further from a satisfactory adjustment than before.

Negotiations with Scates off. He has no title to the land, and can give no security for the making me a title.

Mr. Zavala is sick. Young Zavala arrived this afternoon on his way to the army.

Wrote to W. M. B. by Hale.

Monday, March 28, 1836.

Weather cloudy and rainy. Zavala is better to-day. Carson sick, health bad generally. They complain much that Houston does not write to them.

One of the Mexican prisoners has been set at liberty, he being recognized as a friendly citizen. The others are sent to Galveston Bay to work on the fortifications. Col. Stanley sent to Galveston Bay.

Mr. Gritton arrived here this evening from San Felipe. He is an Englishman; was secretary to Almonte when he visited Texas in 1833; is now employed as translator to the Executive. Says Almonte is the son of Padre Morelas, a priest, or cure; that he always passed for the nephew of the priest. He is now about thirty-one years of age; was brought up in the country house of Pouche & Bean, of New Orleans. He is now with the invading army.

No satisfactory arrangement of the loan yet. The negotiation becomes more and more embarrassed. Thomas is the great stumbling block.

Tuesday, March 29, 1836.

The steamboat *Cayuga*, Captain Harris, came up this afternoon. The sound of her steam made my heart leap like the voice of an old friend. I had not heard the sound before for two months. Mr. Savage came as a passenger in her. Zavala is again very sick. Hardiman has arrived, which will again retard the negotiations for the loan. He must be made acquainted with it.

The probability that Fannin is cut off becomes every day nearer to certainty. Houston is falling back to the Brazos. Colonel Houston, the Quartermaster General, arrived to-day, on his way to Galveston.

Wednesday, March 30, 1836.

This morning Zavala returned home to recruit his health, and his son proceeded to the army; Sage and Norton went down in the boat with him, to proceed to the United States in Morgan's vessel, to sail Saturday, April 2.

Houston has certainly fallen back to the Brazos and encamped opposite to John Groce's, about eight miles above San Felipe.

Savage also went down in the boat with Zavala to Lynchburg.

At length an agreement or compromise for the loan is signed—all the signatures are to it except Zavala's and Potter's.

Rusk is very sick to-day. He would have gone to the army but for his illness.

Dr. Grant, who commanded a party of Texans, has been surprised and cut off. Colonel Ward also has been decoyed from Goliad and cut off (said to have been entrapped by a man named Ayres). *Mistake.*

The present clerks in the Executive Department are: Dr. Southerland, John D. McCloud, Elisha M. Pease, Willis A. Farris, Edward Gritton, translator; * * * Hill.

Wrote to T. Green.

Dr. Neblett went down to Lynchburg.

Thursday, March 31, 1836.

Some difficulty still existing about the loan contract. The Cabinet still has it under consideration, and some modification is suggested by Thomas.

Weather very warm—quite summer heat.

Friday, April 1, 1836.

At length the loan matter is concluded. Rusk has started for the army. The town of San Felipe has certainly been burnt, houses, goods and all. The inhabitants on the west side of the Brazos are all breaking up, leaving their homes and flying to the east. Houston's retrograde movement causes great discontent. A general impression exists that he ought to have fought the Mexicans at the Colorado. His army is said to be diminishing.

This evening Captain Briscoe arrived from the army. Reports the Mexican army were seen yesterday at noon, within three miles of San Felipe. An engagement expected. The Cayuga is to go down in the morning, and the *Kosciusco* waits to take Hall and dispatches to New Orleans. Wrote to W. M. B. and Mrs. Gray.

Saturday, April 2, 1836.

Very warm weather. No news from the army all day. The *Cayuga* detained until a late hour. Secretary Carson went down on her, intending to go to the United States—in bad health. Conrad also went in her, Hall, Hardiman's family, and many others.

An additional article has been made to the loan contract, by which, beside the premium of thirty-two leagues, we have the privilege of taking the $180,000 in lands at 50 cents per acre. (See contract.)

Dr. Neblett returned at night. Says the prairie near Lynch's resembled a camp meeting; it is covered with carts, wagons, horses, mules, tents, men, women and children, and all the baggage of a flying multitude. The people of the Brazos and Colorado are all leaving their settlements with their movables, cattle, negroes, etc.

I last night sat up until 12 o'clock, writing, and waiting for my room-mate, Gritten, to come in, but he did not come. I this morning learned he was arrested by an order from General Houston, charging him with being a spy. He is in custody. I went to see him. He is much chagrined, but declares his innocence; attributes the charge to private malice. The arrest is said to be founded on some intimation or charge contained in a pencil note from Captain Mosely Baker to General Houston. He demands that he be sent to the army. This the Executive will not do. He was some time since appointed collector at Copewood by the late provisional government, which was protested against by Governor Smith. He thinks Smith's hand is in his present arrest. He was recently engaged as assistant editor of the *Telegraph* at San Felipe. Was in Mexico when Austin was imprisoned there. Has a wife and child there. Knew he was regarded with suspicion by the Texans, and since he has been here asked for a passport to leave this country, but was requested to stay and act as translator to the government, and was engaged in translating the Constitution when he was arrested.

He requested me to ask the President to take some order for his accommodation, and that he might be allowed to write to his friends. I did so, and it was promptly granted, but with the restriction that his letters must be perused by the Executive.

Sunday, April 3, 1836.

This has been a most delightful day. The wind sprang up from the north early in the morning, and continued to blow gently and pleasantly until night, when it became calm. The moon rose bright and clear, and all nature looks tranquil and lovely.

Ready to start all day, but Triplett and Dr. Neblett are not ready, and I wait for them till to-morrow morning. It is Easter Sunday. Wrote to Mrs. Gray.

Gritten has been examined by the Executive. They have determined to send him to Col. Morgan's for safe keeping, and not to the army. He gave me a letter for S. F. Austin, in the United States, to be forwarded to him if I should not have an opportunity of delivering it.

The intelligence from the army contradicts the report of the enemy being near San Felipe. They have not left the Colorado as far as is yet known. Houston's army said to be 1,500.

It is now said, on the authority of De Leon, that Fannin's party fought from 4 o'clock in the evening till next morning, when finding he had but thirty men left, he hoisted the white flag and surrendered. They were taken to Goliad and shot.

The Mexican army are now said to have crossed the Colorado at the old Tuskarit crossing, which indicates an intention to bear down towards Brazoria.

Monday, April 4, 1836.

My horse strayed out on the prairie last night, and it was found that he and others were stolen; but having borrowed another and gone in quest of him, I found him about three miles off. On my return to town, found that my friends, Triplett and Neblett, had left me for Lynchburg. I rode there by myself. Stopt at Earle's and got a bowl of milk, and also at Atkins' and got a drink of milk. Passed a number of people on the road flying from the invasion, and seeking a place of safety east of the Trinity. At the ferry were large crowds, all seeking a passage across for the same purpose, with their wives, children, negroes, horses, carts, wagons, and droves of cattle. These they were trying to force to swim across the river.

Found Triplett, Neblett and Dobie about to start in an open boat to Morgan's. I joined them, leaving our horses at Lynch's. The wind was ahead, and we were bad oarsmen, having but one man along to assist us. None of us knew the river except Dobie, and he imperfectly, so we ran on shoals several times; attempted ineffectually to use our sail, and finally reached Morgan's at 11 o'clock at night, having been more than five hours on the water, and sailed a distance of only ten miles. The steamboat *Cayuga*, which left Harrisburg about the same time that we left Lynch's, hove to in the stream just as we touched the shore. Got a bowl of milk and bread at Morgan's, and slept there.

Tuesday, April 5, 1836.

The steamboat *Cayuga*, being bound for Galveston Island, we all proposed going in her, but after various detentions it was announced that she had not wood enough for the trip, and to enable them to wood we must wait here all day, and the boat would start at moon rising. Triplett, Dobie, Neblett and myself then took the sailboat and crossed San Jacinto

Bay, to a piece of land owned by Scott. Went ashore to examine it. Beautifully diversified with prairies and islands. The land rich, but baked very hard. Returned late to dinner. Walked with Morgan to see his orange grove, and the new town of Crockett that he means to lay out. He lives at a place, formerly called Clopper's Point, now by the tasteless name of New Washington. He apologizes for the name by ascribing it to the will of some gentlemen in New York, who have become interested in the new city.

Went to bed, with the understanding that the boat was to start in the night.

Wednesday, April 6, 1836.

We were called up this morning at 4 o'clock by Morgan, but the boat did not get off until near 8 o'clock. In about an hour we met the schooner *Flash*, belonging to Morgan—an armed schooner. She had the Secretary of the Navy on board, and a number of ladies from the Brazos; whose husbands were in the army, seeking safety in flight. The steamboat was turned back, to tow the schooner over the flats. After much difficulty, we returned to New Washington. In a little while two boats with lugger sails came by with the Texan flag flying. They were hailed and informed the Secretary of the Navy was here. They came to, and proved to be Captain Hawkins, of the *Independence*, Captain Hurd, of the *Brutus*, Dr. Cowper, the navy, Dr. Levy, and some gents from Matagorda, going up to Harrisburg to see the government. They stopt some hours, and dined here. Learned that one of them had taken a small Mexican prize; that a company of ninety men from New Orleans had put into Copano and been made prisoners by the Mexicans, and Mr. Baradere brought information that 500 troops from the United States had come over from Natchitoches, and had crossed the Neches; that not more than 1,000 Mexicans had yet crossed the Colorado, etc.

John Sweeny, living on the St. Bernard, in 1835 worked only eleven hands, made 101 bales cotton, averaging 624 pounds per bale; sold it at his own landing at 15 cents per pound, to Mills & Co., of Brazoria; total, $9,340. Made besides a plenty of corn to serve his family. Mr. Harold, who baled this cotton, gave the above information to Dr. Neblett. Harold thinks the lands on the lower part of the St. Bernard are better than those on the Brazos, as they are higher, and do not overflow. He thinks peach land is superior to cane land, but harder to cultivate at first. Sweeney has about 160 to 200 acres of open land, dwelling house, negro houses, gin house, corn mill; he thinks Sweeny will sell low and on credit; has about 1,200 acres.

The steamboat did not get off until near night. We took passage on board, having Colonel Morgan, Mr. Gritten, etc., on board.

Thursday, April 7, 1836.

This morning found ourselves at Red Fish Bar, a very difficult shoal which crosses the bay about midway, and makes the navigation difficult and dangerous. The Captain had been fearful of passing it in the night, and anchored above it. We got under weigh early, and about 9 o'clock came to anchor in Galveston harbor. We passed to the west of Pelican Island, the harbor being between that island, Galveston Island and Point Bolivar.

In the harbor were lying the Texas national schooner, *Independence*, Captain Hawkins, and *Brutus*, Captain Hurd. The merchant schooners *Pennsylvania* and *Henry*, and the schooner *Shenandoah*, were lying behind Point Bolivar, landing some families from the Brazos, who are seeking safety in flight. These, with our own sailboat, and that of Colonel Morgan, the commandant of the post, made the harbor have quite a lively appearance. Went on board the *Independence*, which found in a most perfect and admirable state of finish, neatness and preparation. Took dinner and wine with the officers, Lt. Gallagher, Melish, Capt. Barbee, of the Marius and Dr. * * *. Mrs. Perry, of * * * was on board. Went also on board the *Brutus*, which was undergoing some carpenter's repairs, and was not in the same state of order that appeared in the *Independence*. Very politely received by the officers, Lts. Robinson and * * *. Mrs. Hurd, the wife of the Captain, and her little child, were on board. She is young, pretty and spirited. Mrs. Fisher, of Matagorda (wife of S. R. Fisher), and her children, were also on board.

Two sails appeared on the opposite side of the island, coming up from the south. They fired a gun, and came to anchor. In a little while a boat came round and reported them to be the national schooner *Invincible*, Captain Jere Brown, and her prize, the brig *Pocket*, of which had been captured off the Brazos Santiago, going in with stores for the Mexican army, shipped by Ligordi, of New Orleans. She has a fine cargo. On board were several noted enemies of Texas, who were well known here, Hogan and Morgue (a Frenchman).

The *Invincible* had also an action with the Mexican schooner, *Montezuma* (now called *Bravo*), on board of which were both Thompson and Davis. They ran the *Bravo* on shore and disabled her, but were unable to get on board by reason of the shoalness of the water, and the fact that there were upwards of 1,000 Mexican troops on the beach. The Texans had only two men wounded and none killed. They lost one officer, Lt. Living, who went on board the enemy before the action commenced, with a boat's crew, to ascertain her character. He was not permitted to return, but when the action began the crew put off with the boat and escaped. The action took place on Easter Sunday, the 3rd instant.

The recital of this intelligence caused great joy in the little squadron, and sundry glasses of wine were quaffed to the success of the infant navy of Texas. The officers all rejoiced at the success of their brethren, and each wished he had had a part in it. Before night, a pilot having been sent off, the prize was brought in and moored above the schooner. I went on board; introduced to Captain Brown, an exceedingly plain and unpretending man. The brig is a fine vessel. Here I again met with Mr. Welsh, whom I had formerly seen at San Felipe and Washington, and who is now purser of the *Invincible*. He is writing letters for the Captain, and is going to Harrisburg with dispatches. It is said that among the papers on board the *Pocket* are some clearly showing her character, giving information touching the defenseless state of Texas, and the best place of attack, recommending the occupation of the ports, etc. From the whole it is concluded that an armed Mexican force may be expected here in a fortnight, and the government is now making efforts to fortify the place, so as to be able to repel them. Colonel Hy. Harcourt is the engineer who is to plan the work, and Captain Stanley, the Englishman, is also here. Colonel Morgan, who is a merchant, and the founder of New Washington, where he lives, has been appointed Commandant of the Post, and is entering on his duties with great zeal and activity.

Friday, April 8, 1836.

We lodged on board the steamboat last night. This morning she returned up the bay. We returned on shore. I took a long walk across the island and around its head by the beach, and enjoyed for the first time a full view of the great ocean; a fresh breeze from the south brought the waves in with a noise resembling a great waterfall. The sight of the breakers, whitecrested, lofty and angry-looking, was truly grand, and equalled the ideas I had formed from reading of such scenes. Saw a great number of birds, cranes, curlews, gulls and pelicans. The latter at a distance resembled companies of soldiers, white and gray; the two colors flock together. Said to lay eggs in vast quantities in the sand on Pelican Island, where they are left to hatch by the sun. Pelicans and gulls lay together indiscriminately, and they hatch successively in proportion to the time at which they were layed.

I gathered a number of pretty shells, thousands of which lay on the beach, and boxed them up to send round for my children.

Triplett and Neblett measured off two sections of ground here, as the site of a future town. It is the site of Lafitte's old fort, the shape of which, and some remains of his operations, in the shape of broken bottles, crockery, bricks, nails, etc., are still visible. The whole island is low, no part that I have seen ten feet above ordinary tide, and I am told has all been overflowed since the settlement of the country. The shores are very shoal, and no part presents a good site for a city. A considerable city must one day spring up on this bay, some-where, but at what point is yet uncertain. Galveston harbor is the best yet discovered; it is a safe one, being locked in by Galveston Island, Pelican Island and Point Bolivar. But at no place can vessel, drawing more than two or three feet approach within two or three hundred yards of the shore.

The island is forty miles long—only three trees on it. No habitation; fine pasturage. A great number of deer on the is-land. Said to have been named after Count Galves, formerly Viceroy of Mexico. An Englishman or American must have stood sponsor for it, as the name has an English termination. The best entrance to the harbor is from the east. (See Canty's chart.) The west pass seems to be but little known. There is believed to be a channel there, having eight or nine feet. It is between the little island of San Louis and the mainland. Galveston was formerly called the Island of St. Louis, but that name is now restricted to a small island lying at the west end of Galveston Island.

In the midst of the island, among the grass, I picked up a piece of pumice about the size of my fist, which had the appearance of having been long afloat; the trituration of the waves and sands, etc., had made it nearly round. It is probable it had floated from the Mediterranean to this place.

Wm. H. Wharton told me in New Orleans that he owned all of this island, having purchased it of a Mexican. A. C. Allen said he and a company of New York owned a league at the harbor, where they intended building a city. Burnett says that it has never passed from the government. (See his argument.) Here will be work for the courts and lawyers.

The new fortification is to be erected on Campeachy Point, at the east end of the island.

NOTE–Captain Hoyt, of the schooner *Pennsylvania*, has been commissioned a Captain in the Texas navy–a vulgar, rude, coarse-looking man. Has a number of families on board his vessel, bound for New Orleans. To the ladies he is said to have been rude; they wish to leave his vessel.

Saturday, April 9, 1836.

This morning we started early for Point Bolivar, having procured a pilot, Captain Smith, of Anahuac, where we designed going to-night. The wind, all this week, has been fresh from the south. We came out around Pelican Island, by the west channel, and then stretched across to Point Bolivar under the lee of Pelican Island; the other would have been the shorter passage, but our pilot thought it would be too rough for our little boat. We found this sufficiently so. As we came up the schooner *Kosciusco* went out to sea through the west channelwind fair and fine. It was calculated she would reach New Orleans in forty-eight hours. Called by the *Pennsylvania*, and took off Lt. Bannister, who wished to go to Harrisburg. At Point Bolivar found a number of families from Brazoria, etc., encamped. Got breakfast among them. Lt. Bannister has a boat here called the *St. Patrick*, in which he proposed we should proceed to Anahuac. After much delay and difficulty we all got on board the *Shenendoah*, which having some stores on board that Triplett wished to get for the government, he had prevailed on the Captain to take his vessel up to Harrisburg. The Captain did not know the bay well, and he wanted our pilot. Some of the families on the Point determined to go to Anahuac, and came on board again, which kept us till after 3 o'clock. We made the run to Red Fish Bar very well; but from ignorance of the channel the vessel there grounded. We cast anchor for the night. The vessel being crowded with goods and passengers, we were compelled to sleep on deck.

Point Bolivar is a much finer site than Galveston, and I think a better situation for a town, but not so safe a harbor. It is a peninsula, divided from the Gulf by East Bay, which runs up towards Sabine Bay, some fifteen miles, and the waters of the two bays approach each other very nearly, and in high tides boats have passed from one to the other. A canal intercourse might easily be opened between them. The land on Point Bolivar is very fine, and higher than Galveston. Some few groves of small wood are scattered on the shores. Some strong salt springs are found between Galveston and Sabine Bays. Frank's works, one * * *, another. Captain Smith examined Canty's chart; says it is a very fair one. Canty was once his mate; is now in the navy; an Englishman, a drunkard, a good sailor.

Point Bolivar would make a splendid plantation and stock farm, destitute of wood and fresh water.

Distance to Sabine Bay * * *. The High Islands (groups of trees) lie between them; lands said to be fine, but low.

Sunday, April 10, 1836.

During the past night it has rained, and a strong norther has sprung up. Our vessel has swung from her groundings, and now rides in the midst of the Red Fish channel, but unable to get out for the head wind. We find our situation very uncomfortable, and Triplett and Neblett wished to set out in our little boat. I thought it imprudent, but did not oppose it, and we embarked, designing to run up to New Washington, and on to Lynchburg, Anahuac being given up. Captain Smith, our pilot, took the helm. I quickly repented the undertaking, and so, I believe, did the rest, for the wind was strong ahead and dashed the water over us so much that all quickly got wet. Some fears, I believe, were also entertained for our safety, and all united in the expediency of making for shore except the Captain, who was much disappointed at the delay, and, said he could have made New Washington. Ran into a cove near Clear Creek, and landed at the home of Mr. Edwards, where we found Mr. Ashmore Edwards and his brother-in-law, Ritson Morris (Jaw Bone M.), a Mr. Aldridge, and Mr. Stanley. We were kindly entertained, and as the gale continued, remained all night. Morris came from Lunenburg County, Virginia; Neblett and he were acquainted there. Edwards is the nephew of Colonel Edwards, of Nacogdoches, and the brother of Monroe Edwards, who imported the Guinea negroes from Cuba about a month ago. (See Fisher's report on the subject.) About fifty of those poor wretches are now here, living out of doors, like cattle. They are all young, the oldest not 25, the youngest, perhaps, not more than 10; boys and girls huddled together. They are diminutive, feeble, spare, squalid, nasty, and beastly in their habits. Very few exhibit traits of intellect. None seem ever to have been accustomed to work. Some of them gave the same names to common things that those I had seen at Edward's did; others gave different names; of course, from different tribes. One girl sat apart and held no converse with the crowd. She is said to belong to a different tribe from any of the rest, and to stand on her dignity. There is a boy also among them, about 14 or 15, a runt, who is acknowledged to be a prince, and deference is shown him. He claims the prerogative of five wives, and flogs them at his pleasure. They are mostly cheerful, sing and dance of nights; wear caps and blankets; will not wear close clothes willingly; some go stark naked. A beef was killed at Morris' home, 100 yards from Edwards', and the Africans wrangled and fought for the garbage like dogs or vultures; they saved all the blood they could get, in gourds, and feed on it. An old American negro stood over the beef with a whip, and lashed them off like so many dogs to prevent their pulling the raw meat to pieces. This is the nearest approach to cannibalism that I have ever seen.

Morris' family have gone to the United States in the *Kosciusko.*

Monday, April 11, 1836.

The gale still continued too strong to make it prudent to venture out in our little boat. Dr. Neblett procured a mule, and he and Morris determined to ride to Lynch's. Triplett, Dobie and I to walk up to New Washington. Smith agreed to bring around the boat as soon as the state of the weather would permit. We expected he would be there before us, but he did not reach there in all the day. We reached New Washington about 2 o'clock. Found here Secretary of the Navy and a number of the persons going down in the steamboat. She put off after dinner, but was obliged to come back, the wind was too strong. Was informed by Dr. Patrick that he had sent a letter by the boat for me, left by Mr. Forbes, who had waited here two days to see me.

Morris' league is a very fine one, on the west side of the bay. He raised 350 bushels of yams or sweet potatoes from one acre, and from the experiment he made in cotton he thinks he raised 3,000 pounds from an acre. It is well diversified with woods and prairie.

Tuesday, April 12, 1836.

The steamboat got off this morning. I succeeded in getting my letter from on board. Forbes has flour, corn, etc., in the Brazos, which he wants to sell. Wishes to get a draft on Parker cashed, and to buy land. (See his letter.) Our boat came in sight early in the day, but before she got up an express arrived from the government, addressed to the Secretary of the Navy, in haste. A skiff was dispatched to meet our boat, which was immediately dispatched down the bay, and our baggage brought up in the skiff. The bearer of the express states that the Mexicans were crossing the Brazos at Fort Bend. Other rumors speak of the murder of families of women and children by them on the Brazos. Morris arrived with a mule and a horse, which he lent to us to go to Lynch's while he went down with the express to Galveston. Dobie and I started with the mule, leaving the horse to Triplett, who was detained by having some clothes in the wash. We got as far as Routh's, where we stopt for the night.

Wednesday, April 13, 1836.

This morning Triplett came by. Dobie borrowed a horse of Routh, and we all proceeded together to Lynch's. Here we found Dr. Neblett awaiting us. My horse was missing, whether strayed or pressed could not tell. Triplett, Neblett and Dobie hastened on to Harrisburg, in order to get a grant from the government of the land they had located on Galveston and Point Bolivar, in which I have taken an interest equal to my interest in the loan. I am left here on foot. Wrote to W.M.B. and to Mrs. Gray.

The report of the near approach of the enemy is confirmed by numerous persons. Here is the Mr. Kuykendall and his family who were reported murdered by them. He was a prisoner, and was saved by a Colonel Bringas, who gave him the following safe passport:

El Col. Juan Bringas, Com'dt jr. el E. S. P'se de la seccion de Van-guardia.

En viatudo de haberse procurando el cidu'o Joseph Kuykendall, y no haber kecho armas contra el Ejercito, se le extiendo el presente resguardo p'a que pueda permanecer tranquilo y sin ser molestado.

Fort Bend, Abril 12 de 1836.

Juan M'a Bring.

His wife had the child of his nephew, six or seven weeks old; the mother was missing, no one knew where. The women had been fired on by the soldiers, and had fled. This poor mother had fallen with fright and weakness, and was reported killed. While they were here the father of the child arrived, not knowing that it was here. He had heard of his wife. She is in the hands of friends.

President Burnett passed on his way home to take care of his family.

I heard of my horse, by Mr. John M. Smith, who has promised me another to ride to where mine is tomorrow.

Mr. Zavala and lady were here this evening. He came home yesterday. It is strange that he and Burnett should both be away from Harrisburg at once.

MEMO.—The child with scalded hand.

Mrs. Turner, of Gonzales, six sons, five daughters; land on the LaBaca.

Triplett and Neblett returned about 12 o'clock at night; missed the President, and did not get their business accomplished.

Thursday, April 14, 1836.

At Lynch's Ferry. After breakfast Triplett and Neblett rode to Burnett's, but he had left home with his family. On their return they sent a messenger down to New Washington to see if he was there, and wrote to him. He promised to meet them next morning at 11 o'clock at Vince's.

The steamboat *Cayuga* came up after dark, on her way to Harrisburg. I went on board for a minute, and got Potter's signature to the compromise loan contract. He desired me to say to Triplett that the government wishes him to proceed to New Orleans with all practical dispatch, as vessels would be there in a short time that would make his presence necessary.

Friday, April 15, 1836.

At Lynch's. This morning Neblett rode out to meet the President and get him to sign the grant for two sections of land on Galveston Island and one on Point Bolivar.

While waiting for these gentlemen and my horse, I wrote to Mrs. Gray and also to W. M. B. an account of Galveston Bay and Island, to this date.

A great number of fugitives from the enemy still continue to pass, and many instances of individual distress hourly present themselves.

The Earl family are here.

The Aikins are also here, Mrs. Aikins with an infant only ten days old. One lady from the west was delivered in a canebrake on her flight.

At night the steamboat came down, Neblett in her, also the President, Hardiman, Thomas, and all the inhabitants of Harrisburg. The schooner *William* and four open boats were in town. There has been a complete evacuation of Harrisburg, and all the people of the neighborhood have fled. A party of Mexicans are said to have appeared in Harrisburg as the steamboat put off. Zavala stopt at his house. Triplett went on board, and Hardiman came off with him, and slept in the bed with me. There has been much difficulty in getting the Executive to sign the grant for land on Galveston, agreeably to their contract. The President at first refused, then assented, but said he must consult his Cabinet. He then signed;

but Hardiman, acting Secretary of State, positively refused. Finally, after coming on shore, he consented to sign for one section, on condition that no more should be asked at this time. They are afraid that the grants will be unpopular, and that they will share in the unpopularity. They acknowledge it is our right, according to the contract, but they are afraid to do right, afraid to be just. (This is not the right stuff to make a republican government of.)

Dr. Harrison also came in the steamboat; the son of general William H. Harrison, who was reported to have been massacred at Victoria. He was taken prisoner, but General Urrea having been Minister from Mexico to Colombia at the time that General Harrison was also Minister there from the United States, out of respect and regard for the father, he protected the son. He was entertained in the General's tent, and was permitted to return to the United States on his parole. The General, on his departure, gave him a fine riding horse, $100, a cloak, and also permission to bring off an American prisoner as a servant. He brought off Ben Mordicai, of Richmond, Virginia, who was thereby saved from the general massacre that took place of Fannin's men. Colonel Garay conducted him away from the Mexican camp, and at parting presented him with his sword. He speaks highly of Urrea and Garay—latter is Governor of Durango, and commands the southern division of the invading army. Siezma commands the center, which is now at San Felipe; the northern division is destined for Nacogdoches, under * * *. Harrison says the report in camp was that that division had proceeded up the Colorado 300 miles, without meeting a white man. It will strike across the upper country to Nacogdoches. He says Urrea was very indignant at the massacre of Fannin's troops; said it was done without his orders or knowledge, and that he intended to resign his command and return to his government as soon as the army reached Brazoria. Speaks highly also of Garay. He also confirmed the report of a revolution or trouble in Mexico, which had caused the return of Santa Anna.

Here also I saw Capt. Holland, who was an officer in Fannin's artillery. He escaped the massacre by his prowess and courage. Captain Wallis was his file leader. Suspecting what was about to happen from his knowledge of the language, he communicated it to Wallis, and proposed that they should make an effort to escape. Wallis declined, and said, "Let us meet our fate like men." But Holland watched his opportunity, knocked down one Mexican, jostled, overturned and ran over a second, and, seizing the 'scopet of a third, wrested it from him and knocked him down, and in the confusion and astonishment that ensued, he ran off. To his surprise and dismay, he soon found there was an outer line of guards, one of whom raised his 'scopet to shoot him. He instantly lowered his piece and fired, and shot off the fellow's skull. As he passed him he dashed the 'scopet on him and continued his flight without any further interruption. He suffered much in his attempt to reach the settlements. Nine of Fannin's men are now known to have escaped.

I this day bought a horse of Geo. B. Wilson for $50, and am now ready to start.

VOL. XI

Saturday, April 16, 1836.

The steamboat went down this morning with the members of the Cabinet in it, and Dr. Harrison, on his way to the United States. He sold the gift of General Urrea to Colonel Houston for $50, including saddle and bridle, and presented the sword to President Burnet.

After breakfast Triplett, Neblett and myself started, intending to go to Jacob Winfree's, on the bay, opposite Anahuac, fifteen miles from Lynch's. Dr. Neblett had got directions from several persons, but they proved erroneous. Instead of taking the right-hand road, we took the left, and went up the San Jacinto, till we crossed Cedar Creek, and then took an easterly course, across the prairie, and after traveling twenty-five or thirty miles found ourselves still twelve miles from Winfree's. It being near sunset, we stopt with some fugitives, among them a Mr. Highsmith, from LaBaca, who kindly gave us part of their supper, and we slept in the open air.

We learned from these travelers that it is reported that 2,000 Mexican troops have entered Nacogdoches, where they met no opposition.

Left at Lynch's Mrs. Splan, her brother, Mr. Douglas, Catlett, Cady, Cazneau, Fleury, the Earles, etc.

Sunday, April 17, 1836.

Breakfasted with the fugitives, and then rode on to Winfree's. There we found Mr. Collins, who had left Lynch's a few days before. Triplett and Neblett have bought Winfree's half league and all the improvements for $600. Mrs. Winfree treated us to some fine buttermilk, and three bowls of fine, ripe blackberries. Winfree not at home.

While at Winfree's a Mr. Thompson rode up, and reported that a troop of Mexican cavalry had that morning been at Lynch's and Zavala's, and it was supposed would come directly on. He was going express to inform the people on the Trinity and at Anahuac. Rode on with Thompson; passing Barrow's we saw Winfree. A short distance from Barrow's we passed a bayou, which was too deep for our horses. The road lay through the bay for one-fourth of a mile. In order to pass it we had to make a wide circle, on a bar formed by the meeting of the waters of the bay and those of the bayou. Thompson piloted us.

At the mouth of the old river of Trinity we found a great many fugitives. The wagons and tents looked like the encampment of an army waited from 1 to 4 o'clock, and found it impossible to get our horses across in the boats. The right to the ferry had been usurped by some agent of the government for the use of the fugitives, who assisted each other in passing. They claim to pass by turns, but there is much squabbling and much injustice. All are now seriously alarmed at the near approach of the enemy, and might here gives right. Those who are flying before an enemy they have not seen are valiant in asserting their right to pass the river, and pistols are shown and oaths sworn without stint. A hoary-headed brute, named Patton, who was taking much authority on himself, without possessing the discretion to use it judiciously, used rude language to me. I note it because he is the first man that I have met in Texas who has used rude and offensive language to me. He was equally so to Dr. Neblett, who had proposed putting the women and children all over first, and then taking over the baggage, while the men should organize a company for their defense. He tauntingly said if a few more scary men would come, it would put them all in confusion.

With some difficulty we swam our horses over, and went on to Wallace's, where we stayed all night while there, Douglass came up and said the Mexicans had crossed at Lynch's; that he went back, after starting, and saw them about the house. A French Creole, of Louisiana, who had come over to buy cattle, also slept here, named Comarsac.

At the ferry we met Major Catlett, Major Cazneau, Fleury and Cady, of Matagorda. These two had been at Lynch's when the Mexicans came there, and saw them. They are going to the United States.

Monday, April 18, 1836.

Left Wallace's at an early hour (50 cents), and proceeded towards Anahuac. At Turtle Bayou found no boat, and could not cross. Attempted to pass the mouth on the bar, but could not find it. Fortunately, some travelers were coming

round from Anahuac, and for $1 one of them showed us
the bar. It was fully a half a mile, and a very difficult way
to find. We got through without wetting feet. Following the
path along the river bank, we reached Anahuac about 11
o'clock. Met a number of people leaving the town, for they
had heard that the Mexicans were coming, and were all
flying. One poor woman, a Dutchwoman, Mrs. Oldbender,
had her all in a bundle on her head, a sucking child in her
arms, a little girl leading and a small boy following. Hers
was a pitiable case. Another woman with a little girl, when
she saw us; took us for Mexicans, and fled to the woods.
We called to her, and that reassured her. At Anahuac we
found Mrs. Harris, our late landlady at Harrisburg, also
J. W. Smith, of Bejar, with his Mexican family, who kindly
gave us breakfast. Here we were joined by Dobie, and at 1
o'clock we all left for the Neches. The inhabitants who were
leaving their homes offered us any stores we wanted, bacon,
sugar, coffee and biscuit. We took some of the latter, and a
tin cup given me by Mrs. Harris. Before night we passed the
place of Taylor White, which he had left in charge of an old
negro, who gave us dinner of milk and bread and corn for
our horses; 62 ½ cents. We here also again overtook Mrs.
Oldbender and her three little children. Each of us gave her
$1. We then struck across the prairies, aiming for a clump
of trees, which we did not reach until after dark. It was an
uncomfortable place, and we had difficulty in kindling a
fire. Slept soundly on the ground, with only our blankets
under us.

Anahuac is on the east side of the bay, just below the
mouth of Trinity. The ground a prairie, almost dead level,
rather higher at the bank than further back. The bank,
high, bold, and the view extensive. The prairie rather poor.
The place is now dilapidated, but must ultimately be one of
considerable business. Judge Chambers has a claim on the
land. MEMO. to inquire of him about the title.

Tuesday, April 19, 1836.

This morning a heavy fog. My horse being hobbled, was grazing near us, but the others were not visible. Dobie mounted my horse and went in pursuit, found them about a mile off. Went on across the prairie, taking our course by the compass. Towards noon approached timber, and striking the road, fell in with numerous fugitives, among them the Mc-Niels, with their African negroes, Catlett, Cady, Fleury and Cazneau. The poor, frightened fugitives had thrown away a great deal of furniture, emptied beds of feathers, bags of corn, etc. We stopt to feed our horses from some corn that had been thrown out. Here we met the report that the Mexicans and Indians from Nacogdoches had come down, appeared on the Cow Bayou, immediately in our route, which raised some apprehensions for our safety, and the practicability of getting to the United States in that direction. Agreed with Catlett and company to lodge with them and travel together for our mutual safety.

Passed through the league of land bought of Scates, called Pine Islands. Stopt at Shoats, and got a dinner of milk and bread. Shoats says the Pine Islands are worth $10,000, but that Scates bought it of him, and yet owes him $115 of the purchase money. His daughter, Mrs. Jackson, who is a fine looking woman, was in great wrath against the Texans for bringing on the war and its consequences, and was eloquent in her vituperation against the members of the late convention, particularly her neighbor, Judge West, whom she called Sawyer West, in allusion to his early vocation, and said he ran off from Washington, after signing the Declaration of Independence, before the ink was dry, and in his panic forgot his hat and coat, and came home bareheaded. Here was a poor woman, a fugitive, with three small children sick with measles. Paid for dinner 50 cents. At night we came up with Catlett and company at Williams'; only one young man at home. Got supper and corn for horses. We all stood guard to-night, each one hour, there being eight of us.

Wednesday, April 20, 1836.

This last night we kept guard by turns, each standing one hour. Mine was the last, from 4 till 5 o'clock. Left Williams' at 7 o'clock; $1. As we approached the Neches, we found there was great uncertainty about crossing the river. The boats were said to have been taken from all the ferries and carried down to the lower bluff. Thither we bent our way; passing great numbers of fugitives, men, women and children, black and white, with all the accustomed marks of dismay. Arrived about noon at the lower bluff. The house is kept by Joseph Grigsby, an old Kentuckian, who was an old acquaintance of Triplett, and seemed very glad to see him.

Grigsby says this is a fine site for a town. Th. F. McKinney has laid out one near it, called Georgia. He says the entrance of the Sabine Lake is always good for eight and a half feet of water, and the Neches for nine miles has four to four and one-half feet, and at the lowest stage two feet; that there is a good landing on the inlet. The league is owned by one * * * McGaffey; that on the Louisiana shore of the inlet, opposite to McGaffey's league, there is also a bluff not yet surveyed by the government. A section would cover all the good land there. This place is built on a firm shell bank. Grigsby is the father-in-law of G. W. Smith, who was a member of the convention. He owns a league of land on Cedar Creek, 200 miles up the Neches, on which there is a mill.

The report of the Mexicans being on Cow Creek is not credited here. It is believed to have been circulated by Rains, McLaughlin, etc. There are many families here waiting to be ferried across the bay, a distance of seven or eight miles, and put on the United States shore. There are at least 1,000 fugitives here, among them Menifee, A. B. Hardin, Smith, Jno. Fisher, all members of the Convention.

Thursday, April 21, 1836.

Triplett, Forbes and Cazneau have determined to go to New Orleans by water, in a vessel, the schooner *Loan*, now lying in the bay, believing that it will be the most expeditious mode. Neblett, Dobie, Catlett, Fleury, Cady and myself determined to go by land, by the way of Beaumont. Started at 10 o'clock. Bill at Grigsby's $2.25. Arrived at Beaumont about 1 o'clock. Passed on the road the Kuykendall family. They have in charge the poor little lost baby, which each carries by turns. I took pleasure in carrying it a short distance to relieve the old man.

At Beaumont we found that all the boats had been taken away by the press gang, as they are called. Found several persons engaged in building boats, with which to transport their families across. We united with Tally, Brook and Haynes, got timber from Rogers, who lives at the place, and sent into the country and bought cotton to calk with. My portion of cost, $1.50. Commenced the work at 4 o'clock p.m. Here we met with Reason Green, of Liberty, who agreed to pilot us through the swamp.

The town of Beaumont consists at present of only three or four houses. It is thirty miles from the head of the bay, and sixty miles from the gulf, thirty miles to Ballow's ferry on the Sabine, 170 miles to Zavala by water, and seventy-five miles by land; to Liberty fifty miles, Nacogdoches 155 miles, by the way of San Augustine.

Here is a custom house, and Captain Rogers is the collector. He is also principal proprietor of the town. He is anxious to get a section of the Pine Island league. He sets up a claim to the league, but says if we will let him have a section of it, which he has set his heart on, he will compromise it, and give us one of the best sections on Trinity in exchange.

Friday, April 22, 1836.

Slept in the woods last night on my blankets. Our boat being finished, they put us across this morning, about 10 o'clock, swimming our horses, and we commenced our journey through the swamp, our guide, Green, leading the way. We had to swim a number of little bayous, running out from the Neches, which is now so full as to overflow its banks, and run out towards Sabine Bay. This is the first instance of this kind of overflow I have seen in Texas. Arrived at Ashworth's ferry, we expected to find a boat, but there was none. The family had left the place. Here we started three runaway negroes, who fled and plunged through a bayou at our approach. One of them had a gun, which he discharged in the woods, in our hearing, probably because he had got it wet.

We went on, and at a wide and deep bayou Green and Catlett swam over with their horses, expecting to find a boat at a landing above, in which our baggage could be ferried. But here again we were disappointed; the boat was gone. Both parties now set to building rafts. We failed for want of tools and loose timber. Green succeeded in making one on which he returned to us, but it was too frail. We now determined to go back to Ashworth's, and take the rails and planks there and build a raft. In this we ultimately succeeded, having to tote the timber two or three hundred yards, to a place where it would float. When it was completed it would carry only two men and a small portion of the baggage, so we had to make four trips, and paddle with sorry paddles against a strong current to a landing from which we could get out of the swamp. While engaged in building our raft, a large alligator, some twelve or fifteen feet long, was discovered cautiously approaching us. One of the party fired a rifle at him. It struck but did not hurt him. He slowly moved off, and remained in sight, as if watching our proceedings, for some time.

As our provisions were short, Fleury took his rifle and shot a fine calf which was with a herd of cattle, at the ferry. I took it on my horse and carried it to our raft.

All these operations took us until 8 o'clock at night, when our last raft load reached the landing. We had our veal cleaned and some of it cooked, which we ate with good appetite, without bread, salt or pepper. We also had coffee, but no sugar nor milk. Having finished our supper, we spread our clothes to dry as well as we could, and lay down on wet ground and amidst briars, and I slept well. My coat and pants were nigh getting burnt up in the night by the fire spreading through the grass, which became dry from the heat.

I this morning, on leaving Beaumont, lent old Kuykendall $10.

Saturday, April 23, 1836.

After breakfasting on veal without bread or salt, and coffee without sugar or milk, we started at half past 7 o'clock. Came to a house where a family named Hatton had lived. The family had fled. Father and son here this morning taking off some corn. Got a feed for our horses, 25 cents. Hatton advised us to go to Pattillo's, where we could get something to eat. Arrived at Pattillo's at 12 o'clock. No one at home. Got corn and fed horses, ground corn and made bread, shot three fowls and cooked them, opened a bee hive and got some honey, and made a very comfortable meal. While here young Hatton also came with a bucket, which he filled with honey from one of the hives. We remonstrated with him, but he said his father wanted it, and it was free for anybody. Green, who knew Pattillo, took a memo. of what we used. We afterwards met Pattillo on the road and paid him $1.50.

We crossed to-day Cow Bayou, Adams' Bayou, Cypress Bayou, and arrived at Ballow's ferry after dark, passing for several miles through the worst road I have encountered in Texas. In one place we came upon a poor ox, bogged in the

229

middle of the road. His head and a small part of his body were above the mud. His yoke had been removed and he left there to die. A horrible death.

At the ferry we found Colonel Wm. G. Hill, late of the San Bernard, who had been to take his family and that of E. Waller to the United States. He is now on his return. Waller, whom I saw at Beaumont, has charge of the negroes belonging to him self and Hill. They are trying to take them up Red River. Hill's address will be Alexandria, La.

Here I found my sorrel horse in the hands of the press gang. I knew him by moonlight, and took possession of him.

Sunday, April 24, 1836.

At Ballows'. Owing to the crowd of families now here, we could not conveniently cross the ferry to-day; bargained for flats to take us over in the morning. Catlett's horse was missing this morning; hunted him all day unsuccessfully; concluded he was stolen; offered him the use of mine, as I had to take both along with me.

This is one of Lafitte's old stations. Ballow is said to have been one of his confederates, likewise old Shote, at the Pine Islands. Here stands an old shed, part of the shelter constructed for the African negroes that he used to bring here. It is now a shelter for cows.

We kept guard all night for the protection of our horses from the press gang, each man standing one hour. About 1 o'clock in the morning Rains came riding up with the intelligence that Houston had had a battle with the Mexicans on the 21st, at Harrisburg; killed 500 and took all the rest, 650, prisoners. Almonte prisoner, Cos killed, Houston wounded. The letter was written with a pencil, signed John Reed, and addressed to Major Caldwell. I do not fully believe it, but others do. It is likely there has been a battle and a victory, but the result is too much wholesale.

Monday, April 25, 1836.

Left Ballow's at half past 7 o'clock; $1.25, ferry $1.00, Dobie 50 cents. Went down the river about one mile, turned the lower point of the island, and ferried up on the other side four miles; landed on the east side of the river; happy to find ourselves once more on Uncle Sam's land, and under the protection of his laws.

The island belongs to the United States, as the jurisdiction of the United States extends to the western bank of the Sabine. It is said to be forty miles long, low and marshy, the trees hanging over into the water. Every place on the low banks on the American side, where dry land could be found, was covered with fugitives, who were eager to hear news, and received the account of the victory with exclamations of joy.

Four miles from the Sabine, stopt at the house of Jas. Lyons, and dined. Decent people. Mrs. Lyons a very pretty woman. Sixteen miles further brought us to Hardy Cowherd's, where we stopt and slept. Mr. Cowherd is from North Carolina; he has a very fine plantation in the midst of a poor country. A good farm house, very neatly kept. He told me his land produced in sugar 1500 wt. to the acre, and in cotton one bale.

Neblett and Dobie went on four miles further to Dr. Robt. Neblett's.

Tuesday, April 26, 1836.

Left Cowherd's after breakfast, at 8 o'clock. Bill, $1. Stopt a short time at Dr. R. Neblett's, who then rode with us to Calcasieu ferry, thirteen miles from Cowherd's. Calcasieu is a beautiful stream, very deep and clear. Dr. R. Neblett says it is the largest river between the Mississippi and the Rio Grande. The public house and ferry is kept by Mr. Rees Perkins; very decent people; decent dinner; dinner 25 cents, ferry 50 cents.

At night we reached the house of Arsen Le Blue Comarsac, the French Creole drover whom we had seen in Texas at Wallace's. He was not at home, but his wife, a Virginian and a sensible woman, received us civilly. He is said to be worth $100,000; their little girl, Minerva, is beautiful; living coarse and mean; could get no corn for our horses, which we had to turn out on the prairie; no sugar in our coffee, no butter, and sour milk, although they said they had 1,000 or 1,200 calves. We slept on the floor in a new house, not yet inhabited, and were dreadfully annoyed by fleas.

Wednesday, April 27, 1836.

Paid Mrs. Comarsac fifty cents, and left her dirty mansion at half past 6 o'clock. Passed a drove of cattle belonging to Taylor White, from near Anahuac; started with 500; said to have lost 170; had now only 330.

Early in the day we were overtaken by a heavy shower of rain, and I got very wet. We reached Miles Welch's cabin in the prairie about 11 o'clock, having ridden twenty miles over poor prairie land. His cabin had only one room, which was kitchen, chamber, parlor and hall, and let the rain in through every part. His wife cooked us a coarse dinner; he refused us corn for our horses; after dinner he gave us corn; bill, 50 cents. Went on over a boggy prairie, and in a hard rain. Crossed a marsh in the midst of an extensive prairie, which is here called Grand Marais. In the evening it cleared up, and the moon shone out. We reached the Bayou Mermentau at 7 o'clock; a beautiful stream, and a good ferry boat. Small house, and rather shabby French style. Andrews, the landlord, a loquacious, vulgar, beastly looking man, but jolly, and civil in his way. Jabbers Creole French and English indiscriminately. His son-in-law, John Moutan, a civil, whiskey-drinking fellow, who was dreadfully afflicted with the hiccough. I dried my dripping clothes as well as I could, and got a good lodging. It rained excessively hard in the night. The thunder resembled the discharge of cannon. From

Welsh's to Mermentau, twenty miles. The journey to-day has been forty miles, hard traveling, through mud and rain. We had woodland on our left all the way, but on the right it was all open prairie, except where we struck watercourses. Distance from the gulf, about thirty miles. Here we got a plenty of corn for our horses.

Thursday, April 28, 1836.

It having ceased to rain, and giving some indications of clearing up, we left Andrews about 1 o'clock. Bill, $2.25. At about six miles distant Cady, Fleury and Catlett left us, to go by St. Martinsville, on the Teche, we continuing lower down, towards Vermillion. In crossing a little bayou, my mulish mustang horse bogged and fell down in the water and I under him, by which I was thoroughly wet, and my saddle bags filled with water. At night we got to Abshear's, eighteen miles, where I did my best to dry my things.

Friday, April 29, 1836.

It continued all the morning to rain hard; heavy showers at intervals. Dr. Neblett insisted on going forward through the rain. I determined to stay and dry my things, so he and Dobie left me. I would not consent to set out in the rain again. I found my watch had got wet and stopt, and the crystal, which I had cracked in the famous passage of the Neches, now came entirely out. So I took a lead bullet and beat it out in size and shape of a crystal, and fixed it in, to protect the hands until I can get a crystal put in.

About 3 o'clock, it being fair, I started, with Asa Abshear for my guide. We encountered a very heavy shower of rain, but I only got my boots wet. In a pond of water in the prairie I discovered an alligator about six feet long, which I rode up to near enough to shoot in the neck with my pistol. The blood flowed, and he did not move much, so concluded it was mortal, and left him. Arrived after dark at the house of a herdsman, a Spanish Creole, named Sebastian Nunez, where we were kindly treated. These herdsmen live very simple and apparently happy lives. They have little intercourse with the world, very little learning, no ambition, and have a ball every Saturday night. Sebastian Nunez and Asa Abshear are both going to a ball tomorrow night.

Saturday, April 30, 1836.

Left Nunez's after breakfast. He would receive no pay, but rode with me to near Perry's Ferry. His brother, at whose house we called, gave me an alligator's tooth. Paid Asa Abshear for piloting me $1.25. Stopt at Berry's, and tried to sell my horse. Left after 12 o'clock, having taken directions from Perry, but the road was by no means plain, and was so interrupted by the numerous houses of the Creole French and Spaniards, herdsmen, that I missed my way, and lost nearly an hour in riding from one house to another inquiring the way. Many of the inhabitants did not understand a word of English. Encountered several parties of men and women going to a ball. One young man pressingly invited me to go with them. About sunset came in sight of the Teche, at the foot of a fine lake, which is said to be two miles broad and five or six long. There is a peculiarity about it; a large part of it is covered by a floating marsh, consisting of a thick growth of grass and weeds, in a stratum of soil of some inches, and tenacious enough to bear men and sometimes horses, under which there is deep water. Sportsmen cut holes through this surface of soil and vegetation and angle through there for fish, which are abundant and fine.

Here begin the sugar plantations for which the Teche is famous. The planters are wealthy, and live in pine houses. The first to which I came belonged to a Madame Cigout and her son, the next to Caesar Dublanc, where I saw a large flock of sheep, and some little boys, who were penning them, rode on the sheep with dexterity; also the beautiful mansion of St. Mark Darby. Here I made another attempt to sell a horse, but young Darby apologized for not making a negotiation on account of his brother-in-law, Dr. Smith, who was lying in the house ill—in extremis. Arrived at New Iberia (or New Town) at dark. Stopt at Buyon's; a neat, small, rural looking house, in the midst of a garden, so unlike a house of entertainment that I was fearful I had been misdirected. The fare corresponded with the entertainment. Found here Mr. Loyd Wilcoxen, a fine looking, gentlemanly man, whose parents emigrated soon after the Revolution from Maryland to Kentucky. He has been twenty-seven years at Attakapas; a cotton and sugar planter. Says he has enjoyed fine health, and his appearance corroborates the declaration. He lives on the Vermillion. Has a place on the Teche, a few miles from Franklin, 730 or 740 acres, which he offers for $10,000, half cash, balance one and two years.

The steamboat *Velocipede*, for New Orleans went down the river soon after my arrival.

Sunday, May, 1, 1836.

Fine, clear morning. Mr. John D. Wilkins, Dr. Neblett's friend, arrived this morning from St. Martinsville, and stayed till after dinner. Mr. Wilcoxen also stayed. It rained hard at noon. The steamboat *Plough Boy* went down on the way to New Orleans. If I had sold my horses I should have gone in her. Wilkins expecting Dr. Neblett at his house, invited me to go home with him, which I did. He lives in the prairie, seven miles from New Iberia. He is uncle to Henry Peebles, with whom I traveled in Mississippi last fall. Is a widower, has a daughter, now at school in Kentucky, and a son who is absent, intending to go to the University of Virginia; one son with him, who is deaf and dumb.

Monday, May 2, 1836.

At Wilkins'. It rained hard all the forenoon, by which I was prevented from going out. Cleared up at noon. Had milk and strawberries for dinner; said he had them from the 1st of April. After dinner rode over the plantation; it is large and in fine order. Went through the sugar house. He showed me a section of cane * * * inches in diameter, the wood of the cane one inch thick. Supposed it was washed on the shore from South America; none such in United States. Returned to New Iberia. Proceeds of crop of I. D. Wilkins, 1835:

32 bales cotton	net $2,098.06
23 bales cotton	net 1,402.51
8 bales cotton	net 477.86
23 bales cotton	net 1,295.43
10 bales cotton	net 499.59
11 bales cotton	net 669.44
107	$6,442 89
6,956 gals. molasses, at 32c	$2,110.72
11 hgds. sugar sold 6th March, average wt. 1138 lbs	net $1,188.98
163 hgds. average wt. 1138 lbs., 185,494, at 12 ½c.	23,186.75
1500 bbls. corn, at $1 per bbl	$ 1,500.00
	$34,419.34

Cultivated:
200 acres in cotton.
90 acres in cane, rolled.
26 acres in cane, sowed for seed, and half the crop of 1836 planted from the tops of last year.

Worked sixty hands in the field.
115 negroes on the place, 18 little fellows, sometimes turned out to thin corn, etc.; the rest are cooks, scullions, etc.

Charges:
115 negroes at $500 each, $57,000,

at int. of 10 per cent	$5,750.00
Land, say $13,000, int. 10 per cent	1,300.00
Interest on land and negroes	$6,050.00
Overseer	800.00
Sugar boiler	318.00
80 p. shoes	80.00
100 blankets	250.00
Clothing, etc	1,000.00
	$8,498.00
Sales	$34,419.34
Charges	8,498.00
Profit	$25,921.34

Tuesday, May 3, 1836.

Fair and warm. On my return from Wilkins' last evening, I learnt that steamboat *Teche* had gone up the river, and would be down to-morrow morning. Could not sell my horses. At breakfast had potatoes as large as turkey eggs, of this spring's growth. Here is a Mr. Stone, a handsome young man from New Jersey; came out to settle his father's estate, and is on his return North. Has a wife and child eighteen months old, and yet the wife looks like a girl of fifteen years. Guyon's bill, $6.25; washing, 50 cents. Left New Iberia at 10 o'clock. It is a neat little place of about twenty-four families. Very little trade. Mrs. Guyon keeps a very neat house. A few miles from New Iberia, stopt at the house of Baron Bayard, a French Creole, and sold him my sorrel horse for $65. A few miles further on stopt at the sugar house of Dr. Solange, and examined the operations. They were boiling the molasses that had been left in the bottoms of the cisterns; six boilers. The first is called *Grand*; the second, *Propre*, and the last one *Batterie*. *Sirop de Batterie* is the molasses taken from the batterie before it is boiled enough to granulate. It is a large establishment, fine house; arrangements seem to be superior. Overseer told me the crops of the last two years did not exceed 320 hogsheads. He expected to make more this year than in the last two years. Passed the splendid estate of Major Fusillier, a rich old French Creole. His house is surrounded by beautiful hedges and groves of orange trees, and his fences are ornamented with more than 300 fine catalpas. Passed the estate of Withrop Hardin, the son of old Lyman Hardin, of Natchez. Fine place. Also the beautiful plantation of a Mons'r Preyeaur. Arrived at Franklin at sunset. Stopt at the Mansion House, kept by James A. Anderson; good house.

Wednesday, May 4, 1836.

At Franklin. I wished to go over to Thibedeauville and see Alex'r Lawson, but was told it would be impracticable, the waters were high, and no ferry boats. I wished to see the father and other relatives of Mr. D. Carlin, who live on the Teche, below Franklin, but the steamboat *Teche* is expected every hour, and if I miss her I may not get another for a week, so I have to abandon both gratifications and wait here for the boat.

Sold my Spanish horse to Mr. Anderson, my landlord, for $36.50. Pretty well sold.

The hands of the steamboat have mutinied and some of them have left her above at Major Fusilier's plantation.

Dined with a Dr. Field, formerly of Virginia; a queer body. Presented to a Mr. Royston, also an old Virginian, now an Attakapas planter; a very picture of rosy health. Saw also a Mr. Saunders, a planter formerly of London County, Va.

Royston says the fair average crop of sugar in Attakapas is 1,500 pounds to the acre, or one and a half hogsheads. Some planters make 3,000.

A negro man at Winthrop Hardin's told that the following is the allowance there of food for the negroes, per week:

1 lb. salt meat per hand,
1 ½ pints molasses per hand,
3 ½ bbls. meal for 50 hands.

Royston says the following is a proper allowance:

1 bbl. corn per month,
3 lbs. meat per week.

Sam'l A. Marsteller, of Virginia, was out here last winter, looking at lands; did not buy, but hired his slaves at Port Gibson.

Also a Mr. Carruthers, from Rockbridge, Va., who they say was talkative and boastful, and left a bad impression behind him.

About 7 o'clock the steamboat *Teche* came down the river, and I took passage in her. Found on board Cady, Catlett and Fleury, Mr. and Mrs. Stone, Major Fusillier and his son, etc. Bill at Franklin, $2. Ten miles below Franklin Judge Baker and wife came on board. She is a daughter of the late James Patton, of Alexandria, D.C. They are hearty looking people, and their three children look well. He says they have never been sick. From all that I saw and hear of Attakapas, my impressions are very favorable, as to fertility, healthfulness, and character of the people. The country, too, is pleasant. The Teche is a beautiful, placid stream, fed from prairies, never overflows; and is always clear; seldom rises more than two feet.

Thursday, May 5, 1836.

Found ourselves this morning in Grand Lake, having left the Teche, through the Bayou Sorrel and Lake Chicot, and are now in Grand River, or Atchafalia. From the Atchafalia we passed into the Bayou Placquemine, which is twelve miles long, to the Mississippi. Entered the great Mississippi at the town of Placquemine, at 1 o'clock. The sight of the noble river, fine plantations and splendid mansions, sure indications of prosperity and plenty, are quite cheering, after coming from the wild country and turbulent scenes that I have lately seen.

In conversation with Judge Baker he informed me that in Louisiana there are two District Courts every two months; parish judge keeps records, clerk attends process, etc. No juries in parish, only small causes tried there; it is also a court of probate. Pleadings are simple. Fees for suit and collection of debts, 5 per cent. All other suits matter of contract. Interest, legal, 5 per cent, per contract, any rate not exceeding 10 per cent. Wife's interest in estates, one-half in all property acquired after marriage, entire in her own maiden property; entitled to one-fourth of usufruct of her husband's original property, if she be poor, and not more than four children—if five or more, a child's part. The parish judge sells the estate and appoints administrator.

In conversation with Captain Dowse, of the steamboat, he told me he was well acquainted with all the waters of Louisiana; says there is an island on the coast called Pecan Island, twenty miles long, of the finest cane land. Would make ten or twelve good sugar plantations. It is surrounded with a mud flat of five miles which makes it difficult to reach. He thinks a bayou from the back part of it connects with the Mermentau; first rate for sugar; much game. It could be reached by a canal dug through the swamp, which he thinks might easily be done.

Arrived at New Orleans in the night.

Friday, May 6, 1836.

Took lodgings at the City Hotel. Neither Triplett nor Neblett yet arrived. The news of the day is, that Santa Anna is among the prisoners taken by Houston in his recent engagement. It is not credited. Saw Dr. Barton and Seth. They have purchased of W. S. Allen about 20,000 acres of Texas land, and have taken the deed in my name, and wish me to give them a power of attorney to sell—so that I am to have nothing to do with it. Not a word said about any other agency in it, or commission! I shall give them the power, but would not give much for their title.

Saw John F. Scott for a few minutes. He is just about departing for Red River, in the *Levant*. Says he will return to Vicksburg about the 20th. Requested him to bring my trunk from Natchitoches, that I left in care of D. H. Vail.

H. M. Thompson and A. C. Cammack, of Mobile, are here.

Find here a number of Texans, officers and others, raising troops. Green, Conrad, Thornton, etc. They fill the bar rooms of the public houses, and make too much display of uniforms, etc.

The crew of the *Invincible* are imprisoned and under trial for piracy, before the U. S. District Court, Judge Rawle presiding. They were captured by order of Com. Dallas. Much excitement prevails among the friends of Texas.

Received two letters from Mrs. Gray, of March 28, April 17.

Saturday, May 7, 1836.

In New Orleans. No news yet of Triplett or Neblett. The crew of the *Invincible* were this evening discharged by the court. They were marched in triumph through the streets and to public houses. This discharge is considered an acknowledgment by the court of the flag of Texas. Great exultation, of course, among the Texans.

Went at night to the St. Charles street theater to see the Italian opera. The piece was *Norma, a Tale of the Druids*. The orchestra is a superior one, and the singing was very fine; but this kind of performance not to my taste; nor does it seem to suit the folks of New Orleans; the house was thin.

Sunday, May 8, 1836.

In New Orleans. Dr. Neblett and his friend, Mr. McKaskele, arrived this morning in a steamboat from the Vermillion. He did not see his friend Wilkins.

241

Wrote to Mrs. Gray.

In afternoon, R. Marye and A. Slaughter called to see me. They, A. M. Cammack, H. M. Thompson and myself walked to see the new city waterworks. A noble affair. A large reservoir of water is raised upon an artificial mound in the upper part of the city, which distributes the water through iron pipes to every part of the city, and can be carried into the third stories of the houses. It is raised from the river into the reservoir by steam power. Took tea at Marye's. Mrs. Blackwell is well and in good spirits.

Monday, May 9, 1836.

In New Orleans. Neblett is much elated with his Galveston city scheme. Thinks he can make a good speculation in it. Says several gents have agreed to take shares in it at $1,000 each, and run all risks.

S. [M.] Williams, James Power, John T. Austin, Alfred Guild, etc., are here. Williams is one of the company that claims a league of land on Galveston, and on our ground. Guild wishes to see some land near Lake Caddo that he purchased of C. and Texas, under the same law that Mason purchased under. He left the deeds with me to examine, and referred me to General Mason. He asks 50 cents per acre.

Tuesday, May 10, 1836.

In New Orleans. Met with Jonathan Ikin, of Leeds, England, whom I had seen in Texas. He is boarding here, and still talking largely of his commercial views. Also met Alfred Penn and Colquohoon (I. R. Triplett's former partner). No tidings yet of R. Triplett.

Wednesday, May 11, 1836.

In New Orleans. By appointment with Guild, we called on General John T. Mason, at his lodgings, in the afternoon, to have conversation with him respecting Guild's title. He had a hack at the door, and insisted on our riding with him. Guild declined. We rode to the railroad depot, took a car, and went to Lake Pontchartrain. Had much conversation about Texan affairs. He said the Convention was entirely mistaken in supposing the law of Coahuila and Texas for the sale of 400 leagues of land had been passed in his favor. That the law was passed before he went to the country, and had no reference to him. He merely acted as the agent of the State in selling 300 at a given price, he having the benefit of all that he could get over that price; that he acted under a power of attorney, and had paid over to the State all the money, according to contract. The purchasers received title from the Commissioner of the State, so that in any event, even if the Republic should succeed in abrogating those sales, he would be harmless. Guild, he says, holds under the same law, and stands on the same footing with those who purchased of him (J. T. M.). Guild purchased a part of the 100 leagues that were not sold by him. He thinks they will all hold good. The clause of the Constitution intended to destroy them is so defective that it will not touch them, even if any act of such a body could destroy them.

We returned to town after dark, and I took tea at Slaughter's by appointment. Present, Marye's family, and Mr. May, of Tuscaloosa, a lawyer, who is now here speculating in city lots. He has been successful, and is a very prepossessing man.

Thursday, May 12, 1836.

In New Orleans. No tidings yet of Triplett. Met John W. Smith, of Bejar, who told me Navarro and Seguin were in the city, at a French house, *"Hotel des habitans et strangers."* Called to see them. Introduced to a Mr. Flores, of Bejar, and a Mr. * * *, of Natchitoches, all Mexicans.

Friday, May 13, 1836.

In New Orleans. Met with Copeland, who looks well. S. Barton says he will recover a lawsuit that he is prosecuting, in which a property worth several hundred thousand dollars is involved, and that he will be immensely rich.

Saturday, May 14, 1836.

In New Orleans. Impatient to be at home, but am prevailed on by Dr. Neblett to remain until Triplett arrives, to try and arrange a plan of operations about Galveston; he, Neblett, being obliged to go to the sales at Chockchuma. I am also desirous of getting the script duly arranged, and reluctantly consented to wait for Triplett, who is hourly expected.

Sunday, May 15, 1836.

This morning there was a grand military parade of the legion. Went with Slaughter to the Episcopal service. A Mr. Wheat, of Marietta, preached. He was formerly of Alexandria, D. C. Has been preaching here for some weeks. Good, sensible discourse. This is the first Episcopal service I have attended since I left home. Walked home with Miss Connolly. Saw Mr. and Mrs. B. Chew. Dined at R. Marye's. After dinner he and I set off to go to Carrollton, but were too late for the cars. Met Mr. Pearce and Miss Shields. Went to the tobacco warehouse which Marye rents this year. It is for sale; he thinks it would be a good speculation.

Neblett went to-day.

Monday, May 16, 1836.

I now learn that Triplett went back to the army of Texas after learning of the battle. He is expected here every day. Invited by Pearce to a family dinner to-morrow with Major Miller, etc.

Tuesday, May 17, 1836.

Dined at Pearce's. Company: Major Miller, Mr. Nicholson, Dr. Kerr, Miss Shields and self. Mrs. Kerr has gone to Alexandria to see her daughter, Mrs. Dr. Davidson.

Presented by Pearce with a ticket to the Italian opera. Went at night, and sat in his private box. The piece was the *Straniera*. Performance similar to that which I witnessed before.

Wednesday, May 18, 1836.

Called to see J. H. Caldwell; invited to dinner next day. Called to see Murat; not at home; left card. In afternoon rode in steam car to Carrollton. Took tea at Marye's.

Thursday, May 19, 1836.

Met Geo. Willis, who is going up to Kentucky in company with Major Sam Lewis. Learned from him that his father has resigned his office, and gone to Virginia, and that R. Carmichael has also gone back.

Dined with Caldwell alone. Received from him a package of papers for his wife. He told me he was about to build a house for her in Fredericksburg, the lot to be purchased of Metcalfe. He has procured from the legislature of Louisiana an act of incorporation for his theater, baths and arcade, with banking privileges; capital, $100,000. Intended going to Europe this summer, but his business will not allow it; is determined to contract his business, and devote all his energies to drawing his vast concern into a compact form.

After dinner I went to the hospital to see G. W. French and Cantwell. The latter seems to be well satisfied; gets $30 per month and board. G. French has graduated, and is looking out for a place to practice. Speaks of Natchitoches. Anxious to make something, so as to be able to help his family.

Friday, May, 20, 1836.

No tidings yet of Triplett. My patience is wearing out fast. In conversation with Lambeth this evening he said he had made a speculation in Texas lands with P. W. Grayson, and that if he could, by a sale of certain property, arrange his business to his satisfaction between this and the time of my going out in the fall, he might possibly risk a further sum in that country with me. Although no positive promise was given, he left me under the strong hope that I should get some business from him.

Saturday, May 21, 1836.

No tidings yet from Triplett, and being tired and ashamed of remaining in New Orleans, and unwilling to return home before his arrival, after waiting so long, I determined to run over to Mobile for a day or two. Took the railroad cars to the lake, and embarked on board the steamboat *Merchant,* Captain Scuyler. Left wharf at 11 o'clock. Lake Pontchartrain is a beautiful sheet of water, and associated with an interesting portion of the late war. Passed the Rigolets while I was at dinner, and entered Lake Borgne. Had to stop in the night at Biloxi, to land passengers and goods, and in approaching the place we grounded. In carrying out an anchor, a man fell into the water; the noise made in giving orders recovering him aroused all the passengers, who in alarm ran on deck, fearing some disaster, but there was no hurt done. One poor lady, in her fright, ran into the gentlemen's cabin, in her night dress. In the morning we reached the wharf at Biloxi, and while landing freight I went ashore to see the place. It is a pretty rural village, built by citizens of New Orleans, mostly as a retreat in the summer months, on a beautiful bank, in the bay of Biloxi. The shores here are white sand, and everything wears a neat, clean and healthy aspect, every way different from the murky banks of the Mississippi.

Passengers, Judge Wright, of Pensacola; Mr. * * *, collector, of Florida; Colonel Hamilton, Mr. Barilli, etc. Colonel Hamilton told me much of the Randleson's, Mr. Lyons, and S. Barton's affair with Williams. (Steamcar, 50 cents; steamboat, $12.)

Sunday, May 22, 1836.

Passed through the Sound Islands, on the outside, Pascagoula, Dauphin Island, Mobile Point, etc. Went up Mobile Bay in the forenoon, through the shipping which lay at anchor some miles from Mobile, to receive cargoes. Should judge there were thirty to forty ships, several English, numerous steamboats, lighters, barges and flats, passing down, some with enormous loads of cotton for the ships, the business of loading not being interrupted by Sunday. The new City of Alabama was pointed out by a passenger, on the east side of the bay; great efforts are making by all sorts of people to get up a speculation in it. I apprehend it will turn out nothing more.

Arrived at Mobile after dinner. Put up at Mansion House. Met Rich'd T. Harmon on the wharf, who walked over town with me, showed me to the Episcopal Church. A Mr. Lewis is the pastor. The church is a good wooden building, amply sufficient for a large congregation. But these people are extravagant in everything. This is a temporary church; they are erecting a large brick one. The Presbyterians are also erecting a new brick church, and the Catholics a still more extensive and splendid one. The congregation was quite large for Sabbath afternoon. An organ, not played, singing poor.

Met Mr. Price, a young lawyer of Richmond, Va.; has been here for some months; tired, and going back. Saw also James Spillman and H. M. Thompson.

Monday, May 23, 1836.

At Mobile. Called to see Hugh Nelson (Misuge, Nelson & Co.). Looks badly, consumptive, but the same unaffected, worthy fellow as ever. Called also to see John Scott, who is doing well here in dry goods line.

There is to-day a general parade of the volunteer company to furnish the quota required by the Governor for the Creek campaign. Three companies volunteered, so no draft will be necessary; only two companies called for. In the afternoon walked with Nelson, and took tea with him at his boarding house. Introduced to a Mr. Champlin Parker, a lawyer from the North, a smart fellow; and to a Mr. Jones, editor of one of the Whig papers. He is from Caroline, Virginia. Saw also today a Mr. Wm. H. Easter, a lawyer, partner of Harry I. Thornton. There are many Virginians here. The town is beautiful and thriving; streets paved with shells, white and pretty, houses very neat, some elegant. Great speculations in real property making. Saw again A. M. Cammack and his younger brother, who is living with John Scott.

Tuesday, May 24, 1836.

John Scott was so attentive as to call on me this morning in a gig, and rode me several miles up the beautiful Spring Hill road, and to the famous orange groves, and the graveyard. Delightful gig roads. Called to see Mr. Labuzan, also to take leave of H. Nelson. Memo. to call on him in Petersburg—about Texas, etc. Tavern bill, $5.

At 10 o'clock took passage again on the *Merchant* for New Orleans. A. C. Cammack on board, also a Mr. Treat, of New Orleans, and Mr. Barrelli, who has now got his wife and child with him. Had a pleasant passage.

James N. Newby is keeping a tavern at Pascagoula Bay. He is employed by the proprietor to keep the house. Steamboat, $12; car and omnibus, 50 cents.

Wednesday, May 25, 1836.

Found ourselves this morning in Lake Borgne. Had no in-cident on the passage. At the Lake House met my Mexican friends, Navarro and Seguin, who had been on a trip to the lake, and returned to town in the car with me. Arrived at New Orleans at 10 o'clock. Found General Houston and his staff here. Also R. Triplett, who arrived only last night. By him received letters from Mrs. Gray of February 12 and 19, February 22 and 29, March 3 and 4; from T. Green, March 7 and March 11; from J. M. Patton, March 15, which had gone to Texas, and missing me there, have been returned.

Had a meeting of the subscribers to the loan at the Arcade. They refused to accept the form of script which R. Triplett brought from the Executive of Texas. Appointed a commit-tee to draft a proper form. They approved unanimously of the compromise.

A. Penn promised me his business in Texas if I should settle there.

Thursday, May 26, 1836.

Cannot get Triplett to give attention to the Galveston busi-ness; too much occupied with his agency. Saw Gail and Th. H. Borden. Saw Alex'r Lawson, took tea with him and wife and her sister at the French boarding house of Mesdames Rigault and Griffon. Pretty and fine child, *white* wife.

Friday, May 27, 1836.

Engaged to-day in writing report, and drawing up the form of script to be reported to-night to adjourned meeting of the loan holders. Meeting held at Arcade. Report accepted and the form adopted. Introduced to Dr. Meux, Sam'l Trompson and Mr. Denton.

Received a letter from A. M. Green, at Vicksburg.

Saturday, May 28, 1836.

Got script printed; also left Barnett's pamphlet at McKean's to be printed. Triplett too much engaged to attend to Galveston.

Met Caldwell (James H.) in the street, and had a long and interesting conversation with him respecting his own family affairs. Spoke kindly of Mrs. Caldwell, but says he never can live with her again. Entered fully into the unhappy difference between them. Says he regards her with the most friendly feeling, although her folly or her errors have destroyed his peace, and had well nigh ruined his fortunes; she shall want nothing; that their children will be worth half a million. He means to take Sophy to England when he goes. I could not help pitying him, notwithstanding his faults, and concluded that had his wife shared his fortunes as a wife should, it would have been better for them both.

Sunday, May 29, 1836.

Called to see Dr. Barton; went with him to B. Chew's. Mr. and Mrs. Chew in fine spirits; their daughter is hourly expected from New York, where she has been at school; promised to call to-morrow and see her before I leave New Orleans.

Went with Mr. May to see Slaughter and Marye. All took tea at Marye's. Spent a pleasant evening.

Penn left to-day for Virginia.

Introduced to a Colonel Owens, of Kentucky, on his way to Texas.

Monday, May 30, 1836.

Sent script to Texas by Gail Borden, to be executed and returned as quickly as possible. Also sent by him the proceedings of the meeting respecting the script.

Settled with Triplett for my twentieth part of the Galveston script, $30 paid in Texas, $66 paid now. It is for Texas script

Nos. 1, 2, 3, 4, 5, 6, one section of which is laid on Galveston Island, where the proposed town is to be. See his receipt.

Called at B. Chew's; saw his daughter, and took leave of the family.

Got from Triplett his plan for the city of Galveston; not satisfactory. Gave him my old Texas script to be left with Brandon, McKenna and Wright, to be exchanged for new script when that shall be received at New Orleans.

Took passage in steamboat *Superior* for Vicksburg. Started at 12 o'clock at night.

Tuesday, May 31, 1836.

Found ourselves this morning below the church of Bonnet Garret; passed General Hampton's fine estate, Donaldsonville, etc.

Among our passengers are Mr. and Mrs. Meader (Clara Fisher that was). She has a fine child, white hair and fair skin, exactly such as I anticipate my Alice will be when I see her.

Wrote to Brander McK. and W., Wm. Christy and R. Triplett about my scrip.

Wednesday, June 1, 1836.

On board *Superior*. Passed Port Hudson, Point Coupee, St. Francisville, Tunica Bend, mouth of Red River, Fort Adams.

VOL. X

Thursday, June 2, 1836.

On board the steamboat *Superior*, Mississippi River.

Arrived early this morning at Natchez. Walked up into the town. Met a Mr. Doniphan, formerly of Stafford. Found by the tavern books that Magill Green had gone up Red River, and L. R. Marshal has gone to the North.

Passed Rodney, Bruinsburg, etc.

Friday, June 3, 1836.

Arrived at Vicksburg at 2 o'clock this morning, and found great difficulty in getting lodgings. At length got a bed at the Mansion House. Found here a letter from Neblett. The Chockchuma sales are postponed, and he has gone home. Saw the Grumps, Jackson, Carter, and Arthur Lee.

Got two letters from Mrs. Gray, one of December 25th and 29th, the other of December 30th and January 3rd; also two from Peter, November 8th and January 1st, and one from Evelina, January 3rd. These have been lying here for five months. Still interesting. Dined and supped at R. Crump's. He promised to see Mallory (who is not now at home), about my mare. He and family will leave Vicksburg in a few days for Virginia.

After night the steamboat *Heroine* came up, on board of which I left at 11 o'clock p.m.

Saturday, June 4, 1836.

Found myself on board of a sorry old boat, and rather indifferent company. Among them a genteel young man named Thompson, a grandson of Jonah Thompson, of Alexandria. He is going to commence the dry goods business in Vicksburg. He is the son of Craven Thompson. He told me F. Catlett's father had abused his son and recalled letters of credit which he had given him in New Orleans. There had been some unfortunate difference between them which Thompson did not understand.

David P. Richardson was also on board, but left us at Providence. I had seen him in Vicksburg, and learned there that he had lately killed a man in some quarrel. The passengers

on board of the boat spoke of it in strong terms of reprobation; they stated that he and a Mr. Daggett were boxing or
wrestling in friendly sport; anger arose, and harsh words followed; Richardson procured a pistol and shot him, unarmed,
and upon that slight provocation. It is doubtless bad enough,
but there are always two sides to such stories, and I have
heard but one. I understood he went to Vicksburg to employ
counsel. His trial was to come on the following week. He has
been married only a few months.

Sunday, June 5, 1836.

Read over and arranged my wife's letters, and commenced
one to her. Passed to-day the mouth of Arkansaw River and
of White River. The day was without incident. I mixed but
little with the passengers. My thoughts and feelings were on
things afar off.

Monday, June 6, 1836.

The boat and passengers both begin to improve. The officers of the boat are very attentive. The steward, an old black
man, is the best steward I have seen on the western waters.
He had been a waiter in a tavern in Alexandria, D.C. There is
on board a Mr. Mills, a Virginian that I cannot find out. He is
a man of good conversation and good address. He says he is a
cosmopolite, but calls Virginia his home. There is also a Mr.
Stone, who is quite civil, a Mr. Rundell and a Mr. Reynolds,
and their wives, Mississippians, going to spend the summer
at the North; also Mr. Slaughter, of Kentucky, nephew of Phil
and Sam Slaughter, of Virginia, a respectable, gentlemanly
man, and a Mr. Jounay, who has the model of a press for
pressing cotton, tobacco, etc.

At 2 o'clock we arrived at Memphis, went ashore to see the
town, and was introduced by Mr. Stone to Niel McCoul, the

son of old John McCoul, of Spotsylvania. He says he is doing well. We had a storm this afternoon, and a hard rain. Owing to the darkness and storm we laid by at night until daylight in the morning. Mosquitoes have been very bad.

Tuesday, June 7, 1836.

To-day we passed the town of Randolph. At night a poor mulatto, who came on board the boat at Natchez, and has exhibited symptoms of insanity, jumped overboard from the stern while the boat was under full way. Two negro women saw him go overboard, and cried out. The boat was stopt, but he was neither seen nor heard after he jumped.

In the night also the boat was struck by a snag, which roused some of the passengers. I must have slept soundly, for I did not hear it.

Wednesday, June 8, 1836.

Found ourselves this morning above new Madrid. Passed Mills' Point, in Fulton County, the first town in the State of Kentucky, ascending the river. Entered mouth of Ohio at half past 3 o'clock. In a conversation with January about his pressing machine, a proposition was made for me to take the agency of it for Texas, I to obtain the passage of a patent law, and to take out the patent as a proprietor, in my name. He first said he must consult his partner as to terms, but at last said he would allow me half of all I could make by the sale of rights. Requested me to call at January & Houston's, in Maysville, and see one of the presses in operation. It is the invention of a Mr. * * * Payne. The firm is Payne & January. Slaughter is the son-in-law of Payne, and concerned in the sale of the patent rights.

Arrived at Paducah, at the mouth of Tennessee River, about 10 o'clock. Some passengers went ashore. Arrived at

Smithland, mouth of Cumberland, about 12. I was asleep. Here Mills, Slaughter and January left us, the former going to Nashville, the latter to their home, Russellville, Ky.

Thursday, June 9, 1836.

Found ourselves this morning between Livingston County, Kentucky, and Pope County, Illinois. About 8 o'clock passed the celebrated Cave in Rock, of which we had a full view. The scenery truly splendid. 9 o'clock, met and passed steamboat *Farmer.* A good looking company of infantry in blue dress and white hats was drawn up on hurricane deck; supposed going to Texas.

Friday, June 10, 1836.

This morning, opposite to Rockport. Passed Troy, in Indiana; Cloverport, Ky.; Stevensport, Ky.; Rome and Leavensworth, in Indiana. No incident worthy of note.

Saturday, June 11, 1836.

This morning found ourselves opposite to Portland. Passed up to Louisville over the falls; arrived at Louisville before breakfast. Put up at Galt House. Saw Hill, Cox, Burnley, Wallace. Dined with Wallace by invitation. Present, his sister, Colonel Floyd and wife, and a Mr. Voorhees. Returned to tea with Burnley. Spent a pleasant evening.

Sunday, June 12, 1836.

At Louisville. Went to the Episcopal Church. Inquired for Judge Brown. He was not there. Found the convention was in session. Bishop Smith preached. Saw Geo. Hancock. Dined with him at Galt House. Saw the Rev'd Mr. Cleaver, Dr. John E. Cooke, Dr. Coit, Mr. Caswell, etc. Found there was an unpleasant state of affairs in the church. The Bishop and his clergy are at variance, and they talk of impeaching him for some unbecoming conduct. Was called upon by a Mr. John Thompson Gray, formerly of Culpeper, now of Louisville, and has become rich. He talks of visiting Texas. Introduced also to a Mr. Beale. Took tea with Burnley and wife.

Monday, June 13, 1836.

At Louisville. Saw Judge Brown. Concluded to dine with him, but he went to Albany, and did not return in time. Hill to-day spoke of Texas land, and gave me reason to believe that in the fall he would give me a commission to buy some. Called with Judge Brown to see Bishop Smith, to whom I had a letter of introduction. Saw Mr. Wm. English, of Pittsburg, who married my niece. He has been to St. Louis, and rented a house there; intends removing to St. Louis in the fall.

Tuesday, June 14, 1836.

At Louisville. Saw Mr. * * * Addison, to whom I had a letter of introduction from Mr. Hanson. Saw also John B. Shepherd and Mr. Hume. Left Louisville at 10 o'clock in the steamboat *Ben Franklin*, for Cincinnati. Passengers, Mr. and Mrs. Floyd and daughter. A fine boat, and a genteel set of passengers. Conversed with a Mr. Thomas, of Cincinnati, who I believe was formerly of Baltimore; lame in his right leg. An intelligent young man, quite literary, and I suspect a lawyer or an editor, or both.

Monday, June 15, 1836.

At Cincinnati before day. Went to Broadway Hotel. Sorry house. Called with Colonel Floyd to see Carneal, where I was introduced to General Harrison. Saw also Irwin, Whiteman, and Rev'd J. T. Brooke; met the latter in the street; and afterwards called and sat with him half an hour. Left Cincinnati at 6 o'clock, in steamboat *Detroit*. Passengers, Mr. Anderson and wife, to whom I was introduced by Carneal, Rundell and wife, Martin, of Philadelphia, Foote and wife, Bell, formerly of Stafford, now of Natchez, John Carpenter, wife and sister-in-law, of Mississippi.

Thursday, June 16, 1836.

Found ourselves this morning below Maysville. Went ashore at Maysville; saw in the warehouse of January and Huston the lever press of January and Payne. Passed to-day the towns of Alexandria and Manchester, in Ohio; Vanceburg, in Kentucky, and Portsmouth, Ohio, Greenupsburg, just at night. Met steamboat *Savannah*.

Friday, June 17, 1836.

Above Guyandotte. Anderson and his party and Bell have left us at Guyandotte. Passed Gallipolis, in Ohio, and Point Pleasant, in Virginia. The steamboat *Detroit*, on which I now am, is a boat of the second class, dirty and uncomfortable. The steward and waiters dirty and rude, and the Captain not agreeable. All the passengers out of humor.

Saturday, June 18, 1836.

Found ourselves this morning above Marietta, sixty or seventy miles below Wheeling. Passed steamboats *Wacousto* and *Tuckaloe*. The scenery of the banks improves in beauty and romance. Very mountainous. At half past 2 o'clock the boat grounded, and we did not get off for some time. At 5 o'clock passed Elizabethtown, the courthouse of the new county of Marshall, in Virginia; a beautiful place. A number of coal banks visible on the shore. They dig the coal out of the mountain side, and run it down to the river through spouts, from which it is discharged into boats. Arrived at Wheeling about 7 o'clock. Here Foote and many other passengers left us. Taverns in the town are all crowded. No place to sleep. Stages all engaged for two or three days. Resolved to go on to Pittsburg in the *Detroit*, as our passage to that place is paid, and we may reach there early to-morrow. I wish also to see my sister and her family, and by leaving Pittsburg on Monday I shall not lose much time. Steamboats *Post Boy* and *Dayton* are lying here. Walked up into the town with Mr. Martin. An active, flourishing looking place. A great many manufactories. Saw on the books of the tavern that Wm. H. Wharton had been here a day or two before and had passed on to Texas.

Sunday, June 19, 1836.

Our Captain told us we should stop only one hour at Wheeling, instead of which he stopt eight or nine, got under way before day. Twenty minutes after 4 o'clock passed Warren, Ohio, Wellsburg, Va.; 8 o'clock passed Steubenville, a beautiful place; 11 o'clock, met *Post Boy*; 12 o'clock, passed Wellsville, Liverpool. 1 o'clock, met steamboat *Monroe*. Country romantic and picturesque. River is becoming very shallow and full of islands. 2 o'clock, arrived at Beaver, where Messrs. Rundell and Reynolds and their wives left us. The vicinity of Beaver is very beautiful. Passed New Philadelphia and Freedom, etc., and the famous station of the Harmonists, Economy. At 8 o'clock came to for the night at Shaw's Town, or Floherty. The steamboat *Roanoke* passed by us up the river.

Monday, June 20, 1836.

Started at 5 o'clock, and in less than two miles grounded, and with all the efforts of the crew could not get off until after 3 o'clock, and not until they took out seventy barrels of molasses, a part of their freight. While we lay there the *Oswego* and *Rufus Putnam* and another boat passed up by us, and a boat whose name I do not recollect passed down. Eight of the deck passengers went ashore, and the cabin passengers tried to get on board the *Rufus Putnam*, but she could not well stop. At length we arrived at Pittsburg, just before night. It is an interesting and beautiful approach, through a highly cultivated and thickly settled country. Pittsburg is shrouded in a cloud of black smoke, arising from the numerous manufactories with which it is filled. Most of their machinery is propelled by steam.

Left my baggage on board, and went in search of Mr. English. Found him and family and my sister ill. They have become more reconciled to Pittsburg, and in doubt whether they will go to St. Louis, after all.

Tuesday, June 21, 1836.

Spent this day in Pittsburg, looking at the various objects of note, manufactories, etc. Saw the machine for planing flooring plank, worth attention, and making biscuits by steam machinery. Went over to the town of Allegheny. Pittsburg is a great workshop. Everybody and everything seems to be hard at work. Saw the Jameses, old Wm. and Young, Mrs. J. and Charles and family. Met Rich'd Williams, of Fredericksburg, who has just arrived out, seeking his fortune.

Left Pittsburg at 8 o'clock p.m. , in the stage of the People's Line; paid $12 through to Baltimore, with a positive assurance on the part of the agent that I should be put into Baltimore in fifty-two hours travel, so that making all reasonable allowance for stopping, I shall reach Baltimore on Friday morning in time to take the 9 o'clock cars for Washington. Do my business there, and get home to breakfast on Sunday morning.

Wednesday, June 22, 1836.

Breakfasted this morning at 7 o'clock at Natton's, having traveled all night, eleven hours, and only gone miles. The stages have moved through the day at a tedious pace. Fine, cool weather, and good horses.

Got no dinner until we reached the home of John Lambert, seventy-three miles from Pittsburg, where we arrived at 7 o'clock; seventy-three miles in twenty-three hours of travel! The people had been waiting dinner for us four hours. And here it seemed we were to be left, the drivers refusing to go further, alleging that their duty lay on the road above. Here were two teams unemployed, and we met another about three miles above, leading, and yet owing to some disarrangement in the teams by reason of running extras, and mismanagement, we were all likely to be left here for the night. After much altercation and argument, however, one of the drivers agreed to take us on until he should meet the stage coming from Bedford, whose regular business it is to take us on. A few miles on the road we met the stage, which took us in, and in which we reached Bedford about sundown. Here we encountered Mr. Carpenter and family, of Mississippi, who had one of the extra stages.

Thursday, June 23, 1836.

Left Bedford as soon as we could change stages, about sunrise. A pretty place. Could see nothing of the famous watering place, which takes its named from the town. Arrived at Chambersburg late in the afternoon. The mail stage in which, we should have gone on to Baltimore had left several hours before, and after getting dinner we continued on to Gettysburg, leaving Chambersburg about night.

Friday, June 24, 1836.

After a most unpleasant ride, reached Gettysburg this morning about 2 o'clock. No stage to take us on to Baltimore. A most uncomfortable place, and a surly, disobliging tavern keeper. Told us there was no chance of getting on until 5 o'clock the next evening. So here are the fifty-two hours exhausted, and I am still thirty odd miles from Baltimore, and not likely to reach it for twenty-four hours yet to come. Got to bed a little before day, tired, with a bad cold, disappointed, and out of humor.

After breakfast I walked out to see the town, and in conversation with the editor of a newspaper, who is a nephew of the late Judge White, of Virginia, I learned that a stage left Gettysburg this morning at 5 o'clock for Fredericktown, which would connect with the railroad line for Baltimore, and put passengers into that city before night. So here is a fine chance lost, by the policy of my landlord, who being a proprietor of the People's Line, kept me in ignorance of the Frederick stage, which started from another tavern. A vile imposition of a vile publican.

In the course of the forenoon Carpenter came along in his extra, and finding my situation, politely offered me a seat with his family, which I accepted, and by that means reached Baltimore about 11 o'clock at night. By the agreement with the agent in Pittsburg I ought to have reached it twenty hours sooner, at least. The whole trip has been one of disappointment and discomfort. The weather was cold and wet, and my cold caused me to suffer much. I lost my great-coat on the Ohio, and suffered for want of it. Stopt at Barnum.

Saturday, June 25, 1836.

Left Baltimore in the 9 o'clock cars, and reached Washington at noon. Here I found Mr. Carneal, of Cincinnati; was one of the passengers in the car with me from Baltimore.

At Washington I found S. P. Carson, who had got better after I left him in Louisville, and having come on by Wheeling, he reached Washington before me. Here also I found T. Green and Dr. Neblett. They are on their way to Philadelphia and New York to try to sell Galveston and the scrip. After going home to see my family I am to join them at the North.

Took the steamboat at 10 o'clock p.m.

Sunday, June 26, 1836.

At daylight this morning we arrived in Potomac Creek, and took the stage for Fredericksburg. We had not gone a mile before a brace of the stage in which I was broke, and we had to wait until the driver could go back for another stage. It rained very hard, and the roads were very muddy. By this misfortune we were delayed nearly two hours, and did not reach Fredericksburg until near 8 o'clock. Found my family *all well.*

Here ends W. F. Gray's record of his first visit to Texas. His return visit is recorded in the next set of journals, beginning in early 1837.

VOL. B I

MEMORANDA OF A TRIP TO THE SOUTH AND TEXAS FROM FREDERICKSBURG, VIRGINIA, BEGUN JANUARY 17, 1837.

Left Fredericksburg at 12 o'clock p.m. in the cars on the railroad, baggage consisting of one large black trunk, one hair trunk, saddle bags, hat box with a hat in it, having a cap on my head, umbrella and sword tied together, a large green blanket with a horse blanket and leggings wrapt up in it (too much by half).

Cash on hand:

In gold pieces	$20.00
Small silver in bag	20.00
Bank notes	10.00
Change in purse	5.80
	$55.80

Arrived at Richmond about 8 o'clock at night. Paid fare, $4; dinner, 50c.

W. H. Finnall started from home with me, expecting we should keep company to New Orleans. Found I could not make my arrangements in Richmond to-night; Finnall went on, and I expect to find him in Petersburg. Saw T. Green, Mr. Ritchie; called at Peyton's, where I saw the Tripletts, Macfarland and wife, Dr. Scott, etc. Macfarland said he was glad I was going to Texas, that he would get me to attend to some business for him.

Wednesday, January 18, 1837.

At Richmond. Saw at Triplett's a Mr. Wm. Ross, of * * *, Va., who had a brother, Reuben Ross, who served in some military adventures in the Mexican Revolution, and he says had his account settled by the Mexican government. Balance due him for advances and services, $31,000; that the Mexican government had made him a grant of land on Red River, which had been confirmed by Coahuila and Texas; that R. Ross was murdered in Texas, and never located his grant; that his widow and four children are now living in Virginia, and they wish the claim pushed against the government of Texas. She is a sister of Fleming B. Miller, who is now absent from Richmond, but expected here to-morrow. He is in favor of giving me the claim, but she will do nothing without the advice of Miller and Ross. Referred him to T. Green and J. R. T., who I have requested to arrange a bargain for me, if they can.

Got copies of letters from T. Green. Dined there with Mr. Ritchie, who gave me a letter to B. T. Archer.

Received from T. Green a letter of credit of $1,500, and a check for $300; exchanged a part of the latter thus:

$20.00 of Alabama, 5 per cent	$1.00
155.00 of Alabama, 4 per cent	6.20
105.00 of New Orleans, 2 ½ per cent	2.62
$280.00 By which I gained.	$9.82
9.82	
$270.18	

Paid for candy and apples, 25c.

Wrote a note to W. H. Macfarland, apologizing for not calling to see him, etc. Left for Petersburg at 12 o'clock at night. Fare, stage, $2.50.

Thursday, January 19, 1837.

Petersburg.–Lodging and breakfast, 75 cents. Left on railroad at 9 o'clock. Fare to Blakeley, sixty miles, $3. Finnal had left. Found in the cars Hay Taliaferro, son of H. Taliaferro, of Rose Hill, Jas. H. Williamson, one of Lomax's law class, now a lawyer of Hicksford, going to Alabama; Taliaferro Hunter, going to see young Garnett who is engineering; a Mr. Shindles, from Jefferson County, going to Cheraw; a Mr.

Bullen, from New York, going to Augusta, etc., etc. Arrived at Blakeley at 3 o'clock. Dinner, 50 cents. Paid fare to Fayetteville, $13. Supper at Enfield, 50 cents (having previously passed through the old, dilapidated village of Halifax, which lies on the south side of the Roanoke).

Stopt at * * * to change horses and warm. Here we met the stage from the south, in which was passenger Captain Bolton, of the U. S. navy, with whom I had gone down the Mississippi last winter, who recognized me, and had to tell me his name. (I lack *individuality*.)

Friday, January 20, 1837.

Breakfasted at Lewisburg (courthouse of Franklin County, North Carolina), 50 cents. Dined at Raleigh, capital of the State, 50 cents. Population, * * *. Pretty inland town. New capitol just erecting, of freestone; handsome building. Weather cloudy, damp, gloomy; country poor and dreary. Ate no supper. Roads from Raleigh to Fayetteville very bad; had often to get out and walk for fear of upsetting, which Captain Bolton had advised we should do.

Saturday, January 21, 1837.

Arrived at Fayetteville at 8 o'clock. Found the stage had left us, it being sent off by Saltmarsh, the contractor, without a passenger, just before we arrived. Here we have to stay until chance shall give us a seat in the stage, as the passengers who may come on to-morrow will have the preference over us; so says Mr. Saltmarsh, by whom we have been badly treated, and who is a very rude, ill-bred fellow.

Fayettville is on the Cape Fear River. Has been severely burnt, and appears in a decaying state. They are now much elated at the prospect of revival by reason of railroads, etc.; five very neat churches, Roman Catholic, Episcopal, Presbyterian, Baptist and Methodist. Visited the Donaldson

Academy; pretty and flourishing institution. In the evening
100 guns were fired for the passage of a railroad bill. Wrote
to Mrs. Gray .

Met here L. L. Stevenson, of Staunton. Paid him clerk's
fee, bill for copy of record, Brook v. Beverley, from Staunton,
$2.37. Tavern bill, $2.25. Barber and boots, 25 cents.

Sunday, January 22, 1837.

The mail from Raleigh not arriving in time, we left Fayetteville at 7:30 o'clock, Taliaferro, Bann and Williamson. Day
clear and cold. Mr. Saltmarsh also in company. Dinner at
Dunsville, 50 cents (toddy, 10 cents). Just before night stalled;
quarrel between Saltmarsh and his driver. He said it was the
driver's fault; had he gone the right road he would have gone
clear; if his horses could not pull that load, they could pull
nothing. With the assistance of some blacks we at last got off,
but a few miles further the shackle broke, and we narrowly
escaped upsetting. Then the discerning Mr. Saltmarsh said
nothing could stand such a load as we had, and that he ought
to have left us at Fayetteville. With some difficulty and labor
we got a pole under the stage, and thus got on to the next
stage. Supper at Cheraw, S.C., 50 cents—on southwest side of
the Pedee.

Monday, January 23. 1837.

Breakfast at * * *, 50 cents. Supper at Columbia, 62 ½
cents, in a large, imposing looking room, with no fire place
nor stove; very uncomfortable. Servant said they never had
a fire in that dining room, to prevent gents from sitting too
long at table.

Fare to Augusta, $8. Extra for heavy baggage, $8. Here
commenced a system of iniquitous extortion. I shall long
remember this headquarters of nullification and extortion.
Contractor J. McLean, agent Stalker. Here we left poor Williamson sick.

Tuesday, January 24, 1837.

Breakfast, 50 cents. Passenger from Columbia to Augusta, a Mr. Hope, of the house of * * *; said he had been the clerk of Nat. Richards. Arrived at Augusta about 1 o'clock.

Paid fare to Columbus, Ga., $22. Extra for baggage, $10. Barber and tailor, 25 cents.

Left Augusta about 4 o'clock. At the tavern we took in three new passengers, two of them Mr. and Mrs. Bradford, of Mobile; but finding we had a very heavy mail at the postoffice, they were required to remain, and we went on with only Beeson, Taliaferro and myself, and a Mr. Ward, a stage agent. Supper, 50 cents.

Before reaching Ward's home, the stage sunk into a swamp, where we left her and walked on to the stand. Another stage was sent on, which took off the baggage, and we again proceeded.

Wednesday, January 25, 1837.

Passed the village of Sparta, a dirty place. The tavern a perfect receptacle of filth. Breakfast at Milledgeville. A poor, paltry looking place. The tavern the vilest, dirtiest place that I have yet seen. The capitol is an imposing looking building, of the mixed Gothic order, but the grounds and offices around it rude and neglected. The whole makes a bad impression upon a traveller.

Supped at the little town of Macon. Here Mr. Bunn stopt, and Taliaferro and myself had the stage alone.

Breakfast, 50 cents. Supper, 50 cents.

Thursday, January 26, 1837.

Breakfasted at a roadside tavern, kept by one Williams, about 10 o'clock. Passed the new village Talbotton. After riding twenty-five miles, stopt at Hurd's, where they wished us to dine, but we declined. Here we took in four young ladies, going ten miles to pay a visit, two of them Misses Hurd, a Miss Kilgour, and a Miss Almira Elizabeth Smith, a very pretty and chatty young lady, with whom I became sociable. She told me she is a niece of Judge Richard Ellis, of Texas, and that she had a brother killed about six months ago by the falling of a tree across the road as he was riding on horseback.

Arrived about 8 o'clock at Columbus, in Georgia; another vile, dirty place, where we got a poor supper. All the taverns that I have seen in Georgia, except at Augusta, are execrable. Here I was again subjected to the imposition of $10 for my extra baggage from this to Montgomery, a distance of about ninety miles.

Enquired for a steamboat to Apalachicola, and could we have got one going down the next day, we would have gone that way to Mobile. But there was none ready, so we were obliged to take the road again, and submit to all their impositions. Wishing to make all possible haste, we continued in the mail stage, instead of waiting till next day for the accommodation, so we started about 11 o'clock (one hour after time), with a very heavy mail, and the accession of two other passengers, a Midshipman Harris and a Mr. Williams.

Breakfast at Williams', 50 cents; supper at Columbus, 50 cents; fare to Montgomery, $10; extra for baggage, $10.

Friday, January 27, 1837.

About two miles after the first change of horses, in crossing a swamp, not far from Euchee, over a vile Indian bridge of poles, the stage and horses sunk through, and, owing to the slipping of the poles, it being very wet and freezing, they could not move it. We took off the baggage and mail, but all in vain. The driver then took a horse and went for help, and the passengers walked back to the change house, kept by one Mangum, where we dried our feet and clothes, and got breakfast. In getting out of the swamp we all got wet, having to wade some distance, and the cold was so intense that our clothes froze stiff. The ice stood thick on my greatcoat, long after I got to the fire in the house. About 10 o'clock, the driver and his aids having got the stage out, and all things fixed, we proceeded.

To-day we passed over the ground of the Indian depredations last spring, and saw numerous traces of the war, in burnt houses, recent graves, and bleaching bones. We are now in the midst of what was recently the Indian Nation, which extended from Flint River, in Georgia, to Line Creek, about twenty miles from Montgomery, in Alabama. Columbus is on the east side of the Chatahooche River, which divides Georgia from Alabama, and after its junction with the Flint, at the town of Chatahoochee, it becomes the River Apalachicola, and empties into the bay of that name. Everything here is new. The town of Columbus I could not see, it being dark. The village of Talbotton is a very pretty place, not four years old. The village of Tuskegee, in Alabama, is also new and pleasantly situated. It is the courthouse of Macon County. The road from Flint River to Montgomery is a military road, cut by the United States through the Indian Nation. It might, with very little expense, be a fine road, but is now out of repair, and abominably bad.

Supped on the road about 10 o'clock, and arrived at Montgomery a little before 4 o'clock a.m. Could not get in at the Montgomery Hall, and had to go to the Planters Hotel, a very inferior house.

Saturday, January 28, 1837.

After a few hours sleep and breakfast, walked over the town, which is prettily situated on the south side of the Alabama River. The business part of the town is on a plain, terminated by a bluff on the river. It is surrounded by an amphitheatre of pretty hills, over which it is already laid out, and some pretty houses are extending. It is a place of considerable trade, and has grown rapidly. A much greater growth anticipated, although it is about to be rivaled by Wetumpka, some forty miles higher up, and at the head of steamboat navigation. Saw Wm. Pollard, young Bell and Rootes, and Mr. Whiting, who is now cashier of the bank here, with a salary of $4,000, and a house, etc.—a snug berth. Fortunately found here the steamboat *Ben Franklin*, to steam for Mobile at 5 o'clock, in which we took passage, with a promise to be at Mobile before daylight on Monday morning.

27th: Breakfast, 50 cents; supper, 50 cents.

28th: Bill at Montgomery, $2. Porter, boots, etc., 50 cents.

Sunday, January 29, 1837.

On board steamboat *Ben Franklin*, going down the Alabama. A gloomy, drizzly day. Fine boat and pleasant passengers. Found on board my old acquaintance, Reuben Thornton, who proved to be a relative of Taliaferro. He went ashore early in the morning, at, I believe, Cahawba.

Became acquainted with General Edwin D. King, of Perry County, Alabama, who has lands in Texas, bought in conjunction with J. [K.] Allen.

H. Field, of Union Town, Perry County, Ala., a nephew of Judge R. H. Field; he went from Petersburg. Handsome young man; married; has just sold out; thinks lands and negroes will fall; intends resting on his arms till times change.

Nath'l Reese, of Benton, a Virginian, formerly a negro trader, now a merchant, thinks well of Texas, and says he and many others in Alabama are only waiting for peace in that country, when all who can sell here will go there to push their fortune. This I find to be a common sentiment here. They are getting out of conceit of Alabama.

The Alabama is a narrow and rapid stream, between steep and high banks, the country not visible from the boats; floods rise fifty and sixty feet; banks mostly stiff clay, running into limestone; much cane.

The Captain charged us $20 fare, but by the adroitness of an old traveler named Dunn, who had made a bargain when he first came on board for $15, and who took care to make it known to the passengers, we all got off for $15 each.

Among the passengers were several of the Florida Volunteers on their return home to Tennessee,:Pillow, Maxwell and Williams, the latter an interesting young man of Nashville, who has been sick for four months, and now looks badly. They all speak badly of Jessup, and well of Call. They say the country of the Withlacoochee is rich and beautiful, but there is a great deal of poor and swamp land in Florida.

Monday, January 30, 1837.

Owing to a dense fog, the boat was obliged to lay by last night, in consequence of which we did not reach Mobile until near 2 o'clock p.m. I immediately transferred my baggage to the steamboat *Mediator*, to sail for New Orleans to-morrow at 11 o'clock; walked up town with Taliaferro; saw two uniform companies parading. Town improving; many buildings commenced since May last. Swamps filling up, etc. Saw H. Nelson, Judge Thornton Smith. Took tea with Nelson at Mr. Ketchum's. He pays $60 per month for board and lodging! Slept on board of the boat. Paid porter 50 cents.

Tuesday, January 31, 1837.

Introduced to Judge Lipscomb, Richard Bullock, and Starke. Called at *Chronicle* office and got a copy of the Texas land office law. Saw Jones, the editor, Rob Grinnan, Dr. Terrell, and Glassell. Glassell has sold his plantation, and wishes to form a company, and make a settlement in Texas.

The following persons are interested in Texas: Dobson & Williams (failed), M. J. Keenan, Richard Bullock, Judge Lipscomb.

Judge Lipscomb told me that Michael Menard had bought the government's right to Galveston, and that David White, of Mobile, was his agent for selling it out.

Saw also R. Ellis, Jr., and introduced to Minge, Nelson's partner.

Pressed by Thornton to stay.

Left Mobile at 11 o'clock in the steamboat *Mediator.* Found that in transferring my baggage from one boat to the other I had lost my greatcoat. Among the passengers were Dr. Inge, of Alabama, and his brother, a Colonel Inge, formerly a Member of Congress from Tennessee. Told me he had read law with S. Barton; that his brother married the sister of S. Barton's first wife; that Barton and his first wife lived very happily, and spoke well of him; lamented the difference that existed between Barton and his present father-in-law.

Wednesday, February 1, 1837.

This morning our steamboat grounded in the Pass Christian, about 1 o'clock a.m., and did not get off until 1 o'clock p.m., by reason of which we did not reach the railroad until sunset. Arrived at the Exchange Hotel, New Orleans, about 8 o'clock. Found here Burnley, Ritchie, Parker, Major W. H. Fitzhugh, Colonel Jno. Walden.

Steamboat from Mobile	$12.00
Board one day	1.50
Porter at New Orleans	.50
Railroad	.50
	$14 50

Thursday, February 2, 1837.

At New Orleans.—Received letter from my wife, dated January 22nd and 23rd, per express mail, inclosing one from C. L. Stevenson to B. T. Archer. Wrote to Mrs. Gray and to T. Green. Saw Dr. Barton and S. Barton; called to see Mrs. Barton. She is now living at Mrs. * * *'s boarding house.

Friday, February 3, 1837.

Called on L. Pearce; invited to dine next day. Called on Captain Ker, postmaster. Dined with Dr. Barton and wife. Called to see J. H. Caldwell; delivered package from his wife. Invited to dine on Monday. Saw Shakespeare; he is much grown.

Saturday, February 4, 1837.

At New Orleans.—Received letters from T. Green at Washington respecting Texas and Santa Anna. Dined at Pearce's *en famille*, with only Wm. Christy. Learned from Christy that he had caused a bill to be introduced into the Congress of Texas for refunding to the subscribers their loan, with 12 per cent interest, in lieu of giving them land. The bill did not pass. I told him such terms would be rejected with scorn. "Well, then," said he, "they will get nothing." He seems to think himself a man of mighty influence in Texas; said his whole time was occupied while there in writing bills for Congress; that he drew up the charter of the Grand Railroad, Canal and Banking Company, for which they gave him one-sixteenth (I think it was) of the stock, which he considered worth $50,000. But with all his influence and consequence he could not induce them to pass a law in his favor, making him a citizen, giving him land, etc. He is a man of infinite self-esteem, and I fear his interference in our matters has been mischievous—it was at least unauthorized; and I learn he has an interest in the Galveston scheme, under Menard, which, of course, places him at war with us.

Dr. Kerr also dined with us; he still preserves his good looks and fine spirits. Mrs. Kerr is at her son William's. Miss Shields presided at the table. She has been sick and looks pale, but still pleasant. Pearce frank, hospitable and gentlemanly.

Burnley has engaged passage for us in the schooner *Texas*, now at the wharf, to sail in all next week.

Sunday, February 5, 1837.

At New Orleans.—Weather has been bad for two days; streets horridly muddy. Attended the new Episcopal church in Canal Street. Inside neatly finished; outside not finished. Bishop Brownell, of Connecticut, preached; he has been officiating here for several months. Congregation large and of respectable appearance; organ good, singing only so so. Met here Aug. Slaughter; promised to call and see him and Marye in the afternoon. Called after church, with Burnley, to see Mrs. Childress, who her husband wished me to become acquainted with. Young, pretty, newly married, a Presbyterian, his second wife, interesting. She had heard favorable report of Mrs. Gray, and hoped they might be neighbors in Texas.

Mr. T. B. Barton arrived to-day, via Mobile. He and his brothers called to see me after dinner, and detained me so long from visiting Slaughter that he had walked out when I called. Saw his wife, and had an interesting conversation with her. Visited Marye; found Betsy M. there. She is to remain there with them. Also found there Martin Picket, Slaughter's partner, and young Labuzan. Young M. is sick with measles. Spent an agreeable evening.

Monday, February 6, 1837.

At New Orleans.–Negotiated with A.H. Wallace & Co. a draft on John Ward & Co. for $1,000; paid them commission for managing, 2 ½ per cent, $25, exchange, 1 per cent, $10. Received net $965 in notes of Commercial Bank. Left with them two other drafts of $1,000 each, to be negotiated when I shall draw on them.

Dined by invitation with J. H. Caldwell. Company, Mr. Caldwell, Shakespeare, Messrs. Finn and Barton, players, and a Mr. * * *. Dinner good, company agreeable; Finn a great punster, and his drollery quite chaste and irresistible. He made some good hits at Barton, who it seemed had suffered from him before. Wrote to Guy Richards.

Wm. F. Ritchie went yesterday to Vicksburg.

Tuesday, February 7, 1837.

At New Orleans. Received letter from T. Green, wishing me to make a publication in the New Orleans and Texas papers respecting the Galveston claim. I dislike putting myself forward in the business; it more properly belongs to Triplett and Neblett, but Green's interest is so great, and I feel so strongly bound to do what I can to advance his interest, that I will do it.

Had a conversation with Yates, who is interested in Galveston, and he admitted that the contract of compromise did authorize us to locate our scrip, and demand patents therefor forthwith. He remarked with much warmth: "Burnett is a damnder ass than I ever thought him." He affects to consider Triplett's letter a surrender of the grant, but it is evident to me he is uneasy about it. Also conversed with A. C. Allen. He treats the surrender as complete, but says he never saw it.

Called to see Mrs. Murat; found Mr. Macrae there; Murat not at home. I had delayed calling on her for several days, in order to accompany Mrs. Dr. Barton. But to-day we were to have gone together; by some accident we missed each other, and she and Mr. T. B. Barton went together. I met them coming out as I went in. This was awkward, and I felt a little unpleasant about it at first, but I believe the fault was my own.

Found in New Orleans Wm. G. Cooke, to whom I delivered letters.

Wednesday, February 8, 1837.

At New Orleans.—Received of Jas. H. Caldwell $43, for Mrs. Gray, her bill for tuition of Sophy in music. The bill had been sent to New Orleans by Mrs. Caldwell. Received my thirty-one pieces of loan scrip from Brander, McKenna & Wright, and gave them a receipt for it. Received also from Wm. Christy the odd one to which I became entitled by lot, making thirty-two in all.

Mr. Crump, a Mr. Latham, and several other gents. arrived from Vicksburg, also Joe Christy, from Benton. Mr. Widgery, from Jackson.

Dr. Neblett also arrived from Vicksburg. He is full of the Galveston scheme, and averse to dissolving our first arrangement, of putting in 100,000 acres of land. He will not return to Texas this winter. I believe he is unwilling to encounter the conflict he would have to sustain there. Both he and Triplett seem disposed to escape from the fire themselves have kindled. Saw General Foote, of Mississippi; he was just starting for the North, via Mobile.

Thursday, February 9, 1837.

At New Orleans.—Introduced to Colonel Gholson, of Virginia, just from Texas. He is pleased with the country, and has entered into many speculations there. Is one of ten original projectors of the Canal, Railroad and Banking Company, and complains of an attempt on the part of the distributors of the stock to leave him out, in his absence. He has looked into our Galveston claim, and considers it good. He asked of Neblett that he might be of counsel for us, should the question ever come to trial in the courts. He also held conversations with Allen on the subject, and says Allen is scared, and has not confidence in their title.

The weather has again become wet and cold. I have had my hair cut, and have taken cold in the head, but, notwithstanding, accepted Dr. Barton's invitation to a seat in his box at the St. Charles Theatre. Play, *"Wives as they were, and Maids as they are."* In the box, Dr. Barton and wife, T. B. Barton, S. Barton, Burnley, and a Mr. Barrow, a member of the legislature. The attraction of the night was Mr., Mrs. and Miss Barnes. Performance dull, or I have lost my taste for such things. All of our company left before the performance was over, except Barrow and myself, who resolved to see it out, which I afterward repented. The orchestra is fine. The glass chandelier is much talked of; said to have cost $* * *, but I was not struck with it as very splendid.

Caldwell has procured an act of incorporation for this theatre, with banking privileges; but the stock was not taken, and the banking part of the scheme has fallen through. Met to-day Colonel Horton, Dr. Everett, and Mr. Gritton, of Texas, Mr. Cunningham, of San Augustine.

Friday, February 10, 1837.

At New Orleans.—The weather is inclement, and the streets very foul. My cold increases, and makes me very uncomfortable. Major Fitzhugh, intending to start for Virginia to-morrow, wrote to Mrs. Gray, put $7 to the $43 received from Caldwell, and sent her $50 in letter per Major Fitzhugh.

Called to see Mrs. Chew; not at home; left card. Had previously seen Mr. Chew in his bank.

Not being able, from bad weather, to see Marye again, inclosed to him the Bond of Bass, which he had given me to collect last winter. Saw Allen at Christy's office. Told him Neblett and myself thought it might be necessary to give public notice of our claim on Galveston. He said very well, if you do we shall reply and say what we think of your title.

Read the correspondence of R. Triplett with the Texan government while he was acting agent (in the hands of Sam Ellis), and made extracts of all he said respecting the loan and Galveston, and sent them to T. Green. Am surprised to find he never advised the Texan government that the contract of compromise had been signed by the lenders in New Orleans; on the contrary, he speaks of the difficult task he had "between the two parties," and leaves the impression that the contract had been rejected by them, when in fact they unanimously and cordially approved the contract, and signed it. The form of scrip which Mr. Triplett brought over they did object to, and Mr. Triplett himself was the first to object to it, although he had written it himself, and he wrote the letter directing him to have it printed, etc., which Burnett, etc., only signed. I apprehend that all the difficulty which has existed in this matter has grown out of the singular part which Triplett has acted in it, and the fact that we were not represented in Texas. Wrote T. Green in full on the subject.

Saturday, February 11, 1837.

At New Orleans.—The weather still cold and wet. My tooth aches, and all my head is affected with a neuralgic pain, which disorders me much. Called on Dr. Powell to get my tooth drawn. Could not find him. Obliged to keep my room. At night soaked my feet in a bucket of hot water. Went to bed with a fever, head dreadfully disordered; perspired freely.

Bought two copies journals of Texan Congress at $2 each. Sent one by mail to T. Green.

Sunday, February 12, 1837.

At New Orleans.—The pain in my head a little mitigated; my face is swelled. Went to see the Bartons. T. B. Barton and Mrs. Dr. Barton went off in steamboat to St. Francisville. Weather clear and cold. Called again at Dr. Powell's, but could not find him. Dr. Barton told me to keep my room, keep warm and quiet, and eat oranges, and not to have my tooth drawn, as swelling has taken place. Took his advice, and kept my room. Suffered much all day.

Dr. Neblett and Burnley sat in my room at night until I went to bed and left them talking; they then took their departure.

Com. Hawkins was buried this evening.

Monday, February 13, 1837.

At New Orleans.—The weather is fine, and the schooner *Texas* to sail this afternoon. My bad symptoms are ameliorated, but I am far from well; but as my acquaintances are going in this vessel, I resolved to go too.

Paid for greatcoat	$24.00
Life preserver	3.00
Bridle	3.50
Mending shoe	.25
Oranges, etc.	.50
Money belt	2.50
Servant, Helen	.50
Porter and boots and dray	2.00
Tavern bill	38.38

Got on board schooner at night, and then found she would not sail until to-morrow; returned to hotel; to be on board at 9 o'clock in the morning.

Wrote to T. Green and my daughter.

Wrote also during the last three days and to-night to Geo. Taylor, E. G. Booth, David Dunlap. I called again this morning to see Dr. Powell, and found he had changed his lodging; found him at his new abode, sick in bed (at 11 o'clock a.m.), and found that he was married last night to the lady of the house, a Mrs. Mitchell, who kept a boarding house. Introduced to *Mrs. Powell*, a pleasant, good-looking woman, tall, and rather large, frank, free and unaffected—a phrenologist! The Doctor looked at my tooth and advised against drawing; said the nerve was sloughing, and told me to get gall nut, scrape it fine, and put into the hollow tooth, and confine it there with cotton, which being very astringent, would destroy or dry up the nerve, and it would probably trouble me no more. I followed his advice, but fear, from the offensive discharge that issues from my nose, that the swelling has broken within, and that bone of my face will be carious, and cause me much pain and trouble. This is a distressing idea, on the point, too, of going on shipboard to encounter a disagreeable voyage, and to travel in a country where no good medical or dental aid can be expected.

Tuesday, February 14, 1837.

Morning damp and lowering. Tavern bill for lodging, supper and breakfast, $2.50. Called at postoffice. No letters from home. On board at 10 o'clock, and weighed anchor at 11, with a head wind. The Captain failed to secure a tow-boat to take us down the river, and none are going to-day.

Passengers, twenty-seven; only eight berths. Burnley had undertaken to secure berths for himself and our party, but failed to do so, and we are doomed to lodge in the hold; but Mr. Arnest, who had a berth, kindly gave it up to me, and roughed it himself as he best could. Among the passengers are John T. Gray, of Louisville; Geo. Crittenden, of Kentucky; Wm. Boyd, of Suydam & Boyd, New York; Col. Wm. A. Hill, of Tennessee; Dr. Lynch, a beastly old miser, of Tennessee; Captain W. Walker and Dr. Ramsay, of Texas; Amos Clark, of Evansville, Indiana; John Funstall, C. R. Balfour, Alston; A. Armstrong, Brown, Williams, Clements, B. C. North, Wm. Beardslee.

Only got about twenty-five miles down the river, and hauled along shore for the night. Some of the passengers went on shore and stayed all night at the house of a Creole, among them B. C. and Boyd.

Wednesday, February 15, 1837.

Beating down the river all day. Weather cold, wet and uncomfortable. My head still disordered, and situation on board uncomfortable. Laid to at night along shore.

Thursday, February 16, 1837.

Arrived early in the day in the Southwest Pass. Wind strong from northwest; not fair to go to sea with. Captain cast anchor, and determined to await a fair wind. Went on shore to the pilot's station, with several other passengers, and stayed all night. B. C., Boyd, etc., played cards. I wrote letters and journal. Wrote to J. F. S., Dr. N. and A. H. W. & Co., and to Mrs. Gray, which will go up to New Orleans to be mailed.

Friday, February 17, 1837.

After breakfast this morning the Captain sent his boat for us, and at 11 o'clock he got under way and stood out to sea, under a stiff breeze from the north. When about starting a pilot came alongside and offered his services, which the Captain refused, whereupon he demanded half pilotage, $6, which our Captain had to pay. The wind blowing strong and veering to northwest, we bore down to the south; finding it freshening and taking us out of our course, attempted three times to tack by luffing and failed; the boat stood away before the wind; gibed and attempted to get back to the river; in this he failed. At sunset found we were fifteen miles to leeward of the pass; again gibed and bore away to westward as much as he could. The wind veered to the east, and that night we had a fine run. The rough sea to-day brought sea sickness on all who were not old sailors. For the first time in my life I experienced the horrid feeling. Lay in my berth all night without throwing up.

Saturday, February 18, 1837.

At sea.–Continued our course to the west all day. At noon Captain got an observation of the sun, and pronounced us ninety miles from the pass. Distance from the Mississippi to the mouth of the Brazos, 370 miles. Sick all day; could not eat nor hold up my head.

Sunday, February 19, 1837.

At sea.–It fell calm during the last night, and continued so all this day, warm and cloudy, a high swell in the sea, the effect of the two past days blow, and the vessel rolled and flapped her sails all day, to the great annoyance of the passengers. Sick all day; ate a little dinner and felt better; could eat no supper.

Monday, February 20, 1837.

At sea.–Calm and cloudy. Captain could not get an observation. Impatience begins to manifest itself on all who are not too sick. A few light breezes gave us some hope, but they did not seem to help us on our course much. There was barely wind enough to keep the vessel on her right tack. The swell being less to-day, my feelings improved a little, and I again ate a little salt meat at dinner. The fare is bad, and all hands are grumbling.

Tuesday, February 21, 1837.

At sea.—A light breeze sprang up in the night, and we found ourselves at daybreak moving briskly along in a fog, and within the sound of breakers, which the Captain supposed was the pass of Galveston, and not being able to see the shore, he bore away more to the south. We had had so much calm weather that we could scarcely believe we had reached so near our destination. We must have drifted a great deal by means of the Gulf Stream while we thought we scarcely moved. About 10 o'clock discovered land, and a house on shore. No one could tell where it was.

After standing off and on for some time, the Captain concluded he had passed the Brazos, and put back. About 4 o'clock we descried the houses of Velasco and Quintana, and shortly after we were off the mouth of the river. The wind set strongly on shore, the surf ran high, with a great noise, and we now knew that it was these same breakers we had heard at daybreak, having then been off the mouth of the Brazos. The Captain concluded that the pilots could not come out, and determined to run in without one. He mistook the pass, and ran his vessel on the bar, where she thumped awfully. The squaresail sheet parted and the sail fell on deck, the jib sheet also parted, the vessel rolled on the bar, broached to, and several swells dashed over her broadside and was near sweeping the decks before the mainsail could be lowered. It was an awful moment; the Captain himself quailed, and the boldest held his breath for a time, for they thought the vessel would be a wreck, where many others had been before. The wreck of the *Flora*, of Middleton, lay a few hundred yards from us, having foundered on the same bar a few months before.

By great exertion the mainsail was lowered, she obeyed the flying jib, and again got before the wind, and after a few more shakes which made her crack, she passed over the bar, and we floated under easy sail into the Brazos, passed Velasco, and rounded to at Quintana at sunset.

A number of gents came on board immediately, among them Th. F. McKinney, who lives here, Captain Thornton, and Geo. A. Smith. The two latter are bound to the United States on board the schooner *Byron*, now lying here waiting a wind. Went on shore and took lodgings at Savery's Hotel, a rough, unfinished house, but good, neat beds, and a better table than we have been accustomed to. Right well pleased to escape from the crowded and stinking cabin of the schooner. Burnley and Crittenden went to McKinney's.

I am weak as a child, and sensible that I have fallen off much. My head rolls with the effects of the sea. The house seems to be rolling about over me. I need sleep and am feverish, but before going to bed I penned a letter to my beloved wife, to let her know of my safe arrival.

Wednesday, February 22, 1837

At Quintana.—It rained last night, and is wet and showery this morning. I feel better, but still everything is rolling, and the discharge from my nose, although lessened, is still offensive. Burnley and Crittenden, having got horses of McKinney, left us *sans ceremonie*. Boyd and J. T. Gray both expressed dissatisfaction at Burnley giving us the slip; for myself, I could but feel it also; but, I am not greatly disappointed. Found it impossible to get horses. The steamboat *Laura* is expected every hour, and we must wait with patience for a conveyance to Columbia.

In the afternoon went over to Velasco with J. T. Gray, and saw the fort, Mexican prisoners, etc.

Met Colonel Rob. M. Coleman, who I had known at Washington, a member of Convention. He is now a prisoner, under military arrest, by order of General Houston. From his representation his treatment has been harsh and arbitrary.

He says he is poor, without money, and offers to sell one or two leagues of land in Robinson's Colony; asked $1 per acre; afterwards said he would take 75 cents, and if I would sell it I should have all I could obtain over 75 cents. I feel interested for him, and would like to serve him.

Velasco has about one dozen poor houses, looks old and decaying. It is at the mouth of the river, on the east side. Quintana has four dwelling houses and one store; it is on the west side. The river is about 200 yards wide, and very deep; but the bar without the mouth has not more than six feet at its deepest pass. This will always retard the commercial prosperity of the port. There are no trees of any sort within several miles around.

Thursday, February 23, 1837.

At Quintana.—Fine day; a norther blowing, but not very cold. J. T. Gray and myself invited in to McKinney's. Mrs. McKinney a tolerably good looking woman, but pale, with falling features, looking unhappy. Mrs. Savery also sallow, wrinkled and careworn features. Mrs. Fannin, the widow of Colonel Fannin, and her two children, are boarding at Savery's. She is in mourning, and looks interesting. Not very handsome.

Went over to Velasco again. Found President Burnett living here. Called on him with Dr. Ramsay. Was cordially received and pressed to stay to dinner and partake of red fish, which we did; fish very fine. Mrs. Burnett a good looking woman. She had a stout Mexican prisoner sitting in her room, sewing a piece of cambric. Burnett said he was an excellent seamstress. Had some conversation about the loan. Said Triplett wrote him from New Orleans that the compromise was rejected by the lenders. Here is the mistake. Admitted that the survey and filing of the boundaries of our section on Galveston was valid; said he erred in signing the patent, and that

Triplett voluntarily surrendered it. Another mistake. Thinks Piedras' title worth nothing, and that any is better than Menard's. Asked "Where is the certificate of the Secretary of State of the filing of the boundaries?" I told him I had never seen it. He said: "That is an important document, and ought to be taken care of." *Query*—Did not Neblett surrender it when he obtained the patent? Burnett seems to have very imperfect and incorrect recollections of some of the transactions connected with that business. He thinks the Galveston scrip was purchased by Neblett, and had no connection with the loan. I asked him then how came it to be issued in the name of Triplett. He could not tell; said Hardiman and Thomas were the negotiators, and managed all that transaction. (Hardiman and Thomas are both dead!) I told him I understood the six scripts paid for by Neblett were issued as a part of Triplett's $90,000 of the loan which he had the right of paying up; that it was of necessity issued in that way, the government not feeling authorized to sell land, but they were authorized to compromise the loan and to issue scrip under that loan. He said, "If that be the case, it makes your claim stronger." It is strange that he should not recollect these things more clearly. There is something wrong about it, and this conversation with Burnett rather increases my apprehension that we shall fail in proofs—that documents which are "important" may not be found; that recollections of functionaries which ought to be clear will fail, and they may falsify their own acts.

The *Wm. Bryan* went to sea this evening. Thornton and Smith went in her. Wrote by Smith to Mrs. Gray, T. Green and Jno. Conrad, respecting his son's claims on Texas.

The steamboat *Laura* came down immediately afterwards, heavily laden with cotton for New Orleans, and passengers, furniture, etc., for Houston, whither she is bound, so we cannot go up the river in her.

Friday, February 24, 1837.

At Quintana.—This morning Captain Parker determined to proceed up the river with the schooner *Texas*, and as we could not get horses, we all determined to go up in her. I went over to Velasco again to see Coleman, who expressed a wish to see me before I left there. His object was to request me to say to the President, as from myself, not from him, that he, Coleman, was very anxious for a trial; that his situation was very uncomfortable, and he wished to have a decision of his case, etc. This I promised to do, if opportunity offered.

About 11 o'clock the schooner sailed, and after proceeding a few miles, a turn in the river made the wind head; we then *cordelled* for a mile or two, and finally came to for the night, about five miles from Velasco. Paid tavern bill at Quintana, $4. Passage from New Orleans, $25. Ferryage, 62 ½ cents. Apples, 25 cents.

Saturday, February 25, 1837.

On the Brazos.—Weather fine. Wind still ahead. The Captain took ten of the passengers in his boat and rowed us up to Brazoria, where we arrived about 4 o'clock in the afternoon. A small place, some twenty or twenty-five houses, looking decayed, dirty, uncomfortable. The seat of justice for the County of Brazoria; has been a place of some trade. Soil black, hard in dry weather, soft and tenacious when wet. Stopt at a wretched shell of a tavern, kept by Mrs. Long, widow of Colonel Long, who first settled Point Bolivar, on which she now has some claim. Her daughter, the Widow Winston, married Mr. Stiff, late of Fredericksburg, and he now lives with his mother-in-law. Saw Judge Collinsworth, who received me very cordially, and proffered his friendship and counsel. This kindness increases my already favorable opinion of the man. His court does not sit until November. Salary, $5,000. I fear his habits will prevent his discharging the duties of his office with the credit and ability that his talents and honesty would lead the world to expect of him. Saw also Judge Ben C. Franklin, of the Circuit Court, Winfield, Bland, McCloud. Introduced to Mr. Towns, a young lawyer from Mississippi, formerly from Amelia, Virginia, a prepossessing young man; also Dr. Jones, Dr. Long, Mr. Scott, clerk of the court, W. H. Jack, P. C. Jack.

Sunday, February 26, 1837.

At Brazoria.—It rained all day; the house crowded, dirty and uncomfortable. Some played cards all day, some played music; none seemed aware of its being the Sabbath. Saw Mc-Niel, and delivered to him Freeland's letter; received very politely, and invited to visit him. Mr. Steele, the Commissioner of Robinson's Colony, came up the river this morning, a passenger in the *Watchman*. Brought Jackson's war message, at which we are much surprised; the Texans affect to understand it and regard it as designed to aid Santa Anna in regaining the ascendancy in Mexico, and thus to facilitate the acquisition of Texas.

Monday, February 27, 1837.

At Brazoria.—Called on R. Mills, and delivered Chewning's letter; politely received; said he would cash my drafts on New Orleans for 2 per cent exchange. Found it impracticable to get a horse. Our party chartered two skiffs, and procured men to row us up to Marion, for $2 each. Arrived at Marion about 4 o'clock, having been upwards of six hours on the river, pulling against a strong norther and current; day quite cold and clear.

Stopt at the tavern of Mr. Hall. A perfect shell, dirty and crowded, surrounded by mud; the house in Virginia would not be considered habitable. A carpenter would hardly remove it for it. Yet it rents for $800 per annum. No stables, and scarcely any inclosure around the lot. Found here R. M. Forbes, and Mr. Nibbs, a lawyer, whom I had known last winter. He has bought lots here, and is living in a shanty with his family. Bill at Brazoria, $3.

Tuesday, February 28, 1837.

At Marion.—Fine, clear day. Mr. J. T. Gray borrowed a horse and rode to Columbia. I could not get one, and walked it, two miles through the bottom, road laid out straight, but not smooth. Saw Burnley, Boyd, Dr. Jones, Grayson, Houston, etc. Found D. P. Richardson, acting private secretary to the President. Introduced to Secretary of War Fisher, Secretary of State Henderson, Postmaster General Barr. Saw also Secretary of Navy S. Rhoads Fisher. Boyd and several others had their horses stolen last night.

Had a short conversation with Grayson about the loan. He does not understand it, but is evidently much prejudiced against it. Promised to look into the papers with me.

Saw the Bordens, and got my file of the *Telegraph* completed. They wish to sell the office. Returned in the evening to Marion.

Boarding here, Mr. and Mrs. L. W. Duprey, from Kentucky, and her brother, Mr. J. J. Stevenson, Mr. and Mrs. Townsend, Missouri.

This place consists of about eight or ten houses of all descriptions, mostly shanties. The lots have recently been sold out by J. H. Bell, at $100 each. They are now asking two, three and four hundred for them, unimproved. The tavern lot has commanded a bid of $4,000, which was refused. The place will probably improve, and be a good place for neighborhood business, but can never be a great city. Saw Lt. Woods, of Sherman's company; he has married a Mexican woman; bought lots here, and is improving them, in the woods; a pretty place.

Wednesday, March 1, 1837.

At Marion.—Weather cloudy and drizzling. Borrowed Mr. Nibb's horse and rode with him to Columbia. Saw Governor Smith, now Secretary of Treasury, and Dr. Levi Jones. Boyd and others have recovered their horses. Bell's Indian shot a Mexican. Saw Captain Allen and Captain Harry, of the army. The latter is the Captain of Wm. F. Maury, whom he reported well. Gave him the letters for Maury which I brought from his mother. He is to return to the army to-morrow. Got my file of papers from the printing office. Could not get an opportunity of bringing my business before the Executive. Captain Patton, one of Santa Anna's guards, returned this day from Washington. Left there 4th of February. The President accompanied him home.

Witnessed a trial before a Justice of the Peace, a Mr. Mat. Patton. The culprit had been found in possession of a soldier's certificate for $217, stolen from the auditor's office. Defended by Gibson and Ferris. Committed for trial, bail $1,000. Returned to Marion at night. Can see no horse yet to buy. Capt. Patton came in the *Julius Caesar*. Letters up; none for me.

Thursday, March 2, 1837.

At Marion.—This is the anniversary of the *Declaration of Independence*. A ball is to be given at Brazoria, and some gents were going down from here, but the bad weather prevents them. It rains hard, and the walking is intolerable. Kept the house all day.

Friday, March 3, 1837.

At Marion.—Went to Columbia. Saw Grayson on the subject of the loan. Appointed a conference. Went to Bell's to see a horse that Burnley has for me. Don't like him, but will get Mr. J. T. Gray to see him and pass his judgment on him.

Saturday, March 4, 1837.

At Marion.—Fine, clear day. Rode to Columbia with Mr. Gray. By his advice and Colonel Owens', bought the horse for $200. Dined at Bell's. A good dinner, but no vegetables except potatoes. Bell has a fine place. Beautiful variety of prairie and wood, but his house is mean, made of two log buildings, with an opening between them. No glass windows. Mrs. Bell, a neat, pleasant looking woman. Has only one child at home, a little, blue-eyed girl, about the age of my youngest. Has a daughter fourteen years old at school in Kentucky.

Had a long conference with Grayson about the loan. He admitted the validity of the contract, but would not admit our construction of it, as giving us a right to an immediate location. He also evidently thinks our Galveston grant good, although he is cautious in giving an opinion on it. Says the reasoning of the meeting at New Orleans is strong; that there is force in it, and he will not say it is not right, but inclines to the other idea. Returned after dinner to Marion, in company with Mr. Bell, taking my purchase with me.

Sunday, March 5, 1837.

At Marion—Fine day. Wrote to Mrs. Gray. At length our schooner has got up with our baggage. Also the *Julins Caesar*, *Watchman*, and *Jas. W. Caldwell*. In the afternoon Burnley, Grayson and McKinney came over. I paid the latter for the horse, $200. The horse had belonged to his nephew, and was left with him to sell.

Paid Captain Parker for passage up to Brazoria	$3.00
Paid sailors and steward	1.25
Paid for apples	.25
Horse, as above	200.00

None of the above vessels have brought me any letters. I am without any news from home since 23rd of January.

Saw Edwin Waller and Colonel Wm. P. Hill. Both gave me very cordial invitations to visit them, which I promised to do. Arrived in the *Julius Caesar*, Mr. John A. Parker, Mr. Brook, and Mr. Brokenbrough.

Monday, March 6, 1837.

At Marion.—Discovered that my horse has the scratches; and a Mr. Stoddard says he has the *"Button fearcy,"* a disease that I never heard of before. He recommended bleeding, and doses of burnt coperas. He kindly borrowed phlemes and bled him, and also administered the coperas; also recommended that sulphur be given him, to purify the blood. I have made a bad bargain, got a sick horse at a price that would be enormously high for a well one. Not being able to ride, my first care must now be to get him well, and in travelling order.

Tuesday, March 7, 1837.

At Marion.—The weather is still unsettled and damp. My horse has the scratches badly, and no hope of riding him for some days. Wrote to T. Green; finished letter to Mrs. Gray; wrote to A. Penn.

Paid for three dinners at Columbia, $1.50.

Wednesday, March 8, 1837.

At Marion.—The weather clear and pleasant. Mr. J. T. Gray dined at Bell's with the President, etc. He and several others are preparing to go to the west to-morrow.

Found here a Mr. Evans. Said he is of Pennsylvania; was a fellow student of Arthur A. Morson and Brook Voss. A lawyer; means to remain in the country to practice law. Queer character.

Thursday, March 9, 1837.

At Marion.—This morning Mr. J. T. Gray, Mr. C. R. Balfour, Mr. John Funston, Mr. B. C. North, Mr. Allen Armstrong and Mr. John J. Stevenson set out for the West. The latter goes only to the neighborhood of Matagorda, to view a half league of land, which he and his partner, Duprey, have bought conditionally of John B. Johnson, the clerk of Austin County. I was employed to draw the contract, the first professional job I have got in Texas. Fee, $5.

Ten gentlemen also went down the river, on their way to the United States, among them the two Browns. One of them spoke to me to undertake to sue or collect a debt from the Bordens, if not satisfactorily settled in New Orleans. Our house is becoming quiet and lonely. We have had a bustle ever since I have been here. I am impatient to go, too.

Friday, March 10, 1837.

At Marion.—To-day Burnley, Trigg and Dr. Jones came over, on their way to Velasco. Trigg has purchased a half league of land, and is returning to the United States to bring on his family. Lives at Abingdon, Va. Dr. Jones is going to the United States, to Vicksburg, Mobile, etc. Burnley told me that, in conversation with McKinney, he had admitted the expediency of compromising the Galveston conflicting claims, and between them they had arranged that M. Menard should go on to Richmond, clothed with full authority from the proprietors of the league grant to treat with T. Green, if he shall be authorized by our party, for a compromise. I assented to it, and gave him my written authority to Green to act for me. Wrote to T. Green on the subject, also to Dr. Neblett and R. Triplett, urging them to come into the measure.

Wrote to A. H. Wallace & Co., requested them to purchase for me the following:

Louisiana Civil Code.
Pastidas.
Digest Louisiana Reports.
Archbold's Criminal Practice.
Pothin on Obligations.
Work on Courts Martial.
Scates' Infantry Tactics.
Austin's Map of Texas.
Jefferson's *Manual.*
Mattress and mosquito bar.

Received of Mr. Philemon Waters $500 for my bill on W. G. Freeland, at five days' sight, for which he is to negotiate one of my drafts on T. Green. Wrote to Freeland.

Saturday, March 11, 1837.

At Marion.—Wrote a letter to the President, demanding my scrip. In the afternoon, rode with Parker to Columbia. The President has left town, to spend a few days at Splane's. Saw General Henderson. Inquired at postoffice. No letters from home! Returned to Marion. Weather damp, cloudy and showery all day. Very warm and threatening rain. This night I stript and washed myself all over—the first time I have done so since I left home. Slept in a clean night-shirt; the most comfortable night's lodging I have had in Texas.

Sunday, March 12, 1837.

At Marion.—It rained a storm last night and all this morning. Of course I did not go out. Wrote all the forenoon. Wrote to Peter. Commenced letter to Mrs. Gray. In the afternoon sat a short time in Duprey's room with his wife and Mr. and Mrs. Townsend—pleasant people. Became acquainted with a Mr. Widgen, of Norfolk, Va., also Mr. Tebbett, and Mr. Hubbel, of Mobile, just returning to the United States, after exploring the country for a few weeks. Also a Dr. Porter, of * * *. It is becoming much colder, the wind veering round to the north.

Monday, March 13, 1837.

A severe norther arose last night, and this morning it is very cold. Paid my account to my landlord, Hall, and determined to go to Bell's for a day or two.

Tavern bill	$20.50
Washing, one dozen	1.50
	$22.00

Went up to Columbia. The President has not yet returned from Splane's. Had a conversation with Anderson about the loan. He is very determined that we shall have no priority.

Here is a General Felix Huston, dressed *a la militaire*. He is tall and well made, rather slender. Has the bearing of a proud, ambitious man, evidently making an effort to be free and easy, so as to win popular favor. This is a first impression.

Went to Bell's in the evening. Here are Colonel Owens, Mr. Hobbs, Mr. Gregg, Crittenden, etc.

Tuesday, March 14, 1837.

At Bell's.—Had a long conference with Henderson and Grayson about the scrip. Could make no impression on them. I have exhausted all my argument, and have now only to make my formal demand and receive a formal answer. Went up to Columbia. The President returned about 1 o'clock. Delivered my letter. He said he had no authority to sign the scrip; that he would file the letter and give it proper attention, etc. Could not engage him in a consideration of the subject. Complained of being unwell from drinking some egg-nog made by Mrs. Splane. Returned late to dinner at

Bell's. Found Parker there, who had been out hunting and lost his way. In the evening Burnley and Richardson returned from Velasco, and the President and General F. Huston came down and crowded the house. Much seeming cordiality exists between the two Generals. The President gave up his bed to General F. Huston, and himself slept on the floor. Some of them played cards until 12 o'clock. I slept with Colonel Owens.

Wednesday, March 15, 1837.

The President is sick; no chance to get answer to my letter. Left Bell's, determined to go to Houston City. Burnley, Grayson and General F. Huston rode to Marion. Found Parker could not accompany me to Waller's, and in order to have the company of Colonel Hill, determined to wait until tomorrow. Washed my horses legs, painted his scratchy ankles with white paint, and turned him out.

Thursday, March 16, 1837.

At Marion.—My horse could not be found. Fine day. Spent most of the day hunting him through the woods. Went up to Columbia. Saw Grayson and Henderson, and they promised if my horse came to Bell's to take care of him and let me know it.

Friday, March 17, 1837.

At Marion.—No tidings of my horse. Hunted him in the woods; at night a Mr. Nash told me he had seen him in the woods. Wrote letters, etc.

VOL. B II

Saturday, March 18, 1837.

At Marion.—My horse still absent. Hunted him all the forenoon in the woods, unsuccessfully. Read and wrote. In the evening Mr. Hobbs, whom I had seen at Bell's came to Marion and told me my horse had been at Bell's two days, and Bell thought I had gone to Houston. Wrote to Burnley about my horse, and bargained with Bell's wagoner to bring him over in the morning.

Sunday, March 19, 1837.

At Marion.—Bell's wagoner came over and said my horse had been turned out before he got home, and had not been since seen. Rained all day. I wrote and read.

Monday, March 20, 1837.

At Marion.—Clear weather. Burnley came over and said my horse had not yet come up, and promised to send him as soon as he came. Parker is buying soldiers' rights; bought three of 640 acres each, and some pay for $3.50. In the evening Mr. Hobbs came over and kindly brought my horse. Nearly well of scratches.

Tuesday, March 21, 1837.

Rode to Columbia to inquire into the truth of a rumor that has reached us, that United States has acknowledged the independence of Texas. Found it true. Votes in Senate, 23-19. Appropriation for a minister. Does not give much pleasure to President and Cabinet of Texas. All persons are disappointed. Their hopes have been so highly raised of a speedy annexation to the United States by treaty with Santa Anna, that they can't at once be reconciled to the new state of things presented by the recognition. Texas independent, and compelled to fight her own battles and pay her own debts, will necessarily have to impose heavy burdens on her citizens. Direct and all sorts of taxes will be resorted to—the lands will be taxed. Lands are not considered so valuable now as they were a few days ago; and the squabbles for office and for lands that will take place here among the leaders! The prospect before us is anything but cheering.

Dined at Bell's. Burnley is going to Washington to-morrow, and I agreed to go with him. Returned to Marion. Dispatched letters that I had written to the United States, viz., to T. Green, A. H. W. & Co., and Mrs. Gray, by the hand of Dr. Porter.

Wednesday, March 22, 1837.

Paid Forbes for sack of corn, $5. Paid Hall tavern bill.

Rode to Columbia after breakfast. Burnley not ready to start until after dinner. Wrote to Dr. Meux, about the scrip, etc. No answer yet to my letter; found it was referred to the Department of State. No letters from home! Went to Bell's for dinner. After dinner started with Burnley and Hobbs. Rode sixteen miles to Damon's, at the Mound, an elevated ground of some thirty feet above the level of the prairie; seen at a great distance, looking like a mountain. All the rest of the country here and below, a dead level, dull and uninteresting. Damon not at home. A Caliban-looking fellow, with an unconscionable jaw and chin, named Stout, officiated. A good supper, a fine, large, roasted wild turkey at the foot of the table, coffee, stewed apples, milk, etc. Here we met a Captain Lynch, Dr. Peebles, Taylor Peebles and Judge Baker (Joseph Baker), of Bexar. The latter an intelligent and rather prepossessing young man, apparently twenty-six or twenty-eight years old. He is Chief Justice of the county. A good Spanish

scholar, a Yankee, lived six years in San Felipe, taught school, and edited *Telegraph*.
Bill, $1.25.

Thursday, March 23, 1837.

Left Damon's at half past 7 o'clock. Hobbs and Lynch started before us, Hobbs going to his late purchase on the La Vaca. Dr. Peebles joined us. Dull journey. Arrived about 1 at Thompson's, fed horse, ate dinner. Packed corn with us for food at night. Met Mr. Hudson going below. Dinner and corn, $1.50.

Arrived at Allen's at dark, having traveled full forty miles. At Allen's found Mr. Bliss, of Marion. A pretty looking place, well watered, well diversified with wood and prairie; fronts on Brazos; about 3,000 acres; sold recently to * * * Walker, of Mississippi, for $2 per acre, payment to be made in May. I. R. Lewis, negotiator. I think it cheap. Grace has sold a half league just above at the same price. Allen one of the oldest settlers. Bill at Allen's, $1.

Friday, March 24, 1837.

Left Allen's about half past 7 o'clock. Arrived at San Felipe at 10. Only three or four miserable houses in the place, one good looking home building by Huff. Arrived at Cummins' at 1 o'clock. Took dinner, 50 cents. Cummins in the United States. Miss Rebecca says she has not heard from him since he left home in November last. Here Dr. Peebles left us, his home being close by, on the Brazos. Arrived at Colonel Edwards' after 2 o'clock. Found here Dr. Berry, Steele, Brokenbrough, S. Colquohoon, and a stranger, Howth. Burnley stopt to meet some person expected at night. I went on alone. Arrived at Perry's, on Caney Creek, about dusk, eleven miles from Edwards'. Got a good supper and lodging and corn for my horse. Bill, including breakfast, $2.

Saturday, March 25, 1837.

Left Perry's at 8 o'clock; arrived at John M. Walker's, eight miles, before 10. Walker not at home. Saw Uriah Saunders; he has engaged a man named Lawrence to clear out his league, thinking I would never return. Saw also Sanders Walker; he had also engaged another person (Dr. C. B. Stewart) to clear out his league. The contract was made the day before I arrived. Rode on to Gary's; not at home. My horse was taken sick; went to Gideon Walker's, in search of Gary; had gone to Woodward's; went there; he had gone home. I followed, and when I returned found he had bled my horse in the mouth. He was in much pain. All thought he had the botts. At the instance of Mrs. Gary and a Mr. Henderson, who both said they had seen the Mexicans use that expedient, I exerted myself in slapping his sides and kicking him, which he bore with wonderful quietude. I suppose he was in so much internal misery that he did not regard the external affliction. Gary gave him a strong drench of salt and water, also alum. He had no more appropriate medicines. Towards night he was able to stand up, and seemed free from acute pain. I mounted and rode him briskly over the prairie for a mile or two, which seemed to improve him. He refused to eat corn or to drink water. Hobbled and turned him out on the prairie, and he began to graze. I now concluded he had only had the colic from having eaten too much corn at Perry's.

Saw at Woodward's a Mr. Ryland Clarke Ballard, formerly of Virginia—laborer, blacksmith by trade, and Captain Joseph P. Lynch, who keeps a little store there; had commanded a company in the service of Texas.

Gideon Walker is a Justice of the Peace.

Gary says he is not entitled to a league, his wife having been once before married, and her first husband having drawn a league. He therefore can claim only one-third of a league, and that he wishes to clear out himself. But he offers me a contract which he had made with one Nunly, in lieu of his own. Wrote for him a contract and power of attorney for Nunly to execute, and if he does so I will take it.

Sunday, March 26, 1837.

At Gary's.—A very warm day. My horse seems to be entirely well, but feeble. Bought of Gary his discharge for three months' service, pay, etc., 320 acres of land, for $50, on account of Guy Richards and myself. Went with him to Gideon Walker to get the assignment executed. Found the honest J. P. at work on a wagon (Sunday). Without leaving his work he administered the oath by requiring the party to hold up his right hand while the oath was repeated to him, and signed the certificate on the wagon in the open air, all done in a few minutes. Fee for oath, 12 ½ cents, for certificate, 25 cents.

Also bought of Sanders Walker his discharge for three months' service and right to 320 acres of land, for $50, also on account of G. Richards and self.

Dined at G. Walker's, and then rode to John M. Walker's; he was not at home. Determined to wait his return and stay all night. No corn. Hobbled my horse and turned him out. Walker returned at night. Was unwilling to carry our contract into effect, as he is now able to clear out the league himself. (These Texans are growing smarter than they were a year ago.) He, however, acknowledged it to be a fair bargain, and if I insisted on it he must comply, although a Mr. Stevenson had offered the very day that I arrived to clear out for one-fourth and the labor. We finally settled it at one-third, which I agreed to take, as that is now the common price.

At night I slept in the same room with him and his wife; the same thing at Gary's. No mock modesty about it on the part of the women; they seemed to regard it as a matter of course, and it is no doubt a thing of common occurrence.

Monday, March 27, 1837.

At J. M. Walker's.—My horse has strayed. Walked over to G. Walker's to execute the deed from Jno. M. Walker to myself. Bought of Francis K. Henderson (brother-in-law of J. M. Walker) his certificate of three months service, for $50, on account of G. Richards and self. Returning to J. M. Walker's, found my horse had returned. Set out for Dr. Miller's in company with Captain W. W. Hill, one of the members of Congress for this county, who lives near Dr. M. Passed over ten miles of beautiful country. Rich land, undulating prairie, with a good admixture of clear running streams and wood. Arrived at Miller's at dark; found Burnley there; good supper, good bed, poor log house, like all the rest. Dr. Miller a Kentuckian, intelligent, but plain, lazy and rich.

Tuesday, March 28, 1837.

At Dr. Miller's.—Mr. Chrisman, the surveyor, came in at breakfast. He, Miller and Burnley had business, which would take them some hours. I went on to Washington, where Burnley is to join me at night. Rode through Cole's Settlement, eighteen miles to Washington. A beautiful country. From Washington out through this settlement and on up New Year's Creek, is the finest looking part of Texas that I have seen. Met * * * Evans on the road. He had walked from Marion to Washington, and appeared in defense of a horse thief, who was whipped and branded.

Met also Colonel Jno. P. Coles, who is Chief Justice of the county, returning from Washington, where he had been holding a court of probate. Had a half hour's chat with him on the road. Said this section of the country is very healthful (so said Miller). He had been unfortunate in losing several children, but not from diseases of the climate. His is the only family that has lost children in the settlement—has been here thirteen years. Land will produce thirty to forty bushels of corn to the acre, or a bale of cotton. One hand can make seven to eight bales of cotton. Dr. Miller thinks seven bales to the hand is as much as can be made in Texas, on a fair average of one year with another.

Arrived at Washington at 3 o'clock. Found a considerable increase in building; in March, 1836, there were only about ten families here, now thirty, and several houses building. Put up at S. R. Roberts', who is now a Justice of the Peace, and called Squire Roberts. Saw Dr. Smith, who was very polite, and took me to his house. Saw Scates, who is married to the Doctor's daughter, but did not marry until after their return from the Runaway Scrape. He lamented very piteously his having sold his headright—talked of his poverty, etc.; says the Pine Island league cannot be got without a law suit, and he must give us another. He never got a deed for the Pine Islands, and Menard had laid an eleven-league grant over it. He has authorized Judge Hood to select his headright for him, which he says he will convey to us—but begged me not to say anything to his father-in-law's family about it! I don't like his manner about it, and fear he is not reliable. He spoke of going to his old neighborhood to make contracts for clearing out lands, which I advised him to do, and offered to go halves with him and advance the money required.

Found here a Mr. Blair, of Tennessee, and a Mr. Mitchell, from Orange County, Virginia, who are going in a new corps of Rangers against the Indians on the Colorado. They furnish their own horses and arms, serve a year, receive rations, clothing, $25 per month, and 1,280 acres of land. Pretty good employment for young men without business.

Found at the postoffice a letter written to me by Dr. Barton in March, 1836.

Wednesday, March 29, 1837.

At Washington.—Became acquainted with Mr. W. Gant, Member of Congress for the county; Mr. Merritt, clerk of

the county, and Mr. Shepherd, clerk Circuit Court. Burnley
not arriving, left Washington after 12 o'clock; stopt and chatted with Andy Miller about land, and drank a bowl of his
wife's buttermilk; stopt also at Lat's, and ate some more milk
and bread. Stopt also at the Widow Pankey's and got a gourd
that I had bought of her little son a year ago. Found Nunly,
whose league of land Gary is to clear out, and which he offered in lieu of his own. Nunly seems not disposed to let me
have it. Would not go to Walker's with me, but said he would
see Gary on Saturday at the sale at J. M. Walker's, and they
would talk it over. Passed on by the Widow Miller's, intending to reach Walker's, but at nightfall got bewildered with the
by-roads, and stopping at the Widow Singleton's to inquire
the way, was invited to stop for the night, which I did. Kindly
treated in a very rude way. The widow has three children, her
mother and two brothers live with her, fine, strapping young
men. We all slept in one little room.

MEMO.—A great many widows here in Texas. Nunly was
working the land of the Widow Kiggins. The maiden name
of Mrs. Singleton was Harber, or Harbaugh. They would
receive no pay for my entertainment. Rude hospitality and
unaffected kindness are the characteristics of the old settlers that I meet with. It is only in retired country places that
one will meet with much of these virtues. The new race are
adventurers, sharpers, and many of them blacklegs. The ob-
serving of the old settlers are sensible of this, and lament it
with mortified and indignant feelings. They say they had no
occasion for locks in Texas until within the last two years,
and now no property is safe. None of the offices of the new
Republic are filled by the old settlers; they are crowded out
by newcomers, who assume a consequence to which they are
not entitled. The old men see and feel this with deep but
smothered mortification.

Bill at Washington, $2.12 ½ .

Thursday, March 30, 1837.

After breakfast, left the Widow Singleton's, rode by James Walker's, to John's; not at home. Went on to Gary's; not at home. Wrote a letter for him, which left with his wife. Set out on my return to Columbia. At 1 o'clock reached Perry's, where I got a slight dinner, 25 cents. Arrived at Edwards' quarter before 5 o'clock. Chatted with him a few minutes, and rode on to Cummins', where I found Dr. Peebles, who is said to be courting Miss Rebecca. Bill, $2. Tooth brush, 37 ½ cents. Gave Gary's children 50 cents. Wind south, drizzly and uncomfortable.

Friday, March 31, 1837.

A cold norther. Burnley arrived this morning to breakfast, having reached Edwards' soon after I left there. Also joined by Major Steel and Mr. Martin, of Washington, and a Mr. Sinks, a newcomer from Ohio. Dined at Allen's, 25 cents. Slept at Cole's, on the Bernard. Bill at Cole's, $1.50.

Saturday, April 1, 1837.

Norther continues. Left Cole's at 8 o'clock. Burnley and self arrived at Damon's about 2 o'clock; the others fell behind, and did not overtake us. Dinner at Damon's, 50 cents. Arrived at Columbia after sunset, where I found a letter just arrived from Mrs. Gray, Peter and Eve, written from the 26th of February to 1st of March, the only one I have received from home since I have been in the country. Rode with the President to Bell's, where I stayed all night. Slept in the same bed with D. P. R.

Sunday, April 2, 1837.

At Bell's.—Fine day, indeed, the weather has been fine on all my journey except the drizzle on Thursday and the norther on Friday. My horse was turned out last night, and could not be found until dinner time. Paid the negroes 50 cents for hunting him. The President had an attack of *cholera morbus* last night, and is laid up all day. Introduced to Colonel A. Somerville, who, with Wm. Boyd dined here and then set out for Matagorda. Mr. and Mrs. McCormick, Mrs. Bell's sister, arrived to dinner. Also dined here, R. R. Royal, and * * * Kerr, of Matagorda, land agents.

After dinner, rode to Marion; called on the way to see J. A. Navarro, who is still at Columbia, with his brother, Eugene Navarro. Found there Dr. Allsberry, who married a Miss N., and who told me he intended opening a boarding house at Bexar, and acting as land agent, a business that I have thought of myself. Howard has been to the army, and says soldiers' claims are higher there than they are here.

Monday, April 3, 1837.

Set out for Brazoria, in company with J. A. Parker; called at Bell's for Crittenden. Arrived at 1 o'clock, after the court had taken a recess. Stopt at Mrs. Long's. Court sat after dinner. Grand jury discharged after presenting gambling as a growing evil which calls for the civil authority to arrest. Recommended either suppression by law, or restricting by taxation. In the present state of the country, the latter will probably be most judicious. It could not be suppressed entirely, and a penal law would not be enforced. Public opinion must first be operated on, and then penal laws may be safely attempted. In the meantime, the Republic needs revenue, and the gambling offices may be made to contribute, and by licensing some the number may be reduced.

Tuesday, April 4, 1837.

The lawyers practicing here are mostly young men; the judge is young, and all the proceedings are loose, and not very ceremonious. Presented my license to the judge, who ordered it to be recorded, and a license issued to me to practice in the "District and Inferior Courts of the Republic."

This afternoon Dr. Archer arrived, to whom I presented my letters. Politely received. He appears in behalf of Captain Sude, charged with murder, in shooting Lieutenant Sprowl, at Velasco. Trial to-morrow.

A report came this evening that two brigs and two schooners have appeared at the mouth of the river; supposed to be Mexicans. It produced a little sensation, but no action.

Finished letter to Mrs. Gray, to go by first opportunity.

Ben C. Franklin, Judge of Second Judicial District.
Augustus M. Tompkins, State's Attorney.
W. P. Scott, Clerk District Court.
Robt. J. Calder, Sheriff County of Brazoria.
Geo. McKinstry, Chief Justice of the County of Brazoria.
Wm. T. Austin, Clerk of County.

Lawyers.

Wm. H. Jack, Wm. W. Franklin, Patrick C. Jack, Rob't J. Townes, Henry P. Brewster, Colin De Bland, Geo. B. Crittenden, John A. Wharton, Branch T. Archer.

Introduced to Silas Dinsmoor, Chief Justice of Matagorda; Sweeny, of the San Bernard; Russell, one of the Justices of the County of Brazoria.

Wednesday, April 5, 1837.

At Brazoria.—Trial of Snell continued. The business of the court draws to a close. Jury dismissed. Determined to ride

over and see Edwin Waller. Left Brazoria at 4 o'clock. My
first unfavorable impressions not removed by this visit. Had
my blanket stolen, and got an inferior one in its place. Bill,
$7. Cutting hair, 37 ½ cents. Ferry, 25 cents.

To Waller's ten miles across Bayliss' Prairie, on east side
of Oyster Creek. A fine evening. Arrived a little after sunset.
Waller out in the fields. Introduced myself to Mrs. Waller,
a fine looking woman, some thirty odd years old, ladylike,
plain, unaffected, has four children, three rough, rude, untu-
tored sons, the oldest * * *, and one daughter, the youngest,
a spoilt pet. The home an exceedingly rude, open, double
log cabin, with two shed rooms, furniture pretty good, and
not in keeping with the house. No glass windows, logs not
chinked. Waller came in about dark. Kindly welcomed; excellent supper; good lodging in a very rough room. It is strange
how people who know how to live better and are able can
content themselves to live in such wretched cabins—but they
have been here only about eight months. Should they continue here, and make a few good crops of cotton, they will
improve their building, or, more likely, will seek a habitation
in a healthier and more desirable region, San Antonio, for
instance, and leave this plantation in charge of an overseer.

Thursday, April 6, 1837.

At Waller's.—Mr. Waller had to go to Brazoria on business.
I remained to write some letters.

Wrote about loan to Geo. Hancock, Thos. D. Carneal,
James F. Irwin, Lewis Whiteman, Paul Anderson, Jas. N.
Morrison, James S. Brander, recommending to them to send
powers of attorney to represent them at the approaching session of Congress.

Had some interesting conversation with Mrs. Waller; she
was a Miss Dashields, daughter of Captain Dashields, of Nor-
thumberland, Virginia; married against her father's wishes.

Is estranged from her father and sister, Mrs. Boysie; has been six years in Texas; neither wrote to nor received a letter from father or sister in all that time. That is bad, but I could not but sympathize with her. Children named Hiram, Edwin, Wm. Wharton and Juliet. They have had much trouble since they have been in the country. She is now reconciled to it, but wants to go back to Virginia to see her connections once more.

Waller returned before night. He says he once bought this place for 50 cents per acre; sold it for $1.25, and bought it back for $6; would not now take $25; works seventeen field hands, eleven of them able men. Has 1,000 acres, 275 cleared and in corn and cotton; calculated on 200 bales of cotton this year. The soil is a stiff, chocolate colored alluvium. Growth live oak, Spanish, etc., and cane. Oyster Creek runs through it, a deep ravine, that looks as if it might once have been the bed of the Brazos, with now only a sluggish, unhealthy looking little bayou in it, the residence of alligators, etc.

The morning had indicated rain, wind from the south, cloudy and warm, a few slight showers. In the course of the day the wind veered around to west, northwest and north, and before bedtime blew hard and cold. Apprehensions of frost, which would kill all the young cotton.

Friday, April 7, 1837.

At Waller's.—The norther is up in earnest. It is excessively cold, and the wind blowing a hurricane. My fingers and toes ached excessively before I could get dressed. Oh, these open houses! What a people to live in such barns! The log huts of the poor negroes are more open than the log stables in Virginia, and some of them have no chimneys. No wonder they sicken and die; the wonder is that any of them live.

Remained until after dinner, the wind blowing a hurricane all day. At 3 o'clock took leave, with a kind invitation to repeat the visit. Passed the plantation of J. R. Jones, Bynum and Sayre, distance called ten miles; took me near three hours to ride it. Horrible road, through the bottom. Arrived at Marion after sunset. Found here J. T. Gray and his party, returned from the West delighted with the country, but he bought nothing; is going back to the United States; not pleased with the government. Found here also a Mr. Stockton, from Kenawha, Va., Peter Minor, from Albemarle, and many other newcomers. A Mr. Hawkins, of Kentucky, late of United States navy, whose father was a partner of Austin, came to look after his property.

Supped at Hall's, but when bed-time came the old rascal told me there was no place for me to sleep; went to Peters', who was also full, and I had to beg a resting place on the floor of Forbes' counting room, where I made out with blankets and overcoats, quite as well as I should have done at Hall's. Resolved to have nothing more to do with such a rude, unaccommodating fellow.

Ferryage at Marion, 25 cents.

The report of the Mexican squadron has blown over. The vessels, whoever they were, have passed on, towards Galveston.

Saturday, April 8, 1837.

At Marion.—A bitter cold morning. Ice was formed in vessels that sat out all night, and all the young plants are killed. Weeds, etc., three feet high were prostrated as soon as the sun came out on them. An old settler who has been in the country ever since 1821 says he has never known anything like it before.

J. T. Gray, J. A. Parker, Mr. and Mrs. Townsend, Funstall, Balfour and many others went down the river to-day, in the steamboats *Yellow Stone* and *Wm. Bryan*, on their way to the United States; to sail in the *Wm. Bryan*. Mr. and Mrs. Duprey also. The *Yellow Stone* proceeds around to Houston, and I shipped my two black leather trunks by her, to care of Smith & Allen. My hair trunk I shall leave here to be sent by some other opportunity.

Sold to Captain West, of the *Yellow Stone*, a draft on A. W. Wallace & Co. for $1,200, on account of my drafts on John Ward & Co. Wrote to them to cash my two drafts of $1,000 each, pay my bill for $1,200, and send me the balance to Houston by some safe private hand. See letter. Wrote also by Parker to Mrs. Gray, Jere Morton (with copy of the resolution of Dr. Everett referring loan contract to government ad int.), Geo. Hancock, Th. D. Carneal, J. F. Irwin, Lewis Whiteman, J. N. Morrison, Paul Anderson, J. S. Branden.

In evening rode to Columbia. Got letter from Mrs. Gray, February 10 to 20. Also from W. F. Ritchie, with endorsement of duplicate from R. Triplett to President Houston, December 12.

Postage on Triplett's letter, $1.12 ½, on Mrs. Gray's, 22 ½ cents; mending boots, 50 cents; mending breeches, 25 cents. Bought of Dempsey Pace two discharges for three months, each for $125, on account of Guy Richards and self. Paid Moody for writing deeds, etc., $2.

Returned to Marion at 9 o'clock. Mr. Brooks (new partner of Forbes), kindly got out of his bed and gave it to me, he having another at Hall's. This courtesy increased the prepossession I had already formed for him. He is from Norfolk; lived with Suter; a fine young man.

Houston, July 12th, 1838.

MEMO. to inquire in Virginia for the heirs of Thomas R. Miller, late of Gonzales, who was killed in the Alamo with Travis. He came from Virginia to Texas in the spring of 1830, and never returned from Texas. He was a carpenter in Virginia and merchant in Texas, and acquired some lands.

After his death in the spring of 1836, his brother, Richard Floyd Miller, came into Texas, during the Runaway Scrape, and meeting with Elijah Tate, Wm. W. Arrington and John J. Tinsley, one or other of them had possession of the papers of T. R. Miller, and Tate had two of his negro men; he took from them the negroes and account books and papers, and it is said that he took them to Natchitoches, where, in a drunken or mad frolic he burnt all of the papers, and was himself put in the calaboose. One or more of his brothers, it is said, came to Natchitoches and released him, and took him and the two negroes off with them. Nothing has been heard of them, or of any of the heirs of T. R. Miller, since. His creditors have laid claims against his estate to the amount of about $6,000, and Jos. D. Clements has been appointed administrator. He has about four leagues of titled lands. The court has ordered half a league, one-fourth a league and one-half of a quarter to be sold, to pay his debts. There are some lands due the estate from the government; unless claimed by the heirs they will be lost, and the titled lands being unrepresented in the country by any heirs, are in danger of escheat. Mr. Clements is now in Houston, from whom I have these particulars. He is here on the business of the estate. He has written to the heirs in Virginia, but does not know their residence; is informed by one Lewis that they live in Nottaway. Mr. Clements gave bond in $20,000. Cannot get the lands from government without a power of attorney from heirs.

Joseph P. Laller was clerk for T. R. Miller, and knew all his concerns. He left Gonzales in consequence of stabbing a man, in winter of 1835. Mr. Clements says there is no danger in his returning, if alive. He can save much of the estate by his knowledge of its accounts; he kept the books. He is supposed to have joined Fannin, and may have been killed. His name was not on the rolls of Fannin's regiment.

J. P. Laller was advertised by Governor Smith January 6, 1836; reward, $150. A translation of so much of the *"Recopela-*

cion" as relates to the land laws was made by Governor White, of Florida, by order of Congress, U. S., and was published in 1833 by Duff Green, in his Volume of Land Laws.

END